THE BULL OF OMBOS

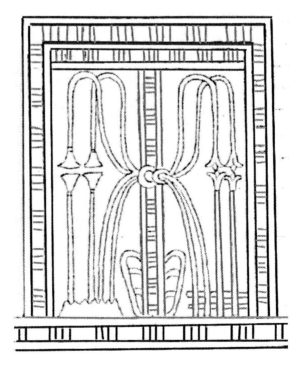

'The origin of the myth of Horus and Seth is lost
in the mists of the religious traditions of
prehistory.'
(Te Velde 1977: 79)

Overleaf: the sema or smaiut - signifying unity, especially of the
'Upper' & 'Lower' (Egypt)

The Bull of Ombos

By

Mogg Morgan

Seth & Egyptian Magick

Volume II

Mandrake

Published by
Mandrake of Oxford
PO Box 250
OXFORD
OX1 1AP (UK)

A CIP catalogue record for this book is available from the British Library and the US Library of Congress.

ISBN1869928873

Contents

Acknowledgements

The anonymous staff of the Sackler Library / Griffith Institute, Oxford, that has been my informal 'House of Life' during the writing of this book. To Robert Jackson, author of *At Empire's Edge: Exploring Rome's Eastern Frontier*, for much invaluable information used in *Pan's Road*, a fictional counterpart to *Bull of Ombos*. To the University of Chicago Press for permission to reproduce the 'Wondrous spell for binding a lover' pages 220-225 below; a translation by E.N.O'Neil of PGM.IV., lines 296-466 from Hans Dieter Betz (1986), *The Greek Magical Papyri in Translation, including Demotic spells*. To the Israel Antiquities Authority for permission to reproduce 'Astarte of the Horns' on page 207. To Kym, amanuensis, proof-reader and editor extraordinaire. To Charlotte, Tristram, Lydia and all at the Bath Omphalos, who by their enthusiasm for some of the ideas in my first book, encouraged me to write more. To my friend and mentor Jan Fries, always a useful sounding board for odd ideas. To Gavin & Astrid. To 'cunning man' Jack Daw, for useful feedback on the practicalities of life. To Payam Nabarz, a mine of information on the cult of Mithras in its various manifestations. To all in the *Tankhem* 'House of Life' and *Black Lodge*, for much valued feedback. To various members of the laterday *Temple of Set*, and *The Storm* for valuable comments, feedback and information.

'Before me in the East Nephthys

Behind me in the West Isis

On my right hand in the South is Seth

And on my left hand in the North is Horus

For above me shines the body of Nuit

And below me extends the ground of Geb

And in the centre abideth the 'Great Hidden God.'

The 'Abydos Arrangement'[1]

'Naqada' Egyptian: Nubt , Greek Ombos

Egyptian time line	Elsewhere
	Neolithic Jericho 8500BC
Egyptian & Nubia Paleolithic 6500BC	Neolithic Mesopotamia 6500BC
Egyptian Neolithic 4500BC Badarian, Merimda	
Naqada I 4000BC	
Naqada II & Predynastic 3500BC	Uruk and invention of writing 3500bc
Naqada III - Early Dynasties Invention of writing	
Pyramid (Djoser) c2650BC	

Correspondences

Number: 7

Jewel: carnelian

Constellation: The Plough (Ursa Major)

Planet: Mercury

Colours: red, gold

Tree: Acacia (Persea for Osiris)

Metal: Iron, Gold

The First Ritual : Drawing down the Plough

Whenever I have need of you
I drawn down the plough
Standing under the night stars,
The canopy clear above me
Searching the heavens for your sign,
An ox moving withershins,
Tethered to a mast of flint
In the northern part of the sky

First I rouse your mate
Who lies sleeping in the earth beneath
Stamping the ground,
So Bat for Bata will awake
Tremors below rising through me
A conduit for the seething cauldron
As the power rises to my belly
My arms upwards piecing the barrier
Separating I and thou

And down it flows
that thing
into me,
or my cup
or via me to my companion
Dizzy now with the elixior
I follow your movements backwards
to the nameless aeon
when none ruled but I

1 Gold in the desert

Naqada is a sleepy little town in Upper Egypt that gives its name to a crucial period in the prehistory of Egypt before the coming of the dynasties. In 1895, William Matthew Flinders Petrie (1853-1942), the 'father' of Egyptian archaeology, excavated an ancient necropolis 7km north of the modern day town. This necropolis belonged to a very ancient city of several thousand inhabitants. With Petrie's usual luck, he managed to stumble upon yet another archaeological find of seismic proportions – not just an ancient city a quarter of the size of ancient Ur, a rare enough find, but the capital of the earliest state established in Egypt.[2] The name of this city, one of the largest of its time, was Nubt, Greek Ombos, the town of Seth, the Upper Egyptian god par excellence. This ancient and lost city of Ombos was often confused with the

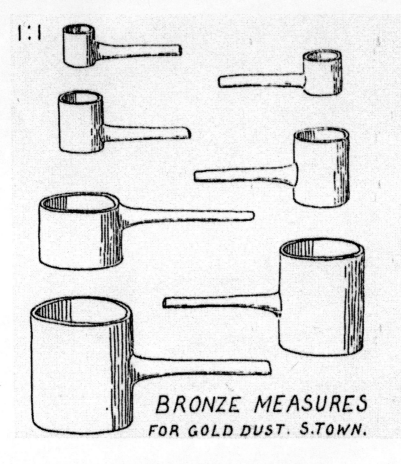

1:1

BRONZE MEASURES
FOR GOLD DUST. S.TOWN.

more familiar Kom Ombo. The reader is advised that these are quite geographically and culturally distinct locations. Jacques de Morgan contradicted Petrie and established the correct period for Naqada, as 'the capital of the earliest state established in Egypt'.[3]

Gold production may well have originated in Naqada. Petrie reported finding a complete set of measures containing binary divisions of the 'uten' a measure of gold dust from ½ to 1/128 when piled.[4] Importantly these measures are based on the Nubian system of dividing the 'uten' for the gold trade. Nubia was one of the largest gold fields of ancient times. And one of the standard weights used in the temples was shaped like a hippopotamus –Seth's animal!

A word on Prehistoric Egypt

The study of prehistoric Egypt took longer than other disciplines to break free from the ideological straitjacket of Biblical theology. Whole periods such as the Palaeolithic were largely ignored, sites were excavated and the results never published or worse, as in the case of Petrie's voluminous field notes, destroyed by his successor Margaret Murray. The late Michael Hoffman, says that very few books written before the 1980s have any accurate knowledge about prehistoric Egypt. Hoffman tells us:

The father of the prehistoric was the pioneer Jacques Boucher de Perthes whose studies of ancient artefacts in association with river terraces along the Somme laid down the basic technique. In general the highest terrace would contain the oldest material, the lowest terrace the most recent. Henry Breasted attempted to apply some of these techniques to the Nile material although the character of the Nile presented peculiar problems of its own.

'The Delta, although marshy, boasted a number of elevated hillocks and a fair amount of dry land in its central and southern parts which supported habitation from early times. Moreover, the deposit of alluvium in the Delta was not uniform, so that at least some prehistoric sites there must still survive near the modern surface. To the south, Upper Egypt, far from being an inhospitable, swampy jungle, was a well drained floodplain that supported with ease Palaeolithic hunters and fishers as well as pre-dynastic and dynastic farmers.'.[5] The Bow was an invention of these late Palaeolithic hunters of =(c12, 000BC), an example of which was found at Jabel Sahabad. This compares with the earliest European bow so far of c7000BC.[6] These hunter-gatherers limited their population much as we in industrial times do, although the methods were drastically different. From this we discover that 'high birth-rates and large populations are not the natural state of man'.[7] I mentioned this, as it's as well to be on the lookout for assumptions that a god connected with abortion or contraception, for example Seth, may not be viewed in a wholly negative light.

Prehistory of the North or 'Lower' Egypt

One of the first discoveries was the Merimda settlement, just north of modern Cairo. These people were fond of using the massive leg bone of the hippopotamus as a doorstep to their huts. This 'practice . .[is] . . .fraught with ritual implications to ward off these beasts, which were later to become personifications of danger in Dynastic times.'.[8] As we shall discover, the hippopotamus was one of the god's Seth's most important totem beasts – and the above use of the animal's bone to protect one of the crucial thresholds shows how ancient is this ritual connection. The hippopotamus, must have been a major food source for these early inhabitants of the Nile valley, supplementing the Bovid diet and indeed symbolic power of their hunter gatherer ancestors.

Other prehistoric and pre-dynastic sites have been found in the suburbs of Cairo. Omari is found at the foot of Gebel Tura and is the source of the Tura limestone used to case the nearby pyramids.[9] Clearly this region is no stranger to human occupation, long before the pyramid age.

Burials in this region are of the same contracted sort as Naqada.[10] Before the coming of the dynasties, Egyptians buried their dead in the contracted or foetal position and not the ubiquitous 'Osiris' position of later times, including our own. In the graves were found semi precious carnelian beads and this may well also be a symbolic connection with what is to come. Carnelian is a red stone that in the *Contendings of Horus & Seth* (see appendix) is used to replace the lost eye of Horus, chewed out and dissected by his brother Seth. In Maadi it may even have been used as currency,[11] which may well explain the occurrence of these same beads in graves from outside Egypt, even as far flung as the British Isles!

The north developed more slowly than the south but according to at least one popular theory, Egypt's first King Narmer eventually conquered it. Narmer unified Egypt, expelling the 'Asiatics', one of the four races of their anthropology, the other three being

1   2

Above: A puzzle: here are two patterns taken from the protodynastic settlement at Naqada. Whilst they share something with the geometric designs of ancient Iran and Mesopotamia, the Egyptian potter has *deliberately* destroyed the regularity of the pattern. The eminent prehistorian in whose work I found this example, says there are many more similar (Baumgartel 1947). When you see it you are immediately aware of the personality of the potter and his or her six thousand year old message to you! The ancient Egyptian mind was very fond of this kind of game and encoded many other examples in dynastic tombs, pyramids and temples.

Humans, Nubians and Libyans. Before this the North showed signs of nascent mercantilism, trading with neighbours in Palestine. Eventually the consumerism and political aspirations of the south came to dominate the situation.[12]

Climate

Rainfall in these very early times was greater than at any time since. Between approximately c7000-3000BC occurs what climatologists call the Neolithic pluvial and sub-pluvial.[13] Rainfall was approximately two inches per annum, that's about the same as modern Cairo and compares with say 30-40in per year in Europe. Even so, two inches is enough to make 'the desert bloom.' Others say these rainfall estimates are too conservative and that it could be as much as 25cm per year. This rain occurred in some kind of relationship to the Nile flood. The Nile never runs dry because it has two sources of water: an annual flood of the Red Nile caused by the Ethiopian monsoon, currently in June/July. In addition the White Nile is fed by the massive headwaters of Lake Victoria in central Africa. In the remote past, rainfall in Egypt proper may have added to the complexity of the system, either by occuring in the winter (January-March) or summer (June-September). Prediction of the coincidence of these natural events was an crucial task for

Neolithic farmers. The Nile, which found a route out of Africa at the beginning of the stoneage, circa 750,000 years ago has not always been benign. The Nile has probably wiped out several early precocious developments with disastrous floods.[14] The duel nature of the Nile, the Red and the White, feeds into Egyptian mythology in many important ways. For example, the Nile god Osiris is, some say paradoxically, drown by his red brother Seth.

Agriculture

'For now at least, it seems as if the food producing revolution occurred in the "red land", [i.e. the desert] many centuries if not a full millennium before it penetrated the fertile Nile bottomlands. So the priority of progress have been reversed and the 'barbarians' were once the wave of the future'.[15]

As I reported in my book *Tankhem*,[16] agriculture starts in the Nabta playa, in Egypt's western desert near the Sudanese border. These people may have been driven by climate change into the Nile's alluvial plain. Environmental changes would be things like the Neolithic pluvial and the lowering of the Nile inundation. These two events may not have happened simultaneously but were within a separation of anything from 200 to 600 years.[17]

Their initial focus of Nile Valley settlement was perhaps a ceremonial complex of some kind.[18] There were several primary centres of ancient upper Egypt, including Nubt - Greek: Ombos, the 'City of Gold', and Nekhen - Greek: Hierakonpolis – 'City of the Hawk'.[19] It was from these primary nodes that an archaic network sprang up, which eventually reaching a critical mass or, to use Renfrew's term, 'multiplier' leading to radical social change.[20] People came together in these places in what is quite a novel way. The best way I can envision it is as the kind of space that existed at one of the free festivals of the 1970s! Lots of nuclear groups coming together for a common purpose but respecting their individual concerns and autonomy.

Naqada

'Gift of the Nile', 'The pyramids built Egypt' or 'civilization without cities' are common enough nostrums that tell us something about the development of Egyptian culture. However modern research now demonstrates that Egypt did have some quite significant cities, some of these founded in prehistoric times. These concentrated settlements were in fact hinterlands of extremely ancient, Neolithic ritual sites.

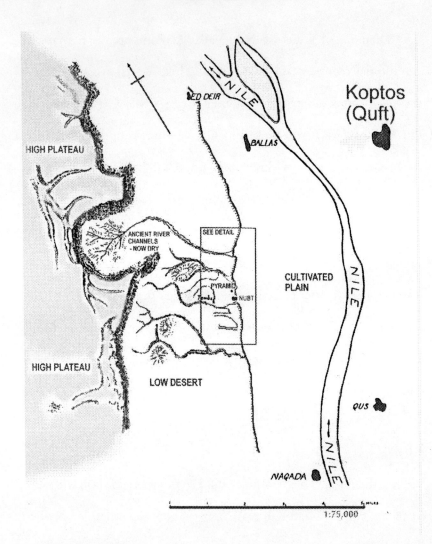

What Petrie and his colleagues discovered at Naqada represents the society built by the descendents of the 'red land' farmers, after they had left their retreating desert pastures, to begin again as near as they dared to the banks of the Nile.

By modern standards Petrie and his colleague Quibell's excavation were botched, recording was haphazard and many important artefacts were lost or destroyed soon after excavation.[21] With hindsight it seems obvious to us that they did not understand the full implication of what they had found. Petrie wrote that 'So far as the whole of the earlier and larger part of the graves are concerned, there is not a single form, material or detail which speaks of Egypt.'[22] Petrie, in very many respects was years ahead of his time and unlike us, had no real conceptual framework of the prehistoric communities of ancient Egypt as a guide. What he found at Naqada, was to his eyes, so different to the dynastic remains that he constantly refers to them as the 'new race', some kind of immigrant group or colony. This was all wrong of course, but it took a while for this to filter through and by designating the finds as those of a 'new race' Petrie more or less guaranteed they would be less interesting to scholars of the time and would thus in effect be reburied and ignored by his contemporaries. It also meant that the collection was restricted to three major collections – the

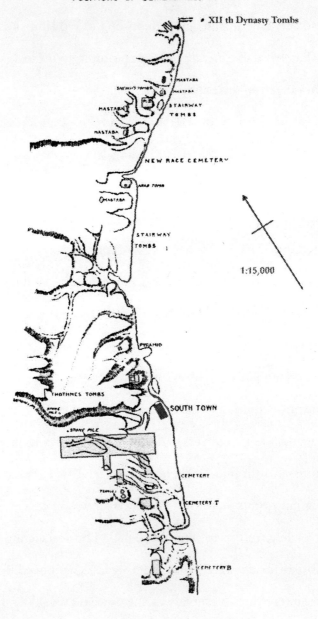

Detail from the map on the previous page

Ashmolean in Oxford, The University Museum in Philadephia and Petrie's own museum at University College, London.[23]

Petrie had to work very hard to maintain this theory of a foreign invasion, completely expelling the native Egyptian population, supposedly occurring during a time known by Egyptologists as the first intermediate period. (That is approximately 2200BC to 2000BC – i.e. between the 5th and 11th Egyptian dynasties.). Even with one eye shut Petrie keeps finding counter examples to his theory, and many later commentators think that Petrie's failure to complete a full documentation of the site was in part an admission that his earlier theory was untenable. A full report would need to include the larger tombs, mysteriously elided from the first publication, and which are parallel in scale and ideology with 1st Dynasty mastabas (tombs). The Naqada necropolis shows the beginning of a trend of segregating burials along class lines, something that became so characteristic of the dynastic Egyptians and the cult of Osiris.

As the dig proceeded Petrie wrote that those classes of foreign things are no isolated matter but belong to a large population spread over the whole of Upper Egypt.[24] The cemeteries found by Petrie at Naqada were so large that they represented a land of the dead, foreshadowing the western lands of Egyptian mythology.[25]

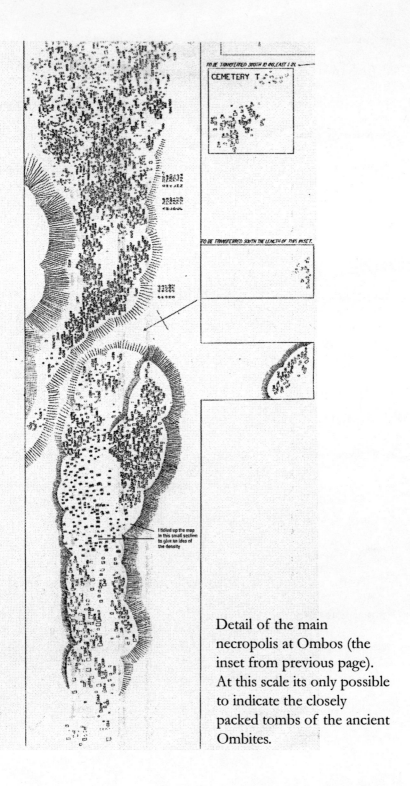

CEMETERY T

I tidied up the map in this small section to give an idea of the density

Detail of the main necropolis at Ombos (the inset from previous page). At this scale its only possible to indicate the closely packed tombs of the ancient Ombites.

Petrie wrote: 'The longer we worked, the more we marked the distinction between these immigrants and the regular Egyptians and the longer we searched in vain for a single object of the many kinds known in Egyptian graves – the headrest, the canopic jars, the pottery, the amulets, the scarabs, the coffins – without finding a single example, the greater appeared the historical gulf between the two people'.[26]

It was Jacques de Morgan who, returning to Naqada two years after Petrie, found the so-called 'degenerate wavy line pots' in direct association with dynastic artefacts. This proved them to be the end point of a stylistic development from pre-dynastic to dynastic times. Which meant that the occupants of the Naqada necropolis could not be some new race but were the direct ancestors of the pharaohs.[27] Naqada must have been one of the major sites from about 4000 - 3000BC in Egypt. The most important Upper Egyptian prehistoric culture is nowadays named after Naqada: the Naqada Period.

It just hadn't occurred to Petrie that such differences could occur within the same culture. He might have considered the radical differences between Catholics and Protestants, which we know has nothing to do with alien migrations by Catholics to Britain? I'd remind you that we were once all Catholics but not one pre-

Reformation Catholic Church remains in the hands of its original congregation.

Ancient Egypt did not have a useful equivalent to our own Latin derived term 'religion' (The nearest is Hem Neter, 'service to the gods'). Even so I hope you will understand my meaning if I say that ancient Egypt was polytheistic and did not have one unified religion or culture. Petrie's fateful walk through the desert led him to the cult of a Hidden God, whom ruled in an ancient city, later deserted. Its inhabitants left materials ranging from the flint tools of the first inhabitants to votive stele in a Temple of Seth left by several kings of the earliest dynasties right down to the time of Ramesses the Great.

Notes

1.   See Lami (1981). Currivan (2004) thinks that geomantic
     orientation is based on linguistics – ie. head to northern
     delta, feet in the first cataract (South); right hand the west;
     left hand the east.
2.   Baumgartel (1970 : 5)
3.   Baumgartel (1970 : 5)
4.   Petrie (1896b : 67)
5.   Hoffman (1984 : 27)
6.   Hoffman (1984 : 66)
7.   Hoffman (1984 : 94)
8.   Hoffman (1987 : 177)
9.   Hoffman (1987 : 193)
10. Hoffman (1987 : 196)
11. Hoffman (1987 : 203)
12. Hoffman (1987 : 212)
13. Hoffman (1987 : 160)
14. Hoffman (1984 : 29)
15. Hoffman (1984: 239)
16. Morgan (2005)
17. Hoffman (1984 : 311)
18. Hoffman (1984 : 380)
19. Hoffman (1984 : 308)
20. Hoffman (1984 : 303)
21. For an account of the affaire Amélineau, whose
     destructive collecting caused a major scandal in its day see
     Hoffman (1984: 267).
22. Petrie (1896 :18)
23. Baumgartel (1970 :4)
24. Petrie (1896 :60)
25. Hoffman (1984 : 109)
26. Petrie (1896 :59)
27. Hoffman (1984 : 116)

2 Sethians and Osirians compared

The differences between the Sethians and the Osirians are rather revealing. Petrie made a list of the differences between both religious groups, of who if any, the Sethian could claim to be the oldest:

Osirians	Sethians
Inscriptions	Rude marks not grouped
Sculptures	Great incapacity of form
chambered tombs	Roofed grave pits
Tombs in cliffs	Graves in valleys
Coffins	Burial in clothing
Extended burial	Contracted burial

Mummification	Dismemberment
Head rests	Decapitation [and re-assembly]
Weapons, bow/arrows	Forked flint lances
Ground cone-shaped axes	Oval chipped flints
Lug axes	Fine flint knives
Copper edged sticks	Quadrangular daggers
Amulets	Ashes
Globular pottery beads	Cylindrical stone beads
Copper mirrors	Slate palettes
Scarabs	fine flint bracelets
Canopic jars	Jars of fat
Wheel thrown pottery	Hand made pottery[1]

Pyramids

It all started with the chance discovery of small stone circles approximately six feet in diameter, made from small flints. These proved to be remains of Roman or perhaps early Christian hermit cells. There was also a wavy line that seemed to mark the 'Nome' boundary, between Ombos and Dendara.[2] A *Nome* is one of forty-two administrative districts, number of the judges of the dead and probably no coincidence. Interestingly each Nome coincides with one of the enormous temporary lakes caused by the annual Nile flood.[3]

Several random objects had been found on the desert floor, then small tombs in places that tradition Egyptology of the time told them they should not be. Significantly the first burials were found near or in streambeds that were now dry but presumably in earlier times had not been so. The burials were by a watercourse or actually on the water table, a layer of

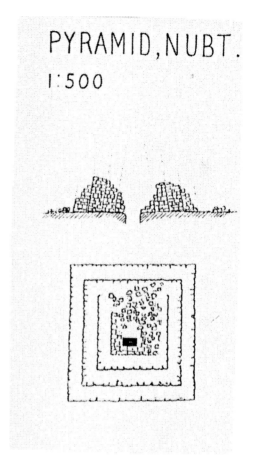

geological shale that lies beneath the top marl and sand that acts as a transmissive layer.

The river Nile, outside of its visible riverbed, flows underground and through this shale layer to a width much greater than what can be seen on the surface. Dig down to this layer and water will gather in the well or depression? This natural water logging would be a well-known phenomenon and would have made mummification difficult if not impossible. But it seems obvious that this was completely intentional. To Petrie it may have seemed 'un-Egyptian' but there are important versions of same phenomena in dynastic Egypt itself, most notably in the Temple of Sety I at Abydos, where the underground Osireion, is resting on exactly this shale layer and as a result forms a natural spring and aquatic burial. This parallel has not, as far as I know, been previously noted.

There may also be a similar intention in the construction of the unfinished subterranean chamber in Khufu's Great Pyramid. Herodotus was told that it was 'Cheops' actually buried in these subterranean chambers, on an island surrounded by water, brought there by a cannel from the Nile.[5] The aquatic nature of the burials is also indicated by the discovery of damage from now extinct white ants.

A remembrance of this is also encoded in the construction of subterranean burial chambers accessible by a long 'well' shaft. These subterranean chambers are placed on the water table and were thus watery places. Mark Lehner in his *Complete Pyramids* tells us that the burial chamber of Senwosret I is now completely underwater, inaccessible to archaeologists due to rises in the water table since ancient times.[5] When first built it lay on the water table and was thus permanently damp and periodically waterlogged.

It could be that all pyramid burials contain an element of this burial by water. Let's remind ourselves of the ways that Seth murders Osiris. It all starts with the donation of a coffin by Seth to his brother. This gift is ambiguous and is difficult to interpret. To the Egyptians, the gift of a coffin helps to guarantee immortality. But when Osiris tries out his coffin, Seth seals the lead box and submerges it in the Nile. This is a good example of an *'historiola', the precedent that causes a spell to work*. Ancient coffins were very often made from lead, and in later times, lead recycled from such coffins was the preferred material for a defixiones or curse tablet. Again it shows the Sethian component both in the content of the curse and indeed the ritual material used for its construction. As with so much in magick, a great number of contemporary practices have extremely ancient precedents – and this use of the 'saturnine' metal is a good example.

Is it a coincidence that lead is also the base metal worked on in alchemy? The term first erupted into the written discourse in an Egyptian context, when the third century Roman emperor Diocletian sought to ban its practice in his re-conquered domain.[6] Gold and lead are both metals with strong Sethian associations, stemming no doubt from his 'Citadel of Gold' - Nubt.

Analysis of this incident yields a crucial key to Egyptian magick. The Osirians view this whole incident with the coffin as a hostile act whereas from the Sethian point of view, it was an ecumenical act, a bow to the Osirian way of death that they as Sethians, did not actually practice with their own dead. This reversal of meaning or intent between both cults is a feature that recurs constantly when studying the dynamics of magick.

The robbed out pyramid of Ombos is perhaps further evidence of how important this place was. It represents the very antithesis of what we might call the Sethian way of death. This elite monument to the dead king may nevertheless have its origins at some transitional stage between both cultures, when the more mercantile and communal Sethians gave way to the Horus kings. Indeed many mysterious features of the pyramids – such as for instance the already mentioned burial on the subterranean aquifers, was perhaps a reminder of the Sethian past.

Petrie recorded that the angles of this otherwise unimpressive pyramid were frequently an even number of retreat on a height of twenty-eight. Twenty-eight has strong lunar associations in the ancient world and its occurrence is no doubt highly significant.

There is evidence here of stone built structures in predynastic Naqada. These predate those of King Den at Abydos, the usual *terminus ad quem* for these techniques. The small sixty foot square pyramid was thought by Petri to be the oldest work he had examined and hence could be pre 4th dynasty! The *tumuli* could also be much older than the conservative pre-roman date. All this stuff largely ignored.

Egyptian death cults?

The cemeteries found by Petrie at Ombos were so large that they represented a land of the dead, foreshadowing the western lands of Egyptian mythology.[7] All Egyptian religion seems bound up with the fate of the personality after death. The Osirians aimed at resurrection in some earthy sphere not too dissimilar to the best of what they were leaving behind. By contrast the original *primitive faith* practiced by the Sethians was focussed not so much on physical resurrection but more on good rebirth! (see below for more on birth imagery). Could it be that this experience of reincarnation was the reason so many Sethian archaisms were secretly encoded into the Osirian cult practice and could never completely be suppressed? You might ask what do I mean – but try to remember how it was when you too believed in reincarnation? Or as it still is in much of south Asia, that the concept is taken as self-evidently true. Put simply, the people of Osiris had concrete memories of the time when they thought and lived as their ancestors the Sethians had – these memories could never be completely denied merely suppressed or coded.

Examples of Ancient Egyptian scepticism about the whole notion of resurrection are not too difficult to find. Known by Egyptologists as 'pessimistic' literature, some view this as part of an as yet elusive Egyptian wisdom literature. It was once fashionable to dismiss 'Egyptian wisdom' as an oxymoron. Egyptians were supposed to be incapable of abstract thought! Nowadays this seems pretty untenable and compositions such as 'The dialogue between a man weary of life with his own 'soul' (Ba)' is a clear counter example. This text that according to Gardiner,[8] is a product of the uncertain times at the close of the sixth dynasty, when various catastrophes were overwhelming Egypt. This is 2200BC but already 500 years, perhaps more, after the construction of the Great Pyramid. The anonymous author writes:

'Even those who shaped granite
to perpetuate in the pyramid
virtues of creation
builders like gods;
their sceptres fell to dust.'

(Translation Reed 1987)

This text has been translated many times since the damaged papyrus was bought from the well-known dealer Anastasi (1780-1857), more famous as the source for the Greek Magical Papyri.[9] It is therefore quite possible that the above text was once a part of a magician's library. Bika Reed is a pupil of the alchemist cum philosopher Schwaller de Lubicz,[9] so should perhaps be treated with a little caution. The original hieroglyphic text was published by Faulkner[10] and there is an assessment of the several dozen other translations.[11]

Is it coincidence that this same 'philosophical' text also contains yet another piece of Sethian mythology? The divine entity IAI is identified by Bike Reed as the ass-eared IAI that does battle with the demon of chaos in the ninth hour of the night. This entity is connected with Seth. Budge felt that it was acting as bait or perhaps as a scapegoat to coax the Apophis serpent to its destruction. The Ass, certainly in later times, is also a Sethian beast. Could IAI be one of the hidden names of Seth? For more data see Budge's translation of the *Book of Gates*, published in Egyptian Heaven & Hell Vol II. Budge based his translation on a transcription of the book as found on the coffin of Seti I, now in the John Soanes museum, London. Belzoni smashed the lid of this magnificent coffin during excavation. More recent translations have had access to a complete version of the text.

The Sethian two stage burial

Less prominent than the high profile necropolises of the Valley of the Kings or Queens, these ancient and often enormous archaic cemeteries have their own significant tale to tell. The maps and plans reproduced above and below show the entire complex, associated urban settlement, and Temple of Seth. Looking at the burials it is possible to begin to understand some of the magical and religious ideas of the people of Seth.

The necropolis was used over a long period of time and some burials are intrusive on top of others. Many tombs are built close to houses, a well shaft descending to the water table, then a southern entrance to small tomb chamber. Children were buried under the floors of the houses, but overall one gets the feeling that the ancestors were kept close by. Objects in the tombs show a marked degree of cardinality – i.e. they are placed at one of the four major directions, the North South axis being most favoured.

The most common laying out position is the foetal, the knees drawn up to the chest, head to the north, facing east. Very significantly, undisturbed graves show the head was removed and placed nearby. It was this feature that led Petrie to say these couldn't be Egyptian burials. Could this be an indication that the people of Nubt thought the dead were somehow a danger to the living? Or perhaps this headless state had some other significance? This headless state immediately brings to mind the lines from a later invocation of Seth discovered amongst the Greek magical papyri, known in contemporary magick as *Liber Samech*. In my earlier book *Tankhem: Seth and Egyptian Magick*, I argued that, although unrecognised by contemporary magicians, this ritual is in fact based upon an ancient invocation of Seth as demonic initiator.

Seth is here called 'the headless demon with sight in his feet'.[12] This was obviously an issue between the people of Seth and the later followers of Osiris. One of the spells in the *Book of Coming Forth by Day* (otherwise known as the *Book of the Dead*, is a protection against decapitation. According to Budge, the most ancient burial customs in Egypt consisted of either dismembering of the body, especially the head or burning. The body was then roughly reassembled, wrapped in a leather bag or exposed as carrion. He speculates this was to do with magick that aims to ward off the dangerous dead. But I say there is more to it than that.

The 'Osirians' who may have been immigrants into the Nile valley, preferred their bodies to remain whole and in the 43rd chapter of what Budge called the 'Book of the Dead' are spells designed to prevent decapitation in the afterlife.[13] This later taboo about decapitation is obviously a bone of contention between the followers of Seth and Horus (defender of Osirian faith).

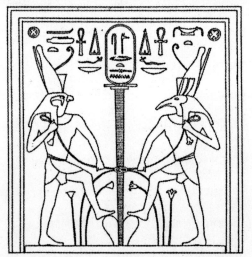

Relief images of
Seth of Nubt and
Horus the Behadit,
from side panels of
enthroned statue of
12th dynasty king
Senwosret I
(Sesostris) c1918-
1875BC. This early
Middle Kingdom
monarch ruled at a
time when military prowess were called upon in campaigns
against the Nubian military culture. Great use was made of the
protection/execration rite - 'breaking the red pots'. His name
means 'Son of Wosret - a local form of the goddess Hathor.
Found along with ten similar examples in the remains of his
pyramid as Lisht. The gods are shown standing on the hieroglyph
of the windpipe and lungs whilst holding the entwined lotus and
papyrus plants, emblematic of upper and lower Egypt -
signifying that both lands are unified in the body of the King.

Seth's companions are known as the Smaiut n Seth, a term that has attracted much attention amongst those with some knowledge of Taoism and Hinduism. The simple meaning of Smaiut, is that when two or more people are of one mind they are said to be breathing together or sharing a breath, a clear enough idea. Hence the hieroglyphic form of 'smaiut' is a windpipe and lungs. Many important stele expressive of this notion of union between two entities, do so by showing them clutching the images of a windpipe and lungs. The political implications of this distinction between being a 'follower' and being a 'companion', literally those who 'breathe together', was obviously as much of an issue to the ancient Egyptians as it is to the contemporary practitioner; where the distinction between the 'rosicrucian' and 'masonic' form of magical organisation is still very relevant. Ask yourself which are you, a follower or a companion?

In the Osirian world, the *Smaiut,* the confederates of Seth are punished by decapitation. It may be that this punishment is something to do with later descriptions of Seth as the 'headless demon' (see *Liber Samech*). Interesting too that the Nome standard and hieroglyphic emblem of Abydos is thought to represent the head of Osiris, found by Isis where Seth had left it on the banks of the Nile. The cluster of ideas around the head and their removal perhaps points to other less negative ideas about the magick of the head – perhaps bearing some comparison to the cult of the head in the European Iron age or Celtic world? Some would argue that the cult of the head was a feature of the Palaeolithic wherever it occurs, including Europe. Michael Dames draws attention to the skull shaped pottery discovered at West Kennet Long Barrow in Wiltshire, UK.[14] Despite more recent academic criticism, Michael Dames' work is, in my opinion, still full of useful symbolic insights.

I've said that Seth has *companions* (Smaiut n Seth) rather than 'Shemsu Hor' those who *follow* Horus. Amongst the companions we might number several upper Egyptian gods with 'Typhonian' sympathies: for example ithyphallic Min later assimilated to the cult of Pan. The goddess Selket, who was the totem of archaic king Scorpion. Sobek the crocodile god, one of whose incarnations provided a toothy end to the archaic pharaoh Menes, or legend has it[15] It's easy to confuse Sobek with Seth, but they were quite separate cults although later priestly equations of the two are intended as an insult.

Petrie thought all Egyptian burials would be laid out in the classic posture of the god Osiris. This position is still widely used in Christian burial, one of many parallels between the cult practice of both religions. But in fact many dynastic burials are also resting on the side, eyes facing east. See for example the Middle Kingdom sarcophagi of 'The Two Brothers' (BM EA 35285) that shows this arrangement. Although here too there are several astonishing hidden elements to the burial.[16]

The standard Sethian position is the foetal crouch, head to south. Professor Hoffman[17] describes it as head south, facing west, with exceptions possibly reserved for outcasts or outsiders. Hoffman doesn't ever discuss Petrie's discovery of head removal and reversal. Another Sethian burial posture, less common is lying on the back, with knees bend up onto the chest. At the time of writing, a rather

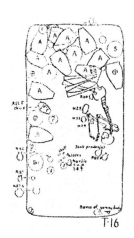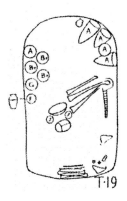

Two sketches from Petrie's notebook of tombs T-16 and T-19. T-16 shows the deposition of the skeleton in the foetal crouch. T-19 the skeleton is disarticulated and incomplete, the skull seems to have been removed then replaced but not in the natural position.

fine pictorial example of this has emerged from the vaults of a
Harrogate museum. Naqada II burials from Medum also had the
head in the north.

The Harrogate Vase

Notes

1. Petrie (1896 :60).
2. Petrie (1896 :11).
3. Butzer (1976).
4. Edwards: (1972 : 86).
5. Lehner (1997 :171).
6. Gibbon (1845 : I.13).
7. Hoffman (1984 : 109).
8. Gardiner (1927 : 24).
9. De Lubizc (1997).
10. Faulkner (1956).
11. Williams (1962).
12. Betz (1986: 103 [PGM V 145]).
13. Budge (1901: p. xxviii).
14. Dames (1996).
15. Hoffman (1984: 289).
16. Reeder (2005).
17. Hoffman (1984: 109).

3 Cannibalism

Now an extraordinary thing. Petrie discovered that 'The whole body was sometimes completely dismembered before burial and artificially arranged'.[1] Which led him to the startling conclusion that the 'bodies were sometimes - with all respect – cut up and partly eaten'.[2] Given the botched nature of the excavations it would be easy to dispute or even ignore Petrie's original impression.

Hoffman throws doubt on the ritual cannibalism thesis, finding a lack of the charring so characteristic, so he says, of marrow extraction. He opts for the thesis that these are indications of human sacrifice of retainers.[3] This is a key moment in the argument and I find myself more on Petrie's side than Hoffman's. Hoffman thinks the occurrence of human sacrifice in the high status cemetery T, is a practice common in early dynastic times, although later dying out and marks the cusp between the primitive institution of the village chief to the more highly organised state and kingship. 'Human sacrifice' he says, 'is a feature of an emerging state[4] rather than a settled one.[5] But why the individual graves rather than 'death pits' found elsewhere?[6]

To me ritual cannibalism fits totally with the desire for good rebirth. It's part of what 'some archaeologists think is this process involving the breaking down of individual personalities, individual people, as they crossed over to the spirit world and entered the community of ancestors'.[7] It has to be said that most modern scholars follow the Hoffman line on Petrie's finds. Despite this I am inclined to side with Petrie. Ritual cannibalism has a clear resonance with the whole eating magick tradition that is so strong a feature of Egyptian magick of all times. This will be discussed in greater detail later, starting with what Ritner calls the divine precedent for this style of magick, the co-called 'Cannibal Hymn' from the pyramid texts:

'The King is one who eats men and lives on the Gods. . .
The King eats their magick, swallows their spirits'
(PT 273-74)

In general among the Sethian burials, the head is removed prior to burial, and used in some unknown rite, perhaps along with the forearms and hands, also removed prior to entombment. The head eventually rejoins the rest of the dismembered body in the tomb, but often not in its natural place or is set looking backwards (facing east). The Nome emblem or standard of Abydos is actually the severed head of Osiris mounted on a pole. There are other examples of this peculiar fetish object that also make an appearance in religious texts such as the *Book of Gates*. In that text, such a fetish is translated as 'The Neck of Ra'. Could such a 'Neck' have been erected as a participant in the archaic funeral feast? They are similar to the Amporites of Solomon's times, the remnants of a great burning (of offerings) at the funeral.

The famous 'wavy handled' jars found in the south of the Naqada graves, show a development or a 'degeneration', depending on your point of view. This might be evidence of a slow impoverishment of the lower classes over time, which might fit with the presence of the so-called high status cemetery T. It is the later variety with 'symbolic' handles that was found in association with dynastic artefacts, and there does mark the end of the sequence.

To the north of the Sethian tombs, Petrie found vessels containing the ash, presumably of a ritual meal of grain and fish.

Also in the grave were some models of the hippopotamus, which after the dog-like 'Seth animal' is one of the most common icons of Seth. Perhaps in this instance, the hippopotamus served to protect the occupant from the dangers of that beast in their journey on, or across the river to the otherworld or rebirth. The hippo here reminding us of the ferryman, the Egyptian 'Charron' Nemty.

Seth as Ferryman

Seth's presence in the boat of Ra, is perhaps the cue to see him to be the ferryman god Nemty, with a similar ambivalent character in myth, open to bribery, and according to the UCL website, shown in formal art exactly like Seth. Actually images of Nemty are very rare, he was though the main deity at the temples of Qaw el Kebir, ancient Tjebu in the tenth Upper Egyptian Nome, Atawla in the twelth Upper Egyptian Nome, pretty much the border between Upper and Lower Egypt, and also at the province of Sharuna.[8]

An episode with the the god Nemty occurs in an ancient text known as the *Contendings of Horus and Seth*. Here's an extract, with the complete version to be found in the appendices:

The Contendings of Horus and Seth

But Seth, the son of Nut, was angry with the Company of Heaven, when they said these words to Isis, the mighty, the god's mother and he said to them: I will take my sceptre of four thousand and five hundred pounds, and I will kill one of you each day. Seth made an oath to the Master of the Universe, saying: I will not contend in this tribunal whilst Isis is in it.

Then Ra-Harakhti spoke to them: Cross you over to the Island-in-the-Middle, and judge you between them, and say to Nemty, the ferryman, Do not ferry across any woman in the semblance of Isis.

So the Company of Heaven crossed over to the Island-in-the-middle, and they sat down and ate bread.

But Isis approached Nemty, the ferryman, as he sat near his ferryboat, and she had changed herself into an aged woman, and she went along all bowed wearing a little ring of gold on her finger. And she spoke to him, saying: Ferry me across to the Island-in-the-middle, for I have come with bowl of porridge for the child. He has been looking after some cattle on the island for five days and he is hungry.

But he said: I was told not to ferry across any woman. But she replied: that is on account of Isis, that that was said?

So he asked her: What will you give me, if I ferry you across to the Island-in-the-middle?

To which Isis replied: I will give you this loaf.

Thereupon he said: What's that to me, your loaf? Shall I ferry you across to the Island—when it has been said to me, Ferry no woman across—for the sake of a loaf?

Thereupon she said to him: I will give you this gold ring. To which he said: Give me the ring. And she gave it to him.

Thereupon he ferried her across to the Island-in-the-middle.

And while she was walking beneath the trees, she looked and she saw the Company of Heaven, as they sat and ate bread in presence of the Master of the Universe in his arbour. Seth looked and he saw her, as she was coming there afar off. Then she uttered an incantation with her magic, and she changed herself into a maiden fair of limb, and there was not the like of her in the entire land. And he really lusted after her.

So Seth rose up, from the picnic with the great Company of Heaven, and he went to overtake her, for no one had seen her except him. He stood behind a sycamore and called to her: I am here with thee, fair maiden.

And she said to him: No, my lord! I was the wife of a herdsman of cattle, and bore to him a male child. But my husband died, and the child came to look after his father's cattle. Then a foreigner came, and he sat down in my byre, and spoke to my son: I will beat you, and I will take away the cattle of your father, and I will throw you out. That's what he said. I wish you would become his protector.

And Seth spoke to her: Shall the cattle be given to the foreigner, while the son of the good man is alive?

And Isis changed herself into a kite, and she flew, and she perched on the top of an acacia. And she called to Seth, and she said to him: Weep for yourself, it is your own mouth that has said it, it is your own cleverness which has judged thee. What ails you now?

And he stood weeping, and he went to the place where Ra-Harakhti was, and he wept. Thereupon Ra-Harakhti spoke to him: What ails thee now?

Seth replied: That evil woman came against me again, that she might beguile me once again, having changed herself into a fair maiden before my face.

Then Ra-Harakhti asked him: And what said you to her?

And Seth told him: I said to her this foreigner's face should be smitten with a rod and he should be evicted and your son put in his father's position.

And Ra-Harakhti said to him: But now look you, you have udged your self; what ails thee now?

And Seth spoke to him: Let Nemty, the ferryman, be brought, and let a great punishment be inflicted upon him, saying: Why didst thou let her cross?—so shall it be said to him.

Thereupon Nemty, the ferryman, was brought before the Company of Heaven, and they removed the soles of his feet.

And Nemty forswore gold to this day in presence of the great Company of Heaven, saying, Gold hath been made to me into an abomination for my city.

Thereupon the Company of Heaven crossed over to the Western Tract, and they sat down upon the mountain. And when it was even, Ra-Harakhti and Atum, the lord of the two lands in Heliopolis, sent to the Company of Heaven, saying: What are you doing, still sitting here? As for these two youths, you will cause them to end their lives in the tribunal! When my letter reachs you, you shall set the White Crown upon the head of Horus, the son of Isis, and you shall promote him to the place of his father Osiris.

Rites of Ombos

All this suggests a meditation. I'm not too sure how you like to do your meditating – maybe if I just tell the story from my own point of view you can see what I'm getting at and put together what you need for your own journey. You might want to look at some similar techniques from other more 'earthy' cultures to help in the construction of your own 'funeral' rite. I've been quite happy to use, at least as points of comparison, material such as the 'Celtic' *cauldron* rites.[9] Don't think of this as a final meditation, but the first of many preliminary sorties into the realm of the dead. At what stage in your journey I can't yet say. But a meditation on the meaning of the Sethian mode of burial will in my opinion yield some profound insights. …

The so-called red 'Goddess of Naqada' - Nephthys or could the
gesture of the arms be intended to represent horns of a cow
goddess like Hathor? Brooklyn museum dated 3500-3400BC (07-
447-505).

The Ombos Rite

My mind sinks back in on itself. I am going back, back a long time ago . . .

I see the ancient glyph of the Meshketyu, the Great Bull, spinning on its axis in the northernmost part of the sky above me. As I watch it spins, counter-clockwise, slowly at first, but soon gaining momentum until it is a blur. Letting go I become aware again of my surrounding. . .

I wake alone in a very tented room, unsure why I am here. I feel warm and comfortable, surrounded by many of my favourite things, viewing the world from a familiar vantage point. An oil lamp burns but somehow I know that even without its feeble light, the room would shine through its own magick – the heka. The walls are lined with new clay pots, some in the shape of animals. I see the familiar outlines of the sacred Hippopotamus, his ample flanks elongated to resemble his Ka, the so-called Seth beast. He is a creature like no other I have known in the physical world. Once again I see myself turning the pages of one of my books, unrolling a scroll, images of him flash into my head.

To the north, above my head, are long conical jars of polished red clay beside others where the red is variegated with black. I see the face of an ancient Goddess known by many names, the earliest is Bat, but later she was called the House of Horus, the Hathor.

Her slender arms are raised and remind me of the horns of an ox, but her hands curve round to cup her breasts. The colour red fills my eye, the colour of Seth. I must be careful not to break these pots or allow others to take them. In times to come these red pots will contain powerful enchantments, anyone who deliberately breaks the red pots will make a most common but effective curse.

Now I see they are filled with the burnt remains of the funeral feast. Has there been a feast? Yes there has been a huge funeral feast, so much food that the groaning table of food defeated the many guests.

In the south, I see wavy handled jars. From their necks the unmistakable aroma of exotic palm oil drifts into my nostrils. My sense of smell is keener than it has ever been before, and the most primeval of memories are awakening. Someone must have gone to a lot of trouble to obtain all these fine things. Would my relatives or friends have done the hard bargaining to obtain such quantities of the scented vegetable fat? It would have to come all the way across the desert from legendary Punt on the West African coast.[10]

My eyes fall on the objects that must have once been so familiar in life. There in the south is the slate used to grind fine malachite cosmetic for my eyes; making them perfect, protecting them from the glare of the sun. The sight of the familiar objects evokes memories from my earliest childhood, when my mother first gave me my very own slate for cosmetics. Little more than a toy, you remember how I spent many hours making pretend eye paint with a little river mud or wet sand. It was such a part of everyone's life that in death a slate of a totally impractical size is there for me, as a remembrance. The sight of it reminds me of all the kinds of cosmetic slate each echoing the many clans that inhabit this ancient town. Most are the standard rhomb or trapezoid the largest of all

Pink limestone funeral vessel, which seems to be a hippopotamus with a canid head very like the traditional Seth beast. Predynastic Naqada II 3600-3250BC BM EA 53888

the clans, almost as many are the double or single headed birds, turtles, hippopotamus or even the elephant.[11]

They are the signs of the mother. You know and love my father but it is the mother's clan that matters most. Her sign is everywhere, from the cosmetic slate to the marks scratched on all our pottery – the pentagrams.

Your hair is again long and luxuriant as it was in your prime when like everyone, male or female, it was held in place with a beautiful comb carved from the bones of a Seth beast, the hippopotamus. Beads of all kinds are there, especially carnelian, a blood red stone that some say represents the eye of Horus damaged by his brother Seth during their many fights.

The thought of a fight makes me reach for my hip, my hand falling on a flint knife. My fingers search for the lineaments that mark it out as a Sethian or Horian, or perhaps they are unsure and the craftsman has successfully blended them together.[12] This knife is special, so distinguished; though copper or even iron is stronger, flint is so abundant and cheap. The desert stone is everywhere in the tools of daily life, the flint sickles used by the harvesters, broken flint knives and tools litter the desert floor and necropolis. But nothing can compare with these exquisite wrought flints that accompany you in your grave. Only a master from a long and ancient

Two further Hippopotamus 'fetishes' from tombs at Naqada, now in the British Museum.

line could have made such a magnificent weapon. Its qualities are

magical and will defend you against every vicissitude.[13] Although

others knives and lances lie nearby, it is on your ancient flint knife

that your hand instinctively falls when any danger looms. And in

the journey to come, there may well be a fight . . .

Notes
1.   Petrie (1897 : 32).
2.   Petrie (1897 : 32).
3.   Hoffman (1984 : 116).
4.   Galvin (2005).
5.   Hoffman (1984 : 261).
6.   Hoffman (1984: 275).
7.   Wallis (2004).
8.   Eighteenth Upper Egyptian Nome.
9.   Fries (2004 : 426sq).
10.   Petrie (1896 :40).
11.   Petrie (1896:43)4 elephants, 15 turtles, 11 birds, 60 double
      birds, 99 etc .
12.   The variety of flint knife is another way of distinguishing
      Sethian from Osirians. according to Petrie the Pitt-Rivers
      ivory knife handle from Sohag, is a blend of both ethnic
      groups.
13.   Petrie (1896 : 50).

4 Temple of Seth

Ancient Ombos, the Citadel of Gold, crouches on a large plateau above the Nile floodplain, and beneath the great escarpment, that separates the Nile from the vast ocean of sand, that is the western desert. It's an obvious place for a settlement, protected from the Nile floods yet within easy reach of the desert roads. Nearby is an ancient ruined pyramid, whose diminutive and ruined state should not blind us to the fact that this may be one of Egypt's first. It's certainly earlier than the great pyramids, and some have speculated on its connection with Peribsen, the second dynasty king, whose name is often linked with the so-called 'Seth rebellion'.

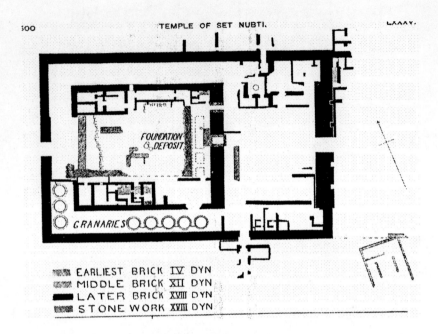

Plan of Temple of Seth from Ombos. The earliest brick structure
is from fourth dynasty and follows the standard east-west
orientation, although one section at the bottom left of the
picture seems to be orientated to the north. The whole is about
250 foot on long axis.

This theory, first propounded by the eminent Egyptologist Newberry, was based on the analysis of artefacts such as the Peribsen stone, now in the British Museum. Interpretation of the stone is greatly aided by a drawing, in which the various elements of early Egyptian titulary are clear – the serekh, or archaic square enclosure – within which are four hieroglyphs spelling the king's name – 'pr-ib-sn' whose name means 'Hope of All Hearts'. Convention stipulates that a hawk, representing Horus should sit atop the serekh, but in this case, the hawk was erased in antiquity to be replaced by a red coloured Seth animal. From evidence such as this Newberry[1] reasoned that there might have been some kind of (temporary) reversal in the otherwise steady rise of the followers of Horus, perhaps some kind of religious or political rebellion[2] although, this kind of reasoning is rejected by later scholars.[3]

Examination of the Egyptian 'Doomsday' book, demonstrates that there were once many temples of Seth through the whole of Egypt, especially in the Sethite districts. Petrie excavated the modest tomb of a prince who was also the chief prophet of Seth(?) Nubti, his name was Bak or Baky.[4]

The temple was rebuilt by Ramesse II and deserted after the Bubastite age of Sheshenq etc. It must once have been a magnificent structure. Petrie[5] describes a magnificent lintel dedicated by

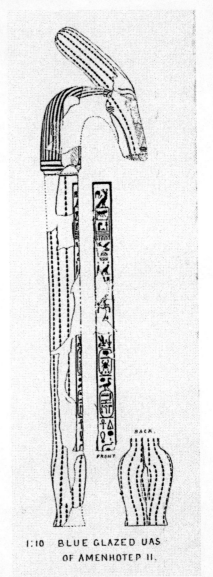

1:10 BLUE GLAZED UAS
OF AMENHOTEP II.

The sceptre or staff is known as a 'was' or 'uas'. As a hieroglyph looking just the same, is pronounced 'was' and means 'power' or 'dominion'. This artefact was reconstructed, with much plaster, from fragments of the turquoise blue glazed ware found by Flinders Petrie in a chamber of the Temple of Seth at Tukh (Nubt) near Koptos. It is decorated with the titulary of Amenhotep II (1427-1401BC) in black down the front of the staff. Two of the cartouches contain his names "Aa.kheperu.ra, Amenhetep. (II) Neter.heq.uast." Its museum number is 437-1895, and it was given by H.M. Kennard. It measures approximately 216 x 48cms.

Thutmose I, one of Egypt's more remarkable military campaigners, sometimes called Egypt's Napoleon. Circa 1493BC he attacked and destroyed the powerful Kerma state in Upper Nubia, beyond the fourth cataract of the Nile. Details of the power, antiquity and influence of the Nubian state is another piece of hidden history, only now being explored.[6] With what we now know of the King's Sudanese struggles, perhaps he was grateful to Seth for his aid in the struggles with Egypt's powerful northern neighbours – I think so.

Wand

Many interesting Sethian artefacts were found in Naqada's Temple of Seth. In the north-west corner of one room he found a pile of blue glassed ware, which when reconstructed proved to be an enormous seven foot high Was sceptre, whose damaged inscription nevertheless shows some variant names of Egypt's 'Napoleon', Amenhotep II. This object is the largest piece of blue faience glassed ware of its time, and is now tucked away in the Victoria & Albert museum.[7] Seeing this object was a scintillating experience. It is such a lustrous blue that even before I saw it, the room was positively glowing, the light reflected off the calligraphy of the divine name *Allah* as executed in the fine ceramics a later period.

The Crooked Wand

The 'Crooked Wand' is the title of a chapter in a recent book.[8] In this book I continue my exploration of the mysteries of Seth first adumbrated in my earlier work on sexual magick.[9] I coined the term *Tankhem,* for this fusion of eastern tantrik and western occultism that is so well represented in the cult of Seth. This is of course, also the essence of Kenneth Grant's use of the terms *Typhonian or Draconian,* of which my own views are an obvious development. I also coined the term 'Setanism' to try to disentangle the cult of the 'Hidden God' from later, admittedly highly interesting but loaded interpretations of the cult of Lucifer or Satan.

Almost as soon as the ink was dry, the 'demon of incompleteness' set to work, and new material turned up. In my opinion this vindicated some of the more enigmatic material in *Tankhem,* for instance the inclusion of an astral temple drawn from Abydos, the chief cult centre of Osiris, Seth's dialectical opposite. This seemingly counter-intuitive move makes sense because *deconstruction* of the cult of Osiris reveals the mysterious cult of the 'Hidden God'.

But for now, I want to add a little to the material on the nature of the wand. In case you've forgotten, Crowley tells us 'The Wand is the principal weapon of the Magus, and the *name* of that wand is the Magical Oath.'

A few months back, I was fortunate enough to have been provided with a very close view of a *Was* sceptre in a most unusual manner. Among the finds at Ombos were the fragments of a colossal *Was* sceptre, discovered in a chamber in the north-western corner of the Temple of Seth. The unpromising pile of turquoise blue-glass ware, was reconstructed with much plaster. It is decorated with the titulary of Amenhotep II (1427-1401BC Egypt's 'Napoleon') in black down the front of the staff. Two of the cartouches contain his names "Aa.kheperu.ra, Amenhetep. (II) Neter.heq.uast. It measures approximately 216 x 48 centimetres.

Many other interesting Sethian artefacts were found in the temple. Naturally I wanted to see them. But again, because of the Sethian connection they have ended up in an obscure and lonely ceramics gallery of the Victoria and Albert Museum!

'It was still only just ten o'clock, and the doors of the museum were just opening to a few early visitors. I smelt the floor polish and I swept through the quiet galleries heading for the restaurant. I picked up a map from reception and looked at it over coffee. None of the rooms mentioned anything Egyptian; I'd have to ask. Confusion at the information desk, they'd never heard of such a thing, was it sculpture, metalwork, how large? I wasn't sure, maybe I'd just explore and see if I could find it, maybe I'd got it wrong.

Parting shot from receptionist, 'try Islamic ceramics, room 182, sixth floor.' Yes, I'll do that.

The lift doors opened onto the deserted ceramics gallery, the words from Oman Khyam flashed into my mind making me smile 'many a beauty destined to bloom unseen.' A quick look at the plan following the narrow gallery to the right, the golden sunlight streaming beneficently from the skylights. The pots aged visibly as I walked, modern, then British, European, Renaissance, now Islamic. I stopped and ran my fingers over a rough terracotta olive jar, Greek or Cretan? I walked on, my eyes falling on the greens and yellows. Now the pots from every case, blue, everything blue, fragments, must be old, special in some way, Arabic writing – the name of God, blue-green patterns, maybe from the wall of an old mosque. I'd reached the final teak and glass cabinet. 'Seth' I thought to myself, 'I know you're here somewhere, I can feel you.' I looked back, gasped, there he was, and my body tingled. In a case in the centre of the gallery, but out of sight until one looked backwards was this god, concealed in more ways that one, truly the 'hidden god'.

The god's inscrutable gaze fell on me, revealing all. Taller than me by more than a foot, his downward curving snout, thick and massive like a hippopotamus. Tiny arms, not the square cut eyes, but a massive domed fez-like head. His body a massive stout column,

THE BULL OF OMBOS

Above: The colossal was scepter from the Victoria and Albert Museum, London. **Below**: 'Magical knife' or wand, from National Museum of Scotland, Edinburgh (with detail superimposed), all photographs by the author.

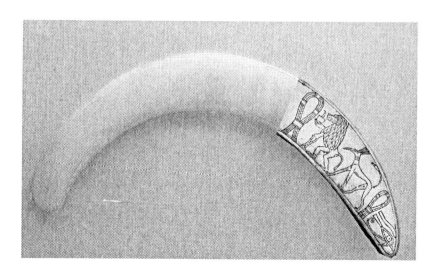

adorned with hieroglyphs, the triple name of a king. The curves of the hips, the stubby legs. Lines of black raindrops flowed over Seth's body. And all over the lustrous faience blue, still stunning after the four thousand years since this sceptre was buried in Ombos, Seth's town. Desert sand and natron. I stared up to the mouth stretched and crinkled into a sardonic smile. My eyes met the hooded gaze of the god, and the words 'Be not unaware of me oh Seth, if you know me then I shall know you.' echoed through the gallery.

Well it was spooky – but calming down I took lots of photographs and transcribed the hieroglyphs into my notebook. The wand's large size helped clarify some of the subtle detail. For instance the forked foot of the wand are actually the stylized rear legs of an aquatic animal. And either side of the head, are two prehensile front legs. So the *Was* sceptre represents a highly stylised, aquatic quadruped. I'll leave it to you to work out what that might be. (see photograph)

There was another wand commonly used in ancient Egypt, and this too bore an image of Seth, as indeed one would expect in operations of a more magical / esoteric nature. Many examples of this kind of wand have been found, and some of the finest are displayed in the more important museum collections. Most museums have numerous other examples of this type of wand in their vaults. This instrument is constructed from a male hippopotamus tusk. The tusk shape shows a clear Sethian association, both from its material and decoration. Its curved nature reminds us of the lunar mysteries that are the secret meaning behind the 'tantrik' contending of Seth with Horus. These wands were used in acts of highly personal magick, the most quoted example being to ward off hungry demons during the critical moments of childbirth and infancy.

Examples of such wands show they were well used and treasured over several generations. The pointed tip shows signs of wear, as if it has been repeatedly used to draw mystical signs, in sand or clay. It is also likely that the wand was used to 'encircle', a primary element of ancient Egyptian magick, as for example in the 'cartouche' inscribed around the name of the King. When the tips broke off from repeated use, the ends were pinned back in place.

Seth

One of Seth's most common epithets is as a denizen of Ombos, to give it its Egyptian name Nubt. "A royal offering to Seth of Ombos, the son of Nut, the mighty one on the prow of the ship and to all the gods in Ombos."[10]

Taken together with the accumulated archaeological evidence of the kind given above, it seems fairly clear that Ombos really is a very ancient centre of the cult of Seth. And this extraordinary archaeological site, deserted in antiquity, does indeed present us with the remains of a temple of Seth. Due to the later ruin of the cult, examples of Sethian temples are extremely rare. And judging by Petrie's write-up, the temple existed there pretty much right from the beginning of Egyptian history, before the coming even of the pharaohs. In fact it spans the transition of Egyptian culture from primitive communism to the kingship model we all know and love as Egypt of the dynasties, that period between approximately 3500BC to the death of Cleopatra. The temple of Seth and its surrounding ancient metropolis, was built and rebuilt many times over this period of several thousand years, changing the orientation to a local west, determined by the orientation of the river Nile at this point. The foundation of the underlying archaic structure still discernable to the expert eye seems to be orientated to the north.

The Temple of Seth of Nubt is situated just north of the ancient settlement (see map). Many interesting Sethian objects were found here, including the man sized Was Sceptre discussed above. The latest structure was dedicated or rededicated during what Egyptologists call the New Kingdom when it received contribution from various kings of the 18th Dynasty. (Thutmose I, & III, Amenhotep II and several Ramessids.[11]

The date of the New Kingdom is sometimes given as (1539-1075BC). Our time line would start here at Naqada, before the unification of Egypt and rise of kingship – a characteristic associated most with the god Horus. Records of these early experiments in monarchy are incomplete, and this is known as the archaic period. As the hegemony of the kings solidifies we call that period the Old Kingdom, during which time the pyramids were built etc. There was some falling apart, a period called the first intermediate, followed by a revived or Middle Kingdom, that again collapsed under the onslaught of an Iron Age culture known as the Hiksos or Shepherd Kings. The rule of the Hiksos is followed by another revival or national liberation bringing a New Kingdom, perhaps culminating in the celebrated 19th dynasty Ramesside Kings.

Interestingly the rededication of the temple took place after the so-called rule of the 'Shepherd kings', themselves renowned for adoption of the cult of Seth. Undoubtedly all Egyptian rulers had a use for Seth's more martial qualities. But despite these new buildings, Seth, as we know, was no stranger to Ombos. The earlier Seth temple is, according to the experts, almost certainly from the

Old Kingdom times of the fourth dynasty and before that into the

dawn of time.

Petrie found that the town of Ombos and its temple was

deserted after the 'Bubastite' age, i.e. when Kings of the 22nd dynasty

(945-715BC) ruled from the Town of Bast in the Delta.

Notes
1.   Newberry (1922).
2.   Newberry (1922).
3.   Te Velde (1967).
4.   Petrie (1896b : PL LXXIX).
5.   Petrie (1896b : 67).
6.   Welsby, & Anderson, (2004) catalogue for *Sudan: Ancient Treasures*, British Museum 9th September 2004 – 9th January 2005.
7.   Room 132, Level six.
8.   Morgan (2005).
9.   Shual (1986).
10.   *Urk.* IV, 1437, 8. quoted in Te Velde (1967: 99).
11.   Baines & Malek (2000 : 110).

5 Seth's Town

Stories concerning the inhabitants of the town still captured the attention of Roman authors such as Juvenal, whose fifteenth satire seems to possess a kernel of truth. In it, Juvenal provides us with a slightly garbled account of the enmity between the inhabitants of Ombos and Dendara.

Juvenal's 15th Satyr:

Juvenal SATIRE XV: AN EGYPTIAN ATROCITY[1]

WHO knows not, O Bithynian Volusius, what monsters demented Egypt worships? One district adores the crocodile, another venerates the ibis that gorges itself with snakes. In the place where magic chords are sounded by the truncated Memnon,[2] and ancient hundred-gated Thebes lies in ruins,

men worship the glittering golden image of the long-tailed
ape. In one part cats are worshipped, in another a river fish,[3]
in another whole townships venerate a dog; none adore
Diana, but it is an impious outrage to crunch leeks and onions
with the teeth. What a holy race to have such divinities
springing up in their gardens! No animal that grows wool may
appear upon the dinner-table; it is forbidden there to slay the
young of the goat; but it is lawful to feed on the flesh of man!
When Ulysses told a tale like this over the dinner-table to the
amazed Alcinous, he stirred some to wrath, some perhaps to
laughter, as a lying story-teller. "What?" one would say, "will
no one hurl this fellow into the sea, who merits a terrible and
a true Charybdis with his inventions of monstrous
Laestrygones and Cyclopes? For I could sooner believe in
Scylla, and the clashing Cyanean rocks and skins full of
storms, or in the story how Circe, by a gentle touch, turned
Elpenor and his comrades into grunting swine. Did he deem
the Phaeacian people to be so devoid of brains?" So might
some one have justly spoken who was not yet tipsy, and had
taken but a small drink of wine from the Corcyraean bowl, for
the Ithacan's tale was all his own, with none to bear him
witness.

I will now relate strange deeds done of late in the
consulship of Juncus,[4] beyond the walls of broiling Coptos; a
crime of the common herd, worse than any crime of the
tragedians; for though you turn over all the tales of long-
robed Tragedy from the days of Pyrrha onwards, you will find
there no crime committed by an entire people. But hear what
an example of ruthless barbarism has been displayed in these
days of ours.

Between the neighbouring towns of Ombos and Dendara
there burns an ancient and long-cherished feud and undying
hatred, whose wounds are not to be healed. Each people is
filled with fury against the other because each hates its
neighbours' Gods, deeming that none can be held as deities
save its own. So when one of these peoples held a feast, the
chiefs and leaders of their enemy thought good to seize the
occasion, so that their foe might not enjoy a glad and merry

day, with the delight of grand banquets, with tables set out at
every temple and every crossway, and with night-long feasts,
and with couches spread all day and all night, and sometimes
discovered by the sun upon the seventh morn. Egypt,
doubtless, is a rude country; but in indulgence, so far as I
myself have noted, its barbarous rabble yields not to the ill-
famed Canopus. Victory too would be easy, it was thought,
over men steeped in wine, stuttering and stumbling in their
cups. On the one side were men dancing to a swarthy piper,
with unguents, such as they were, and flowers and chaplets on
their heads; on the other side, a ravenous hate. First come
loud words, as preludes to the fray: these serve as a trumpet-
call to their hot passions; then shout answering shout, they
charge. Bare hands do the fell work of weapons. Scarce a
cheek is left without a gash; scarce one nose, if any, comes out
of the battle unbroken. Through all the ranks might be seen
battered faces, and features other than they were; bones
gaping through torn cheeks, and fists dripping with blood
from eyes. Yet the combatants deem themselves at play and
waging a boyish warfare because there are no corpses on
which to trample. What avails a mob of so many thousand
brawlers if no lives are lost? So fiercer and fiercer grows the
fight; they now search the ground for stones —the natural
weapons of civic strife—and hurl them with bended arms
against the foe: not such stones as Turnus or Ajax flung, or
like that with which the son of Tydeus struck Aeneas on the
hip, but such as may be cast by hands unlike to theirs, and
born in these days of ours. For even in Homer's day the race
of man was on the wane; earth now produces none but weak
and wicked men that provoke such Gods as see them to
laughter and to loathing.

To come back from our digression: the one side,
reinforced, boldly draws the sword and renews the fight with
showers of arrows; the dwellers in the shady palm-groves of
neighbouring Dendara turn their backs in headlong flight
before the Ombite charge. Hereupon one of them, over-
afraid and hurrying, tripped and was caught; the conquering
host cut up, his body into a multitude of scraps and morsels,

that one dead man might suffice for everyone, and devoured it
bones and all. There was no stewing of it in boiling pots, no
roasting upon spits; so slow and tedious they thought it to
wait for a fire, that they contented themselves with the corpse
uncooked!

One may here rejoice that no outrage was done to the
flame that Prometheus stole from the highest heavens, and
gifted to the earth. I felicitate the element, and doubt not that
you are pleased; but never was flesh so relished as by those
who endured to put that carcass between their teeth. For in
that act of gross wickedness, do not doubt or ask whether it
was only the first gullet that enjoyed its meal; for when the
whole body had been consumed, those who stood furthest
away actually dragged their fingers along the ground and so
got some smack of the blood.

The Satire continues with talk of the 'Maeotid'[5] altar; for if we
may hold the poet's tales as true, the Tauric founder of that accursed
rite does but slay her victims' and the 'eloquent Gaul has trained
the pleaders of Britain, and distant Thule[6] to the Greeks distant
land or island to the North West of Norway which 'talks of hiring
a rhetorician.' At the time Juvenal wrote, Dendera was the centre
of cult of Hathor, Isis and to lesser extent Horus. The satire is
dated to AD127, during the consulship of Juncus. Taken at face
value it seems to indicate that the followers of Hathor and of Seth
were mortal enemies. But I'm inclined to think that the vehemence
of their enmity indicates that things were not always so.

Pharaonic remains

Amongst the Pharaonic remains is a lintel dedicated by Thutmose I (Tahutmes), which was abandoned and destroyed soon after its discovery! Petrie thought it here represents the *Ba* bird of the king, which is said to fly up to leave when the king died. But I think it shows Seth the Ombite and Horus the Behadit (indicated by the

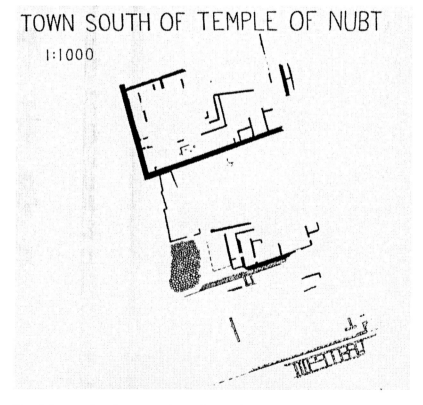

TOWN SOUTH OF TEMPLE OF NUBT

1:1000

Petrie's very inadequate plan of 'South Town', the ancient city, whose inhabitants are buried in the enormous necropolis of Ombos. It is difficult to get any impression of what the Citadel of Seth was actually like apart from it being about a third the size of ancient Ur!

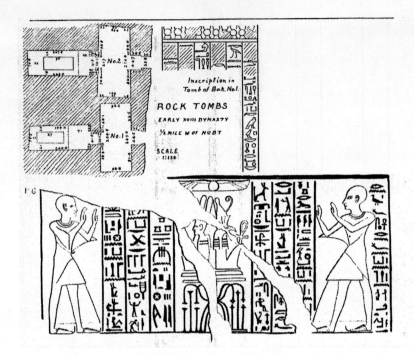

Top: Modest tomb of a prince who was also the chief prophet of Seth(?) Nubti, his name was Bak or Baky. **Middle:** Prince Sen-nefer, devoted to his lord, Makheru. **Bottom:** Temple foundation deposit made by Thutmoses III that included a model ax inscribed 'the good god, Men-kheper-Ra, beloved of Seth of Nubt.' Also a tiny girdle tie carved in ebony.

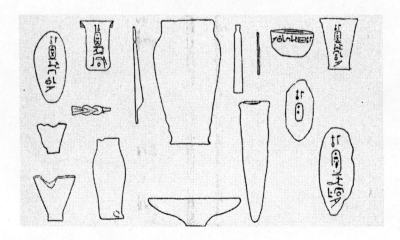

winged disk hieroglyph) giving life to the hawk perched on the *Ka* name of the king. This, as Petrie rightly says, is 'good evidence of the nature of the hawk' which can represent many things - the deified king, the gods Horus, Ra indeed even Seth.[9]

Also found is the fragment of a statue of another thirteenth dynasty king Sen-Nefer. It reads:

> 'May the king give an offering and Seth of Nubt, son of Nut, very valorous, at the front of the Sacred bark; and all the gods who are in Nubt, may they grant the receiving of food that appears upon the altar, of every good and pure thing, the offering of frankincense on the censer daily, to the ka of the hereditary prince, the watchful overseer, loyal to his lord, the steward of …. prince of the southern city of . . . Sen-nefer, devoted to his lord, Makheru.' (Petrie 1896b: 68 PL LXXXIII)

Petrie also discovered a temple foundation deposit made by Thutmoses III that included a model ax inscribed 'the good god, Men-kheper-Ra, beloved of Seth of Nubt.' Also a tiny girdle tie carved in ebony.

Origins of Egyptian Kingship & the 'Naqada' hypothesis

It was once thought that 'many of the most distinctive attributes of the Egyptian concept of divine kingship are not native or restricted to Egypt but belong to a larger – pan-African context.'[9]

However 'archeologically, historically and socially, the social and economic underpinnings of African kingship can be traced to late pre-dynastic and early dynastic Egypt and were not present even in lower Nubia before about 3300BC at the earliest. The institution of divine kingship, therefore was an Egyptian (specifically Upper Egyptian) invention and need not be relegated to some limbo outside of history.[10] Again the supposed occurrence of human sacrifice is a clue to the relative newness of the African kingdoms for 'human sacrifice is a feature of an emerging state rather than a settled one'.[11]

Hierakonpolis in Upper Egypt is an ancient town known in Greek as 'City of the Hawk'. In the Egyptian language this most important of places was called 'Nekhen' city of the 'falcon headed Horus'. This was/is the largest pre-dynastic settlement ever discovered. Now waterlogged by the rising waters of the Aswan dam. It began life as a 'Gerzean' town, and has the oldest standing remains in Egypt, the fort of Khasekhemiu (the last ruler of the II dynasty). Like many Upper Egyptian settlements it was deserted 4000 years ago but continued to receive honours for its connection with Ancient Egyptian kingship and the origin of the 'Golden Horus' name. 'Golden Horus' being an image of Horus perched atop a gold necklace. Bearing in mind the association of Ombos, the 'City of Gold' with Seth, this image of the 'Golden Horus' may well be yet another of the triumphal variety. The celebrated Palette of Narmer, thought once to be Egypt's first king, was discovered here.

Modern research has again rather darkened the mystery, showing that the unification of Upper and Lower Egypt was a lot less neat than the defeat of one king by another.[12] 'Sadly, we do not know for sure where this most graphic piece of evidence, the Narmer Palette, actually came from. It was evidently found near the main (foundation?) deposit, but not actually with the other material. From Green's field notes (Quibell kept none!) it seems to have been found a metre or two away, and Green noted in the 1902 publication that it was found in a place directly associated with an apparently proto-dynastic level, which would date it a generation or two before the unification of the two lands in 3100BC. But two years earlier in the first publication on Hierakonpolis by Quibell, it was labelled as coming from the main deposit, a feature that may be as late as the Middle Kingdom (c2130-1785BC). If we knew for certain that the magnificent palette came from a securely dated stratum then it would be fairly certain that Narmer himself had deposited this monument in the temple of his capital to commemorate his conquests of the north.'[13]

The discovery of ancient Naqada (Ombos) led many to believe that they had discovered the beginnings of the mythological conflict of Seth & Horus, in some kind of socio-political struggle between the people of nearby Hierakonpolis (City of the Hawk) and Naqada, (Citadel of Seth the Ombite). This is known as the 'Naqada hypothesis'. Te Velde, the great Sethian scholar, asks the question how can the historical record of the fashioning of a nation function as a religious myth?[14] This idea has influenced a whole tranche of commentators[15] into the idea that following this political conflict, Seth, a formerly benign god somehow goes bad. Te Velde rightly counters that this 'ignores the possibility that Seth was already malignant, i.e. there is no record of a time before the unification, when Seth had the supposedly pure, beneficent nature.[16] In other words, It's quite likely that danger and passion was *always* a key part of the archaic nature of Seth. Te Velde also finds that 'the idea of historical war between two people does not sit well with the contention between two gods being imbued with homosexuality from the beginning'.[17] Furthermore, one must ask why is war not mirrored elsewhere in the mythology of other Egyptian gods? If anything, we must follow Henry Frankfort who sees the conflict of Seth and Horus as mythological symbols of *all* conflict.[18] Much of the mythology of the contendings, looks not so much like war,

Fragments from a black granite statue of Sennefer, a
thirteenth dynasty king. If you look carefully at the hieroglyphs,
you can see Seth on top of the emblem of a golden necklace - as
worn by Hathor the 'Golden'. Stele starts 'an offering that the
king makes to Seth of Nubt, son of Nuit'. The cartouche is from
the right arm, it reads 'Men-keper-ra' (Thothmoses III) of the
18th dynasty.

as some sort of erotic game. Nevertheless it provided a handy pair of opposites that could be used as a paradigm for other forms of conflict. This all fitted well with the supposed propensities of ancient thinkers to divide things into opposing pairs.

Modern research has also tended to undermine Newberry's thesis of a Seth rebellion. Things are a lot less black and white, it is becoming clear that many important developments in Egyptian culture began at Ombos. The robbed out pyramid is perhaps further evidence of how important this place was, and is, the very antithesis of what we might call the Sethian way of death. This elite monument to the dead king may nevertheless have its origins at some transitional stage between both cultures, when the more mercantile and communal Sethians gave way to the Horus kings. Indeed many mysterious features of the pyramids – such as for instance the already mentioned burial on the subterranean aquifers, was perhaps a reminder of the Sethian form of death. The Osirian cult of the dead is perhaps an indicator of the growing inequality in the division of wealth.

It was once the scholarly consensus to ascribe the unification of the two lands of Upper and Lower Egypt to political and military campaigns led by the first dynastic pharaohs. Recent research has revealed a much more complex process of shifting alliances with

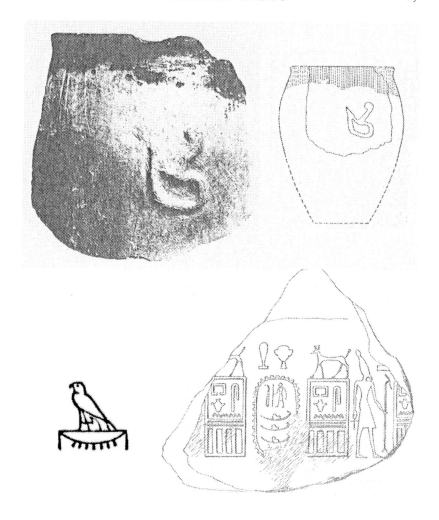

More puzzles: **Top:** a fragment of ancient pottery with the earliest known hieroglyph of the 'red crown' supposedly the Lower Egyptian territory of the followers of Horus. It was found at Naqada, Citadel of Seth in Upper Egypt!

Bottom right: Unbaked clay document sealing from the tomb of Peribsen at Omm el Qa'ab, Abydos. Although called 'King of Upper & Lower Egypt' his Ka name only bears the emblem of Seth. **Bottom left:** hieroglyphic sign for the King's 'Golden Horus' name. It shows a hawk perched on a gold necklace which is also the emblem of Seth of Ombos. There is some debate among scholars as to whether this is an allusion to the hegemony of Horus over Seth (Gardiner).

Verso of the slate palette of Narmer (1st Dynasty) found at City of the Hawk (Hierakonpolis). An artefact of great significance to the Egyptians, in an ancient tradition of use and preparation of eye makeup. This is one of the oldest specimens of Egyptian writing known. The name of the king, written with the nar-fish and the mr-chisel, occupies the rectangle between the Hathor-heads. The other small hieroglyphs give the names or titles of the persons over whose heads they are written; the captured chieftain may have been named Washi (harpoon wa, pool shi). The group at top right was probably intended as explanation of the picture in the centre; at this early date, the gist of complete sentences could apparently be conveyed only by symbolical groups of which the elements suggested separate words. The conjectural meaning is : The falcon-god Horus (i.e. the king) leads captive the inhabitants of the papyrus-land (Ta-mhw ' the Delta'). Information from (Gardiner 1958).

other political entities presenting themselves as candidates for local 'norths' and 'souths'. For instance, 'Naqada' was once itself the capital of the northern part of its ancient territory which is actual in Upper Egypt. Hierakonpolis played a similar role in the southernmost part of the south. Confused, you're not the only one. The traditional 'red crown' of Lower or Northern Egypt, first appear in the archeological record, on a potsherd discovered at Naqada, which is in a territory traditionally referred to as Upper or Southern Egypt. This is also one of the very earliest or archaic hieroglyphs. Also buried at Naqada, is a princess from one of the Northern dynasties, but why should her family make such an apparently perverse choice?[19] It's obvious that the kinship base of developing state is still an open question.

The name of the first Horus king does exhibit a new militarism.[20] Khasekhemui was last of the second dynasty kings (c2775-2650BC) and his cartouche depicts Horus *and* Seth. His tomb at Umm el Qa'ab is said to be 'a fantastic construction'. His 'fort' at Hierakonpolis is similar to one at Shunet el Zebib at Abydos and may actually be a mortuary monument.[21]

Dynastic tombs look like temples perhaps more evidence of the beginning of god-king status. Naqada tombs show differences in status based on wealth but not ontological. At the beginning of the dynasties, Sumerian influence became stronger in Egypt and this, according to Baumgartel[22] is the true origin of the so-called 'palace façade' of multiple niches. In Mesopotamia these are temple designs not tombs. Hence the Egyptian tombs are modelled on temples, not domestic houses. In this, is also an explanation of the confusing number of tomb-temples each member of the new aristocracy possesses - it's all about status.

There has been some argument as to whether the Abydos tombs are 'mere' cenotaphs and the real tombs of the archaic kings of Egypt are at Saqqara in Lower Egypt, near ancient Memphis. However Hoffman thinks that it is more likely that the Saqqara tombs are the cenotaphs[23] although the issue is far from resolved.

Notes

1.   Translated G.G. Ramsay 1918.
2.   The famous statue of Memnon at Thebes, which emitted musical sounds at daybreak.
3.   Oxyrhynchus? And ancient centre of Seth worship.
6   Aemihus Juncus was consul in AD127 which fixes the earliest date for this Satire.
7   The *Palus Maeotis* was the sea of Azov: strangers were there sacrificed on the altar of the Tauric (i.e. Crimean) Artemis.
6   The most distant land or island to the North probably Norway rather than Shetland or Iceland.
7.   It's worth comparing this scene with a similar one found in the pyramid of Senwosret I at Lisht.
8.   Petrie (1896b : 68).
9.   Frankfort quoted in Hoffman (1984 : 257).
10. Hoffman (1984 : 264).

11.   Hoffman (1984 : 261).
12.   The journal *Archéo Nil*, is devoted to predynastic research.
13.   Hoffman (1987 : 129).
14.   Te Velde (1967 : 74).
15.   Griffith (1960).
16.   Te Velde (1967 : 11).
17.   Te Velde (1967 : 39).
18   Te Velde (1867 : 75).
19.   Hoffman (1984 : 324).
20.   Hoffman (1984 : 340).
21.   Hoffman (984: 353), Recent excavations at Abydos
      confirm this supposition (see Galvin 2005).
22.   Baumgartel (1970).
23.   Hoffman (1984 : 287).

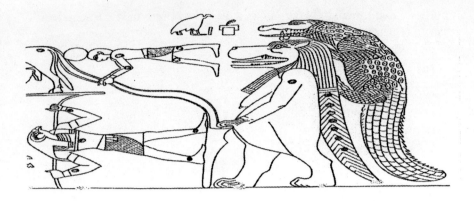

Arrangement of the northern constellations on the astronomical ceiling of corridor II of the tomb of Ramesses VI. Taken from Neugebauer and Parker, Egyptian Astronomical Texts Vol 3 (Texts) p 187 fig 30. In effect this is a detail of the larger scene shown above from Abu Yasin.This Hippo (rrt) holds a flint mooring post, tethering the Bull (Mes) by a chain of gold. The Great Hippo's role like Isis/Sothis, is to prevent the Foreleg going upsidedown in the Duat, holding the fixed point of the universe in its place.

The star maps are amazing - but haven't yet justified the wilder speculations about astrological knowledge in ancient Egypt. The star maps of Edfu are essentially Greek constructions done in an Egyptian idiom. Before that, Egyptian astonomy was focused on the northern constellations rather than the zodiac of our own time.

6 Seth as Bull of Ombos

One incredible important animal avatar of Seth is as the Bull of Ombos. Many bovine images crop up at Ombos, 'in the simplest form those are just a tray with a bull's head, a haunch and some loaves of bread, while some semblance of a tank or trench supplied the idea of water.' Amongst them was found the fragment of a stele with a bull-headed Seth.[1] The decoration of tombs with the actual or simulated crania of the bull (bucrania) can be seen at all periods. Bucrania may well be significant remains of a funeral feast. In the neolithic, feasting was a key means by which surplus wealth was redistributed amongst the tribe. Recent excavations at Kerma in Sudan have exposed an ernormous necropolis. The scale of the feasting can be guessed from indivdual graves where as many as 5000 bucrania adorn the tomb, all carefully arranged by age and sex. The ancient people of what is now the Sudan, also made 'frescoes' of their beloved *dun* cattle. Could this be how amongst them Seth was depicted? Apart from the iconography connected with the bull's foreleg to be discussed below, the image of Seth with a Bull's head or body plays an important role in the religion of ancient Ombos and Sepemeru, both centres of the cult of Seth. Baumgartel's analysis of the predynastic ship 'ensigns' find in the phallic god Min perhaps another candidate for the bull totem, as son and lover of the cow goddess This 'great bull' Ka-mutef 'bull of his mother' was represented by the Z standard or Min's double thunderbolt. In later times this role was appropriated by Horus and shemsu-hor.

Star maps from the tomb of Sety I and elsewhere often show the entire body of a bull tethered to the pole star or held in place by a hippopotamus deity whom we might identify with Tawaret concubine of Seth. In Egyptian star maps discussed below, Hippo is never captioned, prompting some to remind us that they might be separate entities whose distinction is preserved in astronomical monuments.[2]

These icons seems to be carried over into the cult of Osiris in yet another of those examples of negative survival, whereby the images of earlier times become demonic or threatening in another. Te Velde says that the bull's head is often depicted on coffins, in temples, in tombs and significantly as a head-rest. It is also the Apis bull, that carries a mummy to the tomb. In the pap. Jumilhac, Bata, that is Seth carries Osiris on his back in the form of a bull and this is a tradition that dates back to the Pyramid texts and arguable before. Seth as a bull carries Osiris to his grave.

The Tale of Two Brothers

'The Egyptians have the peculiar ability to interpret the same phenomenon from several, and to us, conflicting points of view.' (Neugebauer & Parker 1960: III.191).

'The Tale of Two Brothers' is an account of the conflict between Osiris and his Brother Seth current amongst the members of a cattle cult of Bata, which has strong links with that of worshippers of Seth:

Anpu (Anubis) is the older brother of Bata. They are farmers, Bata spending much of the day with his beloved cattle in the fields. Anpu's wife harbours amorous desires for Bata, who she likens to the 'leopard of the south'. When he rejects her she falsely accuses him of rape. Furious, Anpu tries to kill Bata. But the cattle warn him of the danger and he flees to the 'valley of the acacias'. Bata emasculates himself and tells his brother that from thenceforth he will by magick cause his heart to live in the acacia blossom. If the tree is cut down, the heart will fall to the ground and Bata will die. Anpu will know this because his beer will froth and his wine become cloudy. Anpu must spend seven years searching for the lost heart of Bata. In his new home the nine gods take pity on Bata, fashioning for him a beautiful wife, whom the seven Hathors predict will die by the sword. In due course she is tempted away by the god of the Nile (Osiris), and marries the King. Bata is betrayed and his sacred acacia chopped down. Anpu searches for the heart which has become a seed. Placed in water it revives and returns to Bata's corpse which at dawn is a great bull, a white triangle on his forehead, a mark like vulture on his back, the likeness of a scarab on his tongue. Twice more Bata's former wife betrays him. The bull is slaughtered that she may eat the liver. When from the blood a persimmon tree grows, this too she has hewn down to make a box. When a splinter enters her mouth she become pregnant with a child who becomes the next king. But remembering his previous life this prince Kaoushou has her judged and executed as the seven Hathors had predicted.

Here again we find the motif of castration. An ox is a castrated bull, therefore shares the fate of Seth. The ox is alternatively seen in Egyptian nature history as a bull grown old and therefore of waning fertility and strength.[3] In the Papyrus d'Orbiney of the New Kingdom, there is transmitted to us this story of the two gods Bata and Anubis. Not only the testicles, but also the phallus is cut off. He who does this, however, is not Horus but Anubis, who elsewhere in this papyrus is a form of Seth himself.[4] The motif of castration also appears in the Papyrus Jumilhac,[5] where in a place called Saka, Seth undergoes castration as a bull. His name in this town is Bata. And in a further element of lunar symbolism, the waning moon-god Khons is likened to an ox:

> The moon is his form. As soon as he has rejuvenated himself he is a brilliant (burning) bull, when he is old, he is an ox (shab), because he occasions only darkness. His waxing moon, however, causes the bulls to cover, brings the cows in calf and causes the egg to grow in the body.

The continuation of the image of Seth as bull may also be glimpsed in the cult of Mithras, where its slaughter by the Horus-like Mithras is the cult's core myth, felt by many to also conceal a stellar mystery encoded in the ubiquitous star maps of ancient magick. Interestingly, the tail of the bull killed by Mithras, ends in a form of vegetation often seen in Egyptian images of Seth, and is perhaps some sort of image of fertility of the land.

Anat, another of Seth's consorts, with origins in Canaanite religion, is a cow goddess, and Seth couples with her as a bull.[6] Seth is called a bull, perhaps not because he is a paragon of fertility, but for his strength.

The Aurochs

The aurochs, an extinct bovid, was a sacred beast for many prehistoric cultures, a skeleton of one of these occurs in association with the stone circles of the Nabta playa, near the Sudanese border. The reverence for the aurochs is one good candidate for a universal god form of the nameless aeon. Hence some modern practitioners have found the vibration of the rune 'Uroz' – a powerful way of connecting with the archaic form of Seth.

Notes
1.   Koefoed-Petersen (1948, pl. 43).
2.   Neugebauer & Parker (1960 : 191).
3.   Te Velde (1967: 42).
4.   Te Velde (1967 : 41).
5.   III 18-21 XX 15-18.
6.   R. Stadelmann (1967: 131) quoted in Te Velde (1967 : 37).

7 Hathor

If Seth is a bull or ox (Bata) could Hathor, the cow goddess (Bat), and Seth once have been celestial lovers? Don't you agree that they make a much finer couple than Seth's other partners, Nephthys or Astarte? Interestingly there is a stele from Ombos, recorded by Petrie that shows Seth and Hathor together in harmony, so perhaps relationships between both cults were not always as bad? Elise Baumgartel[1] thought she could identify some of the emblems or 'ensigns' of the ships painted on the many distinctive pots from predynastic sites such as Ombos. What she calls the 'great mother' is a cow goddess, sometimes represented by twin curves, perhaps the same as those featured in the 'ensign' , seen here in a detail from one of those pots from Naqada:

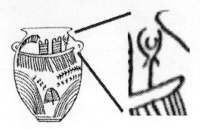

The literal meaning of Hathor is 'House for Horus', just as Isis means a throne for Osiris. Take a look now at the hieroglyphic writing of her name and you can see the Horus hawk perched inside a stylized house. Many of the later names of ancient Egyptian goddesses seem to have this domestic nature - see also Nephthys. The example below comes from the temple for foreigners in Sinai. This association with foreigners being another characteristic shared with Seth.

Because of the oft mentioned lunar associations of the Horus Hawk, it is sometimes speculated that Hathor's name might mean 'lunar mansion'. Incidentally, 'Horus', literally means 'face' rather than 'Hawk'. The common Egyptian word for hawk is 'Bik' not 'Hor' - which perhaps indicates that there is some hidden subtext lying behind Egyptian god names. Hathor's more archaic name: Bat is also the enigmatic standard for Hiw, the 7th Upper Egyptian Nome. The meaning is unknown, a fact in itself indicative of great antiquity.

Hiw was one of those archaic settlements that formed around ritual structures in the landscape of Upper Egypt. You'll find it on the map between Abydos and Dendara. Another name for this place is 'Hut-sekhem' or 'Hut' meaning 'mansion of the sistrum'. The local goddess Bat, is personified as a sistrum shaped object with a human head, bovine ears and horns. This is the archaic form of Hathor. There are graves from Naqada II period at Hiw that contain the familiar image of the baying hippopotamus, cast from red clay.

One such object can now be seen in the Ashmolean museum, Oxford.[2] So here is yet another direct association between archaic Hathor (Bat) and Seth!

Not surprisingly, Bat is a stellar goddess; Schume[3] says the stars associated with include Aldebaran the so-called *red* 'bull's Eye' of Taurus. There is also some connection to the star Sirius. If there really was some relationship between Seth and Hathor/Bat, and this also gives us the true connection between Seth and Sothis –

———————————————

'Set the controls for the heart of the sun'. The oldest prototype comes from the XIth dynasty coffin of Heny at Asyut, c2134-1999BC. However due to its fragmentary nature the astronomical ceiling of Senmut's unfinished tomb at Deir el-Bahri, Luxor is the next best early example. Senmut was queen Hatshepsut's (1503-1482BC) most favoured courtier, possibly lover. This detail shows all the important characteristics of this complex glyph: the central scene with the Northern constellations, Horus (An) harpooning the Bull (Mes), shown with red hoofs and Hippo (Tawaret) holding the flint mooring post surmounted by a red circle representing the celestial pole. The groups of gods to the right and left are the attendant deities, including another form of Seth (Imy-sha) and Isis. Parker says these attendants are deities of the lunar days, which have no obvious connection with the Northern constellations. The twelve circles, subdivided into twenty-four are also connected with lunar festivals. I think the lunar observation could still be connected with the northern constellation as markers of most northernly moon rise/ moon set. Similar observation occur in the station stones of Stonehenge. (Parker 1951; Neugebauer & Parker 1960).

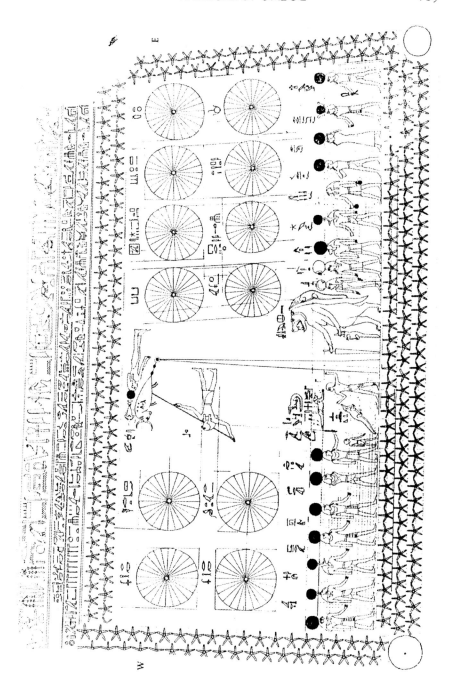

Seth isn't Sothis, the star is his partner, as later it will fulfil a similar role for Osiris. Bat's familiar bovine face and ears appears on one of the most important Egyptian finds, the so-called Narmer palette.

Wherever there is a cow goddess is there not naturally a bull? Further evidence for the pairing of Seth with Hathor, is to be found in an important and complex rite known as the Mithras Liturgi. Following the epiphany of Helios-Mithras, the seven stars of the Plough, step forth as seven bulls, soon followed by seven virgins. These seven virgins have been identified with the seven Hathors of Egyptian cosmology.[4] It's immediately after this that Mithras, a god very much in the Horus mould, places his hand on the shoulder of a young bull, here conflated by the Greeks with the Bear (the later Greek name for the Plough). The initiate, having assimilated himself to the Bear/Plough, becomes weaker as Mithras lays on his hand and must appeal to the god for strength and rebirth.[5]

In the above passage, the magician seems to identify more with the Plough (Seth) than Mithras (Horus). This further corroborates my contention laid out in *Tankhem*, of how Seth does in many ways represent the reality of the human condition.[6]

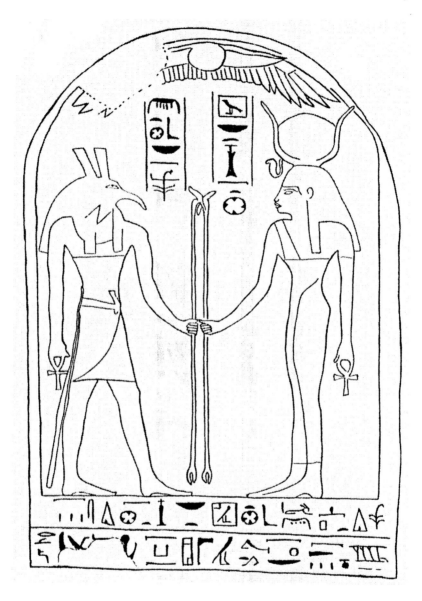

Small Eighteenth dynasty paint and gilded stele of Seth 'Lord of Upper Egypt' and Hathor 'Mistress of Dendara', unearthed near the main group of stairway tombs (Tomb 162) a few feet below the surface in the Temple precinct! Margaret Murray thought the presence of the titulary god and goddess of wine indicated a 'bacchanal' . Analysis of the brick sizes shows the influence of both Sethians and Osirians in various stages of construction and restoration.

Hathor and the Cup or Grail of Babalon

The cup (Tekken) of beer[7] or wine laced with red ochre to taste of blood is surely the prototype for the grail of later legend. It is, along with bread, the quintessential offering of Egyptian magick. The number of examples of its use are too numerous to mention, think only of Omm el Gaab (the 'mother of pots') near the supposed tomb of Osiris at Abydos. There are literally millions of discarded cups strewn across the desert floor. Or think on the discoveries in the secret passageway beneath the Temple of Sety I. In this 'Tunnel of Seth' was discovered the skeleton of a single initiate, who failed to make it to the Osireion, close by lay his offering cup of beer.[8]

Notes:
1. Baumgartel (1970 : 147).
2. Baynes and Malek (2000).
3. Schume (2002).
4. For a version of the Liturgy, see Betz (1986: 51 [PGM IV 475-826]).
5. I'm grateful to Payam Nabarz for drawing my attention to this passage.
6. Morgan (2005).
7. See entry on Beer in the glossary.
8. Morgan (2005).
9. 'The contrast of this text with those in which Isis guards the Foreleg, because it represents Seth, is noteworthy and instructive in demonstrating once again the peculiar ability of the Egyptians to interpret the same phenemenon from several, to us, conflicting points of view' (Neugebauer & Parker 1960: III.191).

The text that separates the Foreleg section from the northern constellations is interesting for its indentification of the former with Osiris: 'Hail Osiris, First Bull: Osiris, bull of the sky, are you . . . The stars of the northern sky, they are your foreleg. They never set in the west of the sky like the decanal stars (baktyw) (but) they travel, going upside down in the night as in the day. Theya re in the following of the Great Hippopotamus (rrt wrt) of the northern sky as your Foreleg, when it foes to the southern sky near the souls of the gods who are in Orion.' Of course it the *off topic* nature of this comparatively late next might be an indication of the fact that Osiris has taken on many of the ancient roles formally held by Seth.

Overleaf: Granite bull sarcophagus from Kom Abu Yasin, now in grounds of Cairo museum (359-341BC). Inner face of lid shows in two strips running from right to left, the positions of Ursa Major for twelve months of the year at sunset, midnight and sunrise. The total rotation anticlockwise should be 180°, but this isn't shown. This suggests a poor copy from an older but lost original. This may also have been copied in the Senmut ceiling, discussed earlier, which also omits the planet Mars. As in so much Egyptian material, it points to a lost golden age. The right hand strip shows a decan list. Five planets, shown as deities in boats, were known to the Ancient Egyptians: Jupiter (Horus of the Two Lands); Saturn (Horus Bull); Mars (Horus of the Horizon); Mercury (Sbq - a name of Seth, meaning unknown) and Venus ('The Star that Crosses'), the latter shown as a goddess. Most of the outer strip that would show the northern constellations is now missing. (Neugebauer and Parker 1960).[8]

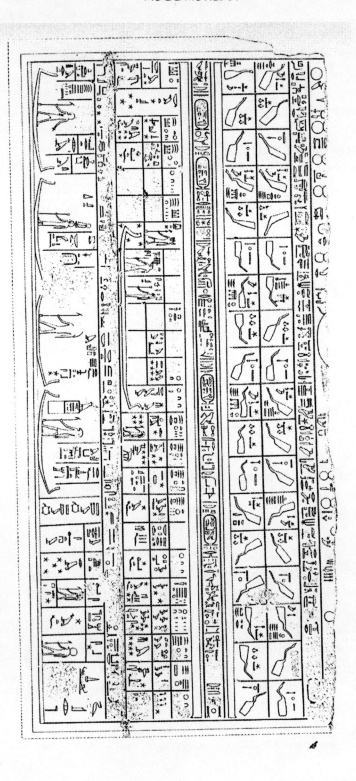

8 The names of Seth

In the Egyptian and Greek sources there are many different spellings and renderings of this god's name. Convenience suggests the Greek version 'Seth' as the most workable.[1] One of the oldest forms of Seth's name may have been *Setesh* or *Zetesh* (s & z were once distinct sounds).

So what does Seth's name mean? Plutarch suggested to 'overmaster', maybe to 'oppose'. Others say it is related to Teshtesh, 'to dismember', sometimes used as a pun on Seth's name. Teshtesh is also the Egyptian name for a griffin, a mythological creature counted amongst the confederates of Seth.

Margaret Murray, Petrie's student and controversial successor, suggested a grammatical original as Se-Bek means 'he who causes to be pregnant', or perhaps 'Se-Tekh' meaning 'who causes intoxication'. Seth and Hathor are respectively the god and goddess of wine.[2] So perhaps the image of the Seth and Hathor found at Ombos mentioned earlier, represent some kind of bacchanalia? Other corroborations of this role, come from later dream manuals, where dreams of craving for drink are seen as Sethian characteristics.

> 'The great lover of women, even though he has at the same time an unadmitted moral orientation, always ready to fight and no enemy of blackmail; he appears as the personification of violence and bad faith.' (Garrot, quoted in Te Velde: 1967:7).

Others have looked at a particular ideogramme, a pictorial sign, that has no phonetic value, but nevertheless helps define the meaning or sense rather than the sound of a word. Ideogrammes are historically the oldest part of the Egyptian language.[3]

Consider the above hieroglyph. Its meaning is unclear, although it is sometimes used as a substitute for the god Seth in Middle Kingdom coffins texts. When used the sign has the sense of separation. The sign itself may represent a carpenter's tool such as a mitre square. Some have suggested this is an instrument for castration, implying that Seth is a eunuch. Te Velde, the great academic authority on Seth, doubts such an interpretation, pointing out that carrying off of Seth's testicles by Horus implies the theft of his seed rather than his masculinity.

A recent piece of research connects this sign in question with *childbirth*. It may seem unlikely, that a god functioning 'as a determinative for words indicating concepts divergent from normal order',[4] should also have an important role in such a normal activity as childbirth, but nevertheless that is what we are going to find later when we look at amulets like the so-called 'fish-tale lance' and the ivory wand.

Egyptian theology is complex, with many hundreds of gods. However, it is possible to recognize family groupings, 'enneads' and 'ogdoads'. Words like 'ennead' or 'ogdoad' may originally have meant nine or eight, but they have come to signify a generic company of gods and goddesses. The major enneads are those of Heliopolis, Memphis, the ogdoad of Hermopolis, the Theban system and the seven fold company of gods of Abydos, as instantiated in the temple of Sety I.

Take for instance, the Heliopolitan Ennead, illustrating as well as any other, Seth's divergent nature. From the primary god Atum-

Ra, arises a pair of gods Shu & Tefnut. They are the primary ancestors; acting as focus of the ancient Egyptian ancestor cult (see *Digital Egypt* for examples). From that nice neat pair of gods, arises, in time, a further pair, Geb & Nuit. And in time, another divine pair, Isis & Osiris. Only this time, the pattern is broken by the irruption of Seth & Nephthys, bursting forth from Nuit's body. So right from his inception, Seth is not born in the normal manner (mshi) but is disorderly, even before he has a name. This fissure continues thereafter with several other gods sharing this disordered birth process. Indeed Horus has no clear female counterpart to share his birth. Hence this whole generation of gods is referred to as the 'accursed', a motif we find repeated elsewhere, as in the Asuras of Hinduism or Aesir of European lore.

Seth's most common epithet is 'Son of Nuit' and this not because he is ever a child, but more an indication of a mother fixation.[5] The mode of his birth perhaps makes him, at least in later times, a natural scapegoat or cause of abortion.[6] Abortion is of course, not so far removed from contraception, which should remind us that Seth, although lord of sexuality is in some respects the enemy of fertility. Although as is perhaps emerging, even if Seth was 'enemy of fertility', was he, especially in his more archaic form, really the enemy of women? You may remember that the first inhabitants of Egypt were 'hunter-gatherers [who] limited their population much as we in industrial times do, although the methods were drastically different. From this we discover that 'high birth-rates and large populations are not the natural state of man.'[7] Seth's involvment in the control of fertility is quite compatible with a function as divine midwife, assisting woman in childbirth. In later times this role laps over into the midwife of knowledge – the divine initiator?

The 'fishtail lance'

The feminine concern of the Ombites is nowhere better illustrated than in an examination of a common amulet known as the 'fishtail lance'. The name is misleading, and stems from Petrie's earlier misidentification of the object as some form of flint spearhead. Previously thought to be an instrument for circumcision, although the provenance of these knives equally in men and women's tombs argues against such a usage. Don Webb, in his groundbreaking book *Seven Faces of Darkness*, favours the idea of this object being an instrument for castration, a echo of the contendings, where Seth is castrated by Horus. This casts Seth in the role of divine eunuch, an idea otherwise dismissed by Te Velde, the main scholarly authority of the mythology of Seth, pointing out that carrying off Seth's testicles by Horus implies rather the theft of his seed rather than his masculinity.

Hoffman was the first to move away from this idea, towards a possibility of these 'fishtail' lances were intended for a ritual connected with the afterlife.[8] Roth goes further and argues they are a variety of small knives used to sever the umbilical cord.[9] Three forms of this 'fishtail' amulet were found in tomb of Khaemwase.[10] We shall encounter this character Khaemwase below in connection with the famous tales of Setna, so relevant to Egyptian magick or Hekau. This Ptolemaic story cycle was attributed to him, although he lived centuries before its composition. Legend has it, that the cycle's eponymous character Setna was based on the life of Khaemwase. He was one of more than three hundred children sired by Ramesses during his long life, sixty-seven years as king. His children needed to work quite hard to stand out from the crowd.

Possessed of a keen interest in the past, Khaemwase was reputed to be an expert in magick. So it is a remarkable coincidence, if that's what it be, that an amulet, which itself has interesting Sethian connotations, should turn up in such a tomb. It's also rather amazing that an important amulet with precedents going back to Egypt's pre-dynastic past, should survive in one of its Middle Kingdom tombs! It shows a continuity of ideas spanning a period of perhaps

2000 years, maybe more. Khaemwase's amulet is carved from red carnelian, a rare and expensive material on a par with meteoric iron, even gold. Its red colour, may parallel the ochre 'red staining' found on pre-dynastic examples.[11]

This object was used as an amulet. I should point out that at least three of these substances have Sethian affiliations. 'Gold', arguable the world's first worked metal, mined in the desert on the eastern side of the river Nile, but also upriver in Nubia. Gold lends its name to the city of Ombos, and incidentally provides us with another connection between Seth and Hathor. The 'tails' of the 'lance' were in later times mutated to resemble the 'curls' of Hathor, thus, further underlining the connection between these deities (see illustration). Blood red carnelian was obviously special to these people and in later mythology was used to replace the eye of Horus, damaged by Seth. The magical association of meteoric iron (beja) stretches back into hoary antiquity and have never ended. For a whole host of reasons, this metal in all its forms, is especially associated with Seth.[12]

So the so-called 'fishtale lance' may well turn out to be, as Roth argues very persuasively, an object used to sever the umbilical cord. The umbilical cord equated elsewhere with Apophis, snake form god of chaos and non-existence:

One of the most famous images of Seth. A Ptolemaic text *Papyrus Jumilhac* relates the rebellion of Seth after the judgement of the gods in favour of Horus and how eventually, in the form of a red dog, he is hunted down, slain and dismembered. 'After he (Horus) cut off his (Seth's) foreleg (khapesh) he raised it to the middle of the sky, deities being there to guard it, the Foreleg (meskhet) of the northern sky, and the Great Hippopotamus (reret waret) holds it so it cannot travel among the gods.' (quoted in Neugebauer & Parker 1960: III.191). So sometimes the same astronomical phenomenon (Ursa Major) is seen variously as the foreleg of a red Bull or Dog depending on the period - but always Seth. The tail of the dog shows the *Pesesh-Ket* knife used for severing of the umbilical cord.

'In birth, differentiation is accomplished by cutting the umbilical cord that attaches the new born child to the primeval waters of the womb, thus making him something separate and specific. The creation of the child mimics the creation of the world, which is accomplished by cutting the snake's body of Apophis in two.' (Roth 1992: 139)

Here we also have an possible explanation of Seth forked tail, a piece of iconography that has puzzled many:

Fourteen days or a half lunation was the time allotted for Egyptian women's confinement after parturition; yet another indication of a possible Sethian associations with the birth process. The moon is a key component in the magick of Seth - an issue explored in some detail in *Tankhem*.[13]

The above drawing shows more detail and leads to the suggestions that the forked tail of Seth is a reflection of his role as divider of Apophis? Apophis or Apep is the colossal demon of 'non-being' who threatens to prevent the god Ra and his retinue from traversing the caverns of the night, and onwards to rebirth at dawn. From this we can perhaps recognise a belief in rebirth and the ultimate demon as that which prevents separation from the mother and becoming our own individual selves. For this reason, the umbilical cord is likened to the demonic Apophis. In later times, Seth maintains his role as an opener of the womb, his role becoming steadily demonised, retaining the negatively perceived role as abortionist, whereas he was formerly connected with childbirth and conception. Of course we are assuming that abortion was always seen as a negative thing. Despite the negative side, recent research shows how persistently woman in classical world resorted to abortion.[14]

Notes

1. For others, consult Te Velde (1967).
2. Te Velde (1967 : 7).
3. For this discussion see sign in Aa21 in Gardiner (1926).
4. Te Velde (1967: 24).
5. Te Velde (1967: 28).
6. Te Velde (1967: 28, 55).
7. Hoffman (1984: 94).
8. Hoffman (1984: 114).
9. Roth (1992).
10. Roth (1992: 138).
11. Roth (1992: 124).
12. In the Greek Magical Papyri, (Betz) 'black blood' is taken by Iathath (ie Seth).
13. Morgan (2005).
14. See (Papparis 2002).

9 Beasts of Seth

In later times, Seth was seen as a beast of ill luck, as also the divine joker, comparable in some ways to Ghede in Voodoo pantheon.   Te Velde (1967: 25).

Over the millennia, various animals were associated with Seth, typically those commonly sacrificed and/or in some other way despised: hence ass, pig, boar, desert dwellers such as the oryx, antilope, gazelle, although the *Lexikon* says the gazelle was also an animal sacred to Isis. The oft mentioned hippopotamus is there in its aspect as a destroyer of boats and of planted fields. The pig was a taboo in Seth's cult. The Greeks later equating Seth with their demon-god Typhon.[1] Other dangerous beasts eventually end up in the 'sethian' fold, although they once have been dieties in their own right. As an insult to the priests of his cult, he was sometimes called Seth but strictly speaking the crocodile is an entirely different god, perhaps not as ancient as Seth. Sobek was held sacred at Ombos despite his dangerous nature where he was one of Seth's 'confederates'. In addition to those already discussed, other beasts forms of Seth are hippopotamus, aurochs, snake and certain fish. Many of these beasts have parallels in the demonology of later times. Margaret Murray wrote about a deity of European demonology known as *Ash*. Murray's speculations have been much criticised by later specialists in European folklore, so some care should be taken here.[2]

Seth as Fish

Oxyrhynchus is the Greek name for an ancient Egyptian capital of the 19th Upper Egyptian Nome. The word means 'long nosed fish' and is presumably a reference to the local cult of the Mormyrus fish. This fish is said to have swallowed the phallus of Osiris, making it impossible for Isis to fully reassemble Osiris after his murder by Seth. Hence a taboo amongst certain Egyptian priests on the eating of fish, in case they accidentally cannibalise Osiris. Not surprisingly this region, whose ancient name was Per-medjed, was a cult centre of Seth, and indeed the Nome ensign discussed earlier, consists of two Was scepters flanking a human foot. The pharaonic remains have not so far been discovered. The motif of a phallus-eating fish lends itself to a physiological and metaphoric interpretation. Physiological in that it again seems to key into the notion of ingestion of the sexual power of the god. The motif also occurs in significant form in Hindu tantrism where one sect, the Nathas,

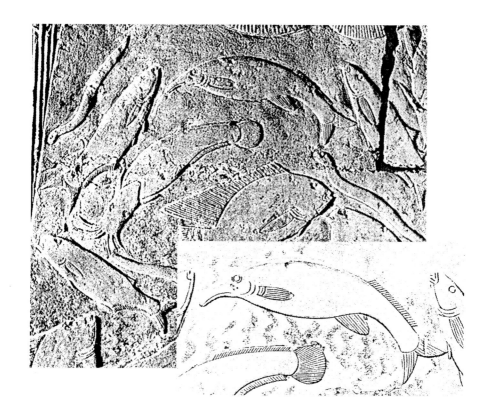

Images of the Nile fish taken from a fishing and hunting scene in the tomb of sixth dynasty King Teti's vizier Mereruka (c2325-2176BC). The Mormyrus fish (see detail) whose long nose resembles Seth appears at the top (Duell 1938: Plate 10). See sketch detail.

received its mythic transmission from a scroll found in the belly of a fish, or in some versions of the myth as a fish that overhears the conversation of Shiva with his consort on the mysteries. We could multiply these references, including the fish imagery connected with Gnosticism and as an emblem of Christ.[3] There is also, the so-called 'money fish' reputed to have eaten the blood money, forty pieces of silver cast into the waters by Judas Iscariot! Catholic priests seem to have reversed the taboo of the Egyptian with their friday fish suppers. Even *Lord of the Rings* uses this motif.

The natural history of the Mormyrus kannamae fish may hold interesting clues to the mythology of Seth. The Mormyrus has a very large brain, which it needs to control an unusual electric organ, which it uses as a type of radar to navigate the murky bottoms of the river. There may well be something significant in the reproductive biology of the fish - millions of spermatozoa and eggs released into the abysmal waters after fertilization in its mouth.

The Hippopotamus as an Emblem of Seth

Within the Naqada graves, Petrie and his colleagues found many thousands of small grave goods, the vast bulk of which were eventually shipped to the Ashmolean museum in Oxford. Common amongst the finds, are images of the aquatic, 'baying'

Hippopotamus, recognised by Petrie as an emblem of Seth.

There are very many inscriptions and texts, that show that the hippopotamus is the most common form adopted by Seth when fighting Horus. Perhaps one of the most famous images comes from Edfu, where 'Horus is the formidable guardian at the gate of the sanctuary, with the testicles of Seth in his hand, a victorious god inspiring the demons with terror. Finally, in the Horus myth of Edfu we find the story of the actual fight and the castration of Seth as a hippopotamus:

> "The seventh harpoon is struck fast in his body and hath spiked (?) his testicles." (Blackman and Fairman 1943: 14 quoted in Te Velde 1987)

One of the ubiquitous Hippopotamus icons found in the graves of the Ombites. This one is from the British Museum but it is very similar to the Ashmolean version.

The relief illustrating this text shows Horus thrusting a seventh harpoon into the testicles of the hippopotamus that represents Seth. It must have been quite a fight! *We can hardly think it correct, though, to assume that this version of the myth was always valid everywhere in Egypt,* and that those data referring to erotic play and the theft of semen leading to a quarrel, are to be regarded as entirely secondary (my emphasis).[5] Te Velde is reminding us that the Edfu myth represents a *sectarian* version of events and that there was an original, more erotic, what we would call tantrik, version of the same incident.

The Hippopotamus is a mean little beastie. Its natural history tells us that it is the origin of term 'sweating blood' because of the blood red secretion that form part of the animal's protection against the sun. No doubt the mention of 'seventh' harpoon triggered some memory. Seven is a number that recurs again and again in association with Seth, so much so that the two words, 'seven' and 'Seth' might well be linked etymologically.

In *Tankhem*, I described one or two ancient rites connected with strong Sethian associations amongst them one, the Heptagramme, comes from the Greek magical papyri and is widely used by contemporary devotees as an opener. The gestures of the Heptagramme rite may well be an enactment of the above scene from Edfu - Horus levelling his harpoon at Seth (as hippopotamus) - and having speared him, lifting him up to the stars. The duty of keeping Seth in his place amongst the stars falls to his 'concubine' Tawaret – the female of the species, whose major role is as protectress during childbirth.

"And after he had cut out his fore-leg *he* threw it into the sky. Spirits guard it there: The Great Bear of the northern sky. The great Hippopotamus goddess keeps hold of it, so that it can no longer sail in the midst of the gods." *Pap. Jumilhac* XVII, 11-12)

This connection is perhaps another indication of Seth's earlier role in this important human activity. It's another example of how Sethian imagery – with heavy bias towards Horus, permeates Hermetic magick. For more details on this rite see various, but *Tankhem*.[6]

Notes
1. Edited from Internet, Social Science Data Lab.
2. Murray (1973) and Mercer (1949:188).
3. Griffiths (1960: 115).
4. Brewer and Friedman (1989).
5. Te Velde (1967: 59).
6. Morgan (2004: 174).

Tawaret, whose name (reret weret) means 'Great Hippo' is the
'Concubine of Seth'. The Book of Day and Night, (time of
Ramses VI) tells us: 'as to this Foreleg of Seth, it is in the
northern sky, tied to two morring posts of flint by a chain of
gold. It is entrusted to Isis as a hippopotamus (reret) guarding it.'
(quoted in Neugebauer & Parker 1960 III.190). It is sometimes
said that the female hippopotamus was regarded as the more
benign of the species, with strong maternal instincts.
The more aggressive males were the hunter's prey. All of which
tends to point up the connection of Seth with childbirth.

10 Seth -
the red ochre god

'There are two meaningful regularities in human evolution,
tool making and the collection and use of ochre'
(Wreshner 1980: 631).

At some point in our evolution we developed colour vision
and thereafter became programmed for the categories
'red, yellow, green and blue.' The discoveries at Olduvai are perhaps
the very earliest evidence for this capacity for perceptual colour
categorization.[1] Red is arguably the most primary of the colours.
Red is the first colour to develop from the black and white vision
of the foetus. It has strong associations with both tomb and womb,
it seems almost self-evident that the red colour of blood is the key
to the power of red, although some have posed the question of
whether blood is so powerful because it is red, rather than the other

way round. For example, why isn't a clear substance like water, or the green of vegetation, equally as powerful as a colour? Ochre has additional element of magical transformation through the agent of fire. The often yellow raw material become the familiar deep blood red. Red, is of course the primary colour of Seth, as for instance in red dog of the *Papyrus Jumilhac* or the red donkey or ass of the myth of Horus of Edfu. The optical contrary of red, is green, the symbolic colour of Osiris.

The Plough

'The constellation of the Great Bear (Ursa Major) is the sign of Seth, as Orion is the star of Osiris and Sirius the star of Isis. In the Papyrus Jumilhac it is related that Horus had cut out the fore-leg of Seth:[2]

> 'And after he had cut out his fore-leg *he* threw it into the sky. Spirits guard it there: The Great Bear of the northern sky. The great Hippopotamus goddess keeps hold of it, so that it can no longer sail in the midst of the gods.'
>
> (*Pap. Jumilhac* XVII, 11-12).

The Bull's Leg

The Great Bear was how the Greek referred to the constellation Ursa Major. The Greeks took over the rulership of Egypt after the defeat and expulsion of the Persians by the Macedonian king Alexander the Great. The relationship between the Greeks and Egyptians was not much better, and has been characterised as a form of apartheid. They obviously grew rich on the great agricultural surpluses and operated a system of repressive tolerance concerning Egyptian religion. Even so, they acknowledged a huge philosophical debt to their Egyptian subjects, although quite how substantial this intellectual exchange might have been is a moot point. Most classical scholars are dismissive, in my opinion unreasonably, of the idea of Egyptian 'wisdom'. More recent studies argue that Greeks did secretly assimilate and perhaps even appropriate many core Egyptian concepts.

In magical texts, despite changes in terminology, the underlying connection with the Hidden God remains intact. If you look through many of the invocations and spells of the Greek magical papyri, you will soon find that the several surviving invocations of the Bear abound in Sethian symbolism. It might be an interesting point to investigate just what the Bear connoted to the Greeks.

The image of the Bull's foreleg has a very ancient lineage and, is to be found in the original cult of the Sethians at Ombos. When Flinders Petrie, the first excavator of the site came across such offerings, he persisted in viewing them as a survival of the 'new race'.[3] But on this point, Petrie's initial analysis has been rejected by many later researchers. Those he thought were foreigners we might call 'Sethians', who, far from being a new race of incomers, should perhaps be seen as the indigenous people of Egypt!

A haunch and / or head of an ox were generally found in the finest of their graves at Ombos. This ancient piece of Sethian iconography marks the beginning of an idea that persists into the Middle Kingdom, the dominant Osirian culture, being formed from the blending of two equally chthonic ethnic groups. From these bovine-offering trays evolved the ubiquitous 'soul houses' found in many a Middle Kingdom Egyptian tomb.

In fact, what we are seeing here is a prime example of the Egyptian veneration for cattle. The late Palaeolithic, Qadan culture (12,000-10,000BC), routinely marked their graves with cow horns.[4] The arm gesture of the so-called 'Goddess of Naqada' (see picture) is arguably a further reflection of this ancient, ubiquitous cattle cult.

Again I must underline my working axiom, that much of the ancient Sethian religion can be understood, by deconstructing the surviving Osirian hegemony.

The same bovine symbolism can be seen at Sepermeru, another cult centre of Seth, which lies in the 19th Upper Egyptian Nome.[5]

The above gritty limestone and stucco stele comes from Qau/ Badari in Upper Egypt. The inscription, much damaged was translated by Mr Battiscombe Gunn reads - 'An offering that the King gives and Seth the mighty(?) .. . . . Elephantine(?) ...... Lord of Thebu within (?) the Aphroditopolis and Antaeopolite Nome.' One the right: 'Made by the mayor(?) of Thebu (capital of the Aphroditopolis nome)'. (Brunton 1930: III 32).

The Nome capital in classical (Greek) times was Oxyrhynchus (modern El Bahnasa). Oxyrhynchus has become famous for its enormous Greco-Roman rubbish dump that has given rise to the new academic discipline of papyrology. Because of the strange fact of an absence of any archaeological remains at Oxyrhynchus, prior to the Romans, it seem likely that the original ancient settlement was in some other, as yet undiscovered, place. It's not unreasonable to hypothesis that Sepermeru was the original capital of this Sethian Nome. Now you might be wondering how we can know so much about a lost settlement? The answer comes largely from a remarkable manuscript known technically as the Wilbour Papyri, but in essence an Egyptian 'Doomsday' book.[6] This book itemises the property of ancient Sepermeru, amongst which are the incumbents of a Temple of Seth, with an associated shrine to Nephthys, built by Rameses II. Among various other residents, is a goatherd for the 'white goats' kept or sacrificed in the temple. As mentioned below, goats were yet another of the traditional enemies of Osiris.[7]

The Egyptian 'Doomsday' also lists a temple to Bata – another manifestation of an ancient cattle cult, whose folklore preserves a view of the Osiris myth common amongst Sethians (See *Tale of Two Brothers* in the appendix).

Not surprisingly, various desert roads radiant from nearby Oxyrhynchus, principally to Bahriya and Siwa. Although nothing survives of any ancient remains before its Greco-Roman settlement, this was obviously an important place in pre-dynastic times. The Nome standard shows a human foreleg or foot, flanked by two Was sceptres (see below). The human foreleg or foot is one of the more common hieroglyphic signs: *bn*[8] 'to place or position'.

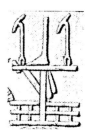

Again this reminds me of the phrase found in the Greek Magical Papyri, where Seth is described as having 'vision in his feet' which is perhaps parallel to the descriptions of his as 'powerful of forefoot'. It was indeed said that Seth killed Osiris by kicking or by standing on him with his iron hoofs. The *Was* Sceptre, fabricated from meteoric iron, and thus both derived from, and capable of holding up the vault of heaven, was yet another weapon used against Osiris.

Notes

1.   Wreshner (1980 : 632).
2.   Te Velde (1967 : 86).
3.   Petrie (1897: 42).
4.   Hoffman (1984: 91).
5.   Te Velde (1967: 89).
6.   Gardiner (1941).
7.   Perhaps considerd so because they eat Osiris, the deity of vegetation.
8.   D58 in Gardiner's sign list.

11 Seth and Horus

Seth's most important, and ancient role in Egyptian religion is as protagonist of Horus. For a time during the third millenium BC, Seth replaced Horus as the major deity of the pharaohs. He also made a comeback during the time of Ramesses II. In mythology Seth and Horus were at war for eighty years, or perhaps 80 days in the year. During these contendings, Seth tore out Horus's left eye. The story of the conflict of Horus and Seth was one of the oldest and most important of ancient Egyptian myths.[1] The concensus amongst Egyptologists, is that the myth concerns a natural event of the waxing and waning moon, and other lunar phenomena such as the eclipse.[2] See for example the well known episode in the Contendings of Horus & Seth, where Seth semen appears on, or from his forehead as the golden disk of the moon god Thoth:

> 'The myth of the creation of the gold disk[3] in the Contendings of Horus and Seth lends itself particularly well to a structural reading. Thus it makes it possible to show that the disk in question is the satellite at the beginning of the night of the full moon and that it was used probably in an old version of the mytb of Horus and Seth as 'arsenal' to the two divinities.' (Servajean 2004 : 148).

Old as all these sources are, they were written when a new cult, that of Osiris, reached a pinnacle from which, it was never to fall. The rise of the cult of Osiris would eventually cause the priesthood to edit out any Sethian material from the ancient sacred writings. Even so, quite a lot is left, although it is often incomplete, hidden or fragmentary. There is one rare and mysterious passage in the Pyramid texts, where the Eye of Horus is said to rest on the wing of Seth. A hint that Seth might also have a bird form, perhaps a peacock.

Horus was no longer the friend or brother of Seth, he turns tearing from Seth his leg and testicles. The severed leg of Seth gives its name to the constellation The Plough, which if you look is very suggestive of a leg and haunch. Horus eventually emerged victorious, or was deemed the victor by a council of the gods, and thus became the rightful ruler of the kingdoms of both Upper and Lower Egypt. In the *Book of the Dead,* Seth was referred to as the 'lord of the northern sky' and held responsible for storms and cloudy weather. Seth protected Re against the Apophis-snake during his night voyage through the underworld. On the other hand, Seth was, in some accounts, a peril for ordinary Egyptians in the underworld, seizing the souls of the unwary. In the *Book of Gates,* a text inscribed on the sarcophagi of many Ramesside kings, most notable Sety I, he plays a more benign role.

Early scholars saw in Apophis an entity connected with absolute evil.[4] Although later commentators seem to move away from this to more a connection with non-being. Whether non-being is the same as absoluted evil is a moot point.

Horus is the falcon-headed god, son of the goddess Isis and the god Osiris. Following the death of Osiris, Isis retrieved her husband's body and summoned the 'generative power' or Ba of the sun god Ra. Ra appears in the form of a vulture complete with erection (Ba is more commonly drawn in hieroglyphics as a Jiburu Stork). From this remarkable interaction, Osiris is sufficiently revived to conceive a son, Horus. This whole scene is shown depicted on a raised relief from the Opet temple at Karnak.[5] The word 'Opet' means 'secret chamber'. It refers to the private and secluded rooms, adjoining the holy sanctuary of Amun of Luxor in the innermost chamber of Amenhotep III's temple. The reclining image of Osiris was originally shown with an erection that had remained intact since for several thousand years, until it was viewed by the erotic explorer Richard Burton. Pretty soon after this, prudish Egyptian archaeologists hacked off the offending phallus!

This conflict between the two gods Seth and Horus, is most often played out in the sexual arena. In the fight between the two gods, the eye of Horus is damaged, becoming 'small', directly as a result of a homosexual act committed on Horus by Seth. This damage to the Eye of Horus is complex and not a simple matter of a violent blow. It goes right to the heart of Egyptian theories of the body and the internal relationship between semen and the eye, perhaps the third eye. It should perhaps remind us, of the kind of physiology so familiar in later magical theories of Hindu tantrism, where conservation of semen, the body's own elixir of immortality, or lack of, is the cause of illness and premature death. The conflict of Seth & Horus gives us a window into a very early form of body magick, that had survived into historic times from the nameless aeons of the Neolithic.

Small statue of Horus 'the royal god', brother, lover and
eventually the enemy of Seth. Horus is the falcon-headed god,
son of the goddess Isis and the god Osiris. Following the death
of Osiris, Isis retrieved her husband's body and summoned the
'generative power' or Ba of the sun god Ra. Shows his typical
fighting posture. British Museum.

The fifteenth day of the moon was known as the 'day of rams' when the moon begins to wane, and thus loses its virile powers – it was on this day, that the ritual of filling the eye was performed. In the *Contendings of Horus & Seth* (see appendix) when Seth is tricked by Horus into eating his own seed, Thoth commands it to show itself, and it appears in Seth's own forehead as a golden disk. So out of the 'contendings', Seth and Horus bring forth the god of peace, Thoth, the origin of the moon. Thoth, personification of magical wisdom, can therefore be seen as the offspring of this erotic interplay between the elder gods; so too can Anubis.

The symbol of the eye of Horus is used to represent fractions of corn or land. Gardiner[6] says it preserves a more primitive kind of fraction obtained by halving. The symbol is derived from Seth's shredding of the eye.

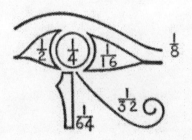

When all the parts are reunited a 1/64th part is absent, which perhaps leads to a meditation on the nature of being and non-being. I remember being shown a stone pillar in India that had 64 facets, each decorated with a particular deity - all save one - which was left blank - as an offering to the god of incompleteness.

'The ritual of completing the eye was carried out not on the 15th day but on the 6th day of the month and paid less attention to astronomical observations than to the symbolism of the parts. On the first day of the month the 1/64th part of the eye was ritually united with its counterpart to form the 1/16th and so on in the following days. Finally on the sixth day ½ was united with the other and thus the eye was filled. The Wadjet eye perhaps shows this overflowing of light/moisture. Ultimately this light is emited by the phallus of Seth.' (Te Velde 1967: 49)

Is there a dialectic between the moon and sexuality? We do find as such in many later 'tantrik' cultures, although the Egyptians saw no shame in the testicles in the way some forms of Buddhism view them as symbols of degenerate sexuality.[7]

Horus (Light) and Seth (Sexuality) must be united or balanced, with, for the ancient Egyptians, Horus on top. Thus the symbolism of Seth & Horus is very primeval and not the result of later historical-political development.

Seth's cult declines after Rameses III and the end of empire. As a god of frontiers, his function is no more and when associated with foreigners, he can hardly prosper as a popular deity. His birthday on the third epagnomal day is largely ignored.

'The negative aspect or complement of reality is no longer
acknowledged let alone celebrated and honoured.'

Te Velde (1967: 67).

What remains of ancient Egyptian body magick is seen again
in Seth's abusive relationship with Anat, the consort given to him
by Neith and the company of gods, as recompense for various
injustices including the loss of Nephthys (see Appendix). Anat
comes to Seth as a man and they have anal intercourse, which later
causes Anat to experience eye problems not unlike those of Horus.[8]
Egyptian medical texts also echo the view that aberrant sex such as

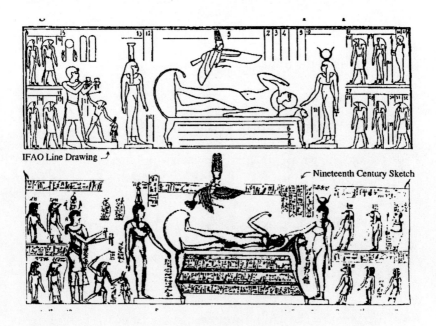

IFAO Line Drawing

Nineteenth Century Sketch

Remarkable erotic interchange between Ra and Osiris in the
Temple of Opet (revival of Osiris) at Karnak. The original was
mutilated by Victorian archaeologists.

rape causes eye problems, literally the semen flows to the eye. Indeed Greek medicine shares a similar schema whereby semen originated in the eyes. So perhaps its true that masturbation will make you blind!!

Meteoric Iron & Seth

Before the so-called age of iron, this metal was an extremely rare and valuable commodity. Almost 100% of ancient iron objects originate from meteorites. Perhaps, we can also say that meteorites are more often found in arid landscapes, where they are less likely to be hidden in dense vegetation. I think I am on firm ground if I maintain that this metal has a universal magical status, see for example the *Kris* knives of Indonesia.

Fascinating too that iron, the archaic substance par excellence, was to be the technology of the future. Under this category of iron, we can also group iron compounds and ores such as haematite and ochre.

Most meteorites *appear* to fall from the northern part of the sky, that which the ancient Egyptians call 'the imperishable stars', the body of Nuit, one of whose children was Seth. Seth's constellation is in fact the northern Ursa Major, known as *meshketyu* by the Egyptians. This is the shape of an adze, a woodworking tool with an arched blade set at right angles to the handle. Sometimes also as Kapesh, a similar shaped sword. It's a natural enough name of the asterism. Such a complex tool would be well suited to manufacture iron. Iron bolts were routinely used to secure temple and tomb doors. The ritual texts associated with these bolts contained the lines to be uttered during the sliding back of the bolt.

'I remove the finger of Seth from the Eye of Horus.'[9]

Te Velde maintains, that in this context, finger can also be understood as a phallus. Meteoric iron was also used for construction of various sceptres including the highly important Was sceptre discussed below. This is a Sethian object par excellence. In some accounts, it is this awesome weapon that is actually used by Seth to kill Osiris. As in the case of later martial gods such as Indra or Zeus, only Seth's hideous strength is equal to the task of wielding such a weapon. When not threatening others, it functions as one of four massive pillars that hold up the vault of the firmament!

Notes
1. Griffiths (1960: 1).
2. Griffith (1960: 126).
3. jtn n nbw.
4. Budge, *Egyptian Hieratic Papyri in British Museum*.
5. Reeder (1998: 72sq).
6. Gardiner (1957).
7. Te Velde (1967: 52).
8. Te Velde (1967 : 36).
9. David (1981). Ritual text from shrines of Sety I at Abydos.

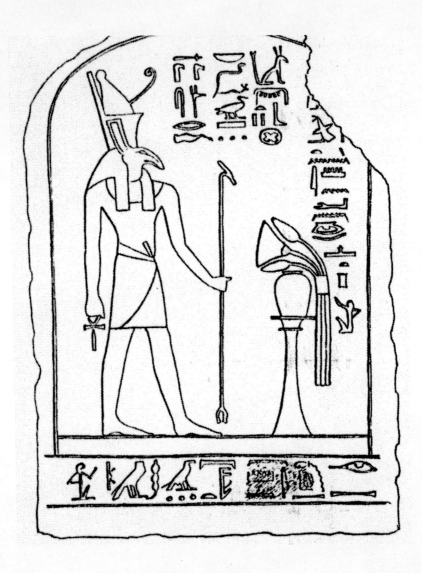

Stele of Amenhotep from Temple of Seth at Ombos. About
quarter size, engraved by Nezem.

12 Opening the mouth

A symbolic or miniature version of the adze is used in the important ceremony of the opening of the mouth. This ritual, which originated amongst the kings of Buto,[1] occurred during the final funeral rites just before burial in the tomb. The mummy was purified with holy water and fumigated with incense. Then followed a bull sacrifice, one of whose forelegs was presented to the deceased. I remind you that the Bull's Leg is another name of the constellation *Ursa Major*, so it's obvious that here we see yet another manifestation of Seth in the sacrificial process. After the sacrifice the *sem*-priest, touches the mouth of the mummy with several magical instruments including the adze,[2] the seven sacred oils, the 'Fishtale' lance or *Pesesh-Ket* knife.

Amongst the magical instruments presented to the mouth of the deceased is the 'Pesesh-Ket' otherwise known as the 'fishtale lance' that as we remarked already, is connected with birth. Could the other tools, especially the adze, have a similar function? After all, is not the opening of the mouth an important part of birth not death? Once again, we find Seth connected with the inner mysteries of birth. The birth goddess is Meshkenet,[3] who has four personifications, like the four bricks on which Egyptian women squatted during childbirth. Her name is derived from 'm sh nt' the place of 'place of causing to alight'. Four humble, and therefore ignored mud bricks are routinely found at the cardinal points of tombs. This underlines the death and rebirth connexion. One's fate was said to be written on the birthbricks by Thoth, (the son of Seth) a kind of predestination that is perhaps alluded to, in famous scenes in the judgement hall of Osiris. The placenta shares the symbolism of the Ka – where 'to join the ka' is a euphemism for death. In the ceremony of opening the mouth, 'sethian' instruments such as 'Pesesh-Ket' knife continues the parallel. The *sem* priest who performs the above ceremony, is one of the most important of the ancient Egyptian priesthood. He is the reciter of the famous

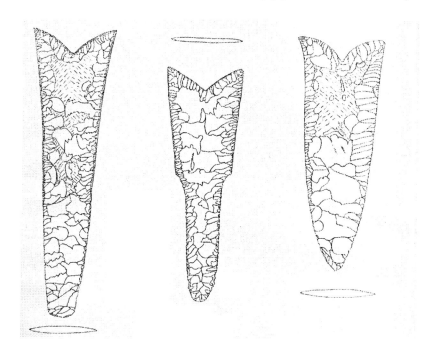

Three archaic examples of the *Peseshket* flint knife found in
graves of the protodynastic site of Naqada (see Petrie 1896a).
Originally termed a 'fish-tail' lance, they have since been
identified from graves of all periods as the knife used in the
ceremony of opening the mouth. Recent research postulated that
they were originally used to cut the snake-like umbilical cord, also
called 'Apophis' - the demon of 'non-being', who is a peril at the
moment of birth or coming forth. The 'sethian' citizens of
Naqada may well have treasured the implement used at their own
birth, and it thus accompanied them to the grave. The canid
form of Seth has such a forked knife attached to his tail (see
earlier picture).

liturgical phrase 'an offering which the king gives'. The distinctive leopard skin dress of this priest is yet another reminder of Seth. The leopard receives its spots as a red hot branding as a punishment.

The earliest precedent for the rite seems to be in the Pyramid Texts, where offering are made into the mouth, included the combined 'spit' of Horus and Seth.[3] The importance of 'spit' and its anagramme 'semen' are explored further in the section on Hekau below.

Closely following, is another bodily fluid, the mysterious *zmjn*, which Roth conjectures may be connected with menstrual blood! Roth has argued quite convincingly that all these objects are connected with birth. One cannot help wondering whether we are also seeing an archaic version of a 'tantrik' rite. It is worth considering that the moon is often associated with the birth. Ancient medical texts tell us that the moon controls the birthing process, and indeed the gestation period is usually measured as nine or ten lunations. Incidentally, one of the groups known in modern times as the Ordo Templi Orientis, stipulates a period of nine months for the completion of its first degree, hence a kind of magical rebirth.

The ceremony of opening the mouth is also used on otherwise inanimate statues to bring them to life. This undoubtedly is one piece of archaic magick that still survives in some amended form in contemporary practice. See for instance 'sigil' magick, where a deceptively simply 'seed' is 'given life', and thereby the ability to act in the subconscious realm.[5]

It is clear how Sethian imagery completely permeates this whole ritual. Do we explain this entirely as part of the atonement by Seth for the murder of his brother Osiris? I maintain that in addition to the components of resurrection and immortality evident in the ritual, it is possible also to see traces of an earlier rite connected with rebirth. Please note the distinction between bodily resurrection and rebirth.

Seth as Murderer of Osiris

'I am Osiris . . . I have fallen upon my side [ie died] that the gods may live on me'[6]

Just as in the death of John Barleycorn, the dying of Osiris is no bad thing. In the earliest strata of Egyptian cosmology, the god Ra is threatened by Apophis, the demon of non-being. In the subsequent cult of Osiris, the role of Apophis is transferred to Seth. Egyptian religious texts contain not a single coherent account of Osiris' murder by Seth, though it was perhaps thought too traumatic or taboo an incident to actually write down. The death of the Nile god by drowning is another paradoxical element to the tale, indicating just how cosmologically disordered is the whole episode. Ritual dramas and folk tales are some of the 'non religious' discourses that do fill in the details. Some of these folk versions of the murder have become very widely diffused as for instance in the story cycle of Patini analysed at length in *Isis in India.*[7]

'Seth not only a murderer and demon of death, but also assists the resurrection of Osiris. This would mean that he is the demonic initiator, who leads his brother to life through death by violence.' (Te Velde 1967: 98)

Notes
1. Egyptian: *Wadjet.*
2. Mercer (1949: 319).
3. No etymological connection with *Meshketyu* – the Plough.
4. Pyramid Text 26.
5. Fries (1992).
6. Coffin Text 168c, 169a, b) quoted in Te Velde (1967: 81).
7. Morgan 2004.

13 Seven

'The number seven figures prominently in Egyptian theology in the seven Hathors who decree fate, the seven creative utterances who begat fate; The seven uraei who guard Re; the seven gates of the underworld palace of Osiris; the seven horns of the goddess of writing etc. This is perhaps influenced by the association with deities of creation and authority, the number abounds in religious and magical literature from the pyramid texts through to the Coptic period . . . Steadily increasing in importance, the symbolism of the number seven acquires cosmopolitan influence in the Hellenistic period from the seven vowels in Greek and Seven planets of Mesopotamian astrology.' (Ritner 1993: 161).

There are said to be seven sacred oils – which as of 2000, no one has yet identified them from the dozens available to the Egyptians. In the famous artefact with seven named depressions, the oil is referred to just as oil, the sevenfold idea a later interpolation. The names do not seem to correspond with any obvious taxonomy, so perhaps they refer to some other, perhaps magical or contextual quality of the oil.[1]

We could add to this litany examples such as the seven steps or workings of alchemy - Tincture, Coagulation, Distillation, Putrefaction, Solution, Sublimation and Calcination. The sevenfold cosmology of Abydos, and of course the Seven Stars of the Starry Plough.

The seven creative utterances are hypostasized as the seven sages or shamans of the primordial cow, those who utter the seven creative words or spells, that bring the world into being. This also provides us with a key axiom of ancient magical praxis – magick revolves around the power of the word that must be uttered or spoken to be effective. In my earlier book *Tankhem* I wrote:[2]

'Other texts describe these very first sacred landscapes, describing buildings that, even for the ancient Egyptians, were a fading and distant memory. The earliest mythologies often talk of the first or primal building. They did not even know the names of the gods that roamed during those days of yore but referred to them cryptically in books such as the 'Book of the Primeval Old Ones' as the nameless gods.

The non-magician tends to focus overly on the surface exterior form of ceremony and ritual, whilst having very little understanding of the inner states implied by these techniques. I like to interpret them using a psychological model. 'The Book of the Primeval Old Ones'[3] tells that in the primeval times, the surface of the planet was covered with water. Below the water, lay the remains of one or perhaps more than one previous creation. The divine entities were without form but not without power. The ancient sages or shamans, call out to these beings, using words of power that they had but recently learnt. There are said to be seven sages or shamans, and this is a motif that seems to crop up all over the place. I have found references to them in Egyptian, Hindu and even Chinese mythology, where they are connected with the constellation the Plough or Great Bear. Apart from any astrological significance, they seem to me to be real personality types, perhaps members of the tribe whose trance awareness is slightly more advanced than the others, and are thus able to say, 'that is a special place, we should build a temple here'.

At the word of the seven shamans, the power quickened and the first cosmic island rose from the waters. On this island, those shamans or seers built the first sacred temple. Perhaps it was these visionaries whose consciousness first emerged randomly from the past. (Interestingly, it was another visionary, Imhotep, who was later to be credited with the creation of the first temple hewn from stone, and was subsequently deified for his efforts.)

Concerning this 'Atlantis' type myth, see for example the Edomite Kings of Judaism, and the Seven Rishis of Vedic religion. Given that the Greeks claimed to have heard of legendary Atlantis from Egyptian priests, it is not unlikely that the extremely ancient Egyptian myth of a failed or drowned creation, is the source of the story. Similar myths abound in several other ancient cultures, and they are the primary myths of magick considered as a religion. Magick is therefore the oldest religion, and the occurrence of activities recognizably magical in almost every other subsequent religion is explained by the fact, that magick has been around for so long.

Notes

1. Nicholson & Shaw (2000).
2. Morgan (2005).
3. Reymond (1969).

14 The Boat

The meditation ended on the point of departure for a journey taken by the soul (Ba). What better means of conveyance than a boat? It is difficult to overestimate the importance of the image of the boat in Egyptian eschatology. Recently discovered petroglyphs in the Eastern desert, underline the fact that from prehistoric times, the people of the region envisioned their gods as riding about in boats.

The image is coterminous with the beginnings of Egyptian art – those miracles hidden away in the museum's first few cabinets, those past that we all hurry on our way to the dynastic splendour. But spare a few moments to gaze upon those yellow ochre pots, painted with such care, with such magical skill, and then deposited in the simple Naqadan graves for the use of the dead.

These boats often have a long bank of oars, which Petrie felt indicated that these people, whom he wrongly surmised were immigrants, had come not from the Nile but most likely from the Mediterranean seaboard where rowing is much more common than sailing. However, the occurrence of Ostrich eggs still used by people of the Sahara as water carriers.[1] And Ostrich feathers, a creature not native to Egypt, suggests a North African provenance. Behind the boat, some see a tree or trees, hills, ports, all perhaps special, otherwise why, asks Petrie, are they depicted? The 'ensign' of the boats also suggests an African origin. Take a look at the following decorated pot from a Naqadan grave. Look closely, and you can see a stylized boat, two gazelles above cabins or seats. The stern cabin has a curvilineal ensign. Elise Baumgartel,[2] Margaret Murray's successor at the University of London, re-examined and reappraised the prehistoric collection. She thought she had identified this ensign as the cow goddess, also termed by Baumgartel as the 'Great Mother'.

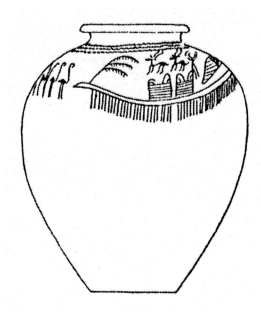

Another pot has the same boat image with two cabins, but this time, the ensign has a 'Z' shape, and multiple 'zzzzzz' are painted below. Baumgartel thought she recognised in this the 'Z' standard or Min's double thunderbolt. This god is son and lover, also the 'great bull' Ka-mutef 'bull of his mother' - who has much in common with Seth's most ancient form.

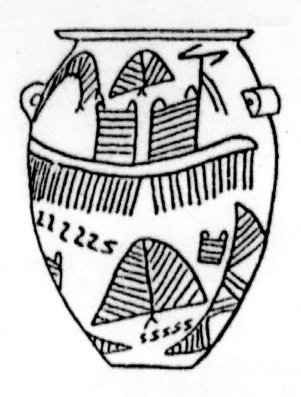

Either way, east or west, they would have arrived not by boat at all, but via the desert and oasis tracks that radiate from Ombos, Abydos, Sepermeru, etc. As I write this, a major exhibition, *Sudan: Ancient Treasures* is touring the world, before returning to its new home in Kartoum. Here indeed is a vast lost civilization, with development paralleling those of the Egyptian culture, and arguably the origin of the many of its feature, perhaps even the original homeland of the people of Seth.[3]

Again the Hidden God – as I write this – I hear a story on the radio. In Harrogate, a vase is taken out of storage where it has languished for many years, due to a slur on its authenticity. For over 30 years it was considered a fake, but recent tests have revealed that a vase owned by Harrogate Museums may well be one of the earliest ever depictions of an Egyptian burial on a ceramic vessel. The vase depicts Egyptian burials prior to mummification - with the body on a boat. It is one of several hundred items of Egyptian artefacts from the private collection of Benjamin Kent, which decorated his home at Tatefield Hall, Beckwithshaw, near Harrogate, until he died in 1968 at the age of 83. The vase was unprovenanced, i.e. it did not come from a scientific excavation but was most likely bought from a dealer during Kent's 'grand tour'. The fine condition and unique nature of the decoration, led to the suspicion that the vase was one of many fakes produced for the tourist market.

The decoration of this classic wavy handled vase is rather extraordinary. It shows an un-mummified corpse, lying on his or her back, in the contracted or foetal position – precisely as was common practice at Ombos, ancient city of Seth. Next to the corpse in the boat is a lattice structure, pavilion or cockpit, surmounted by two *Was* sceptres – perhaps we have here the oldest representation of that archetypical Sethian Icon. In the prow of the boat stands a solitary figure, probably Seth or perhaps the transformed spirit of the deceased. There are archaic symbols, perhaps proto- hieroglyphs, representing the constellations above the boat. Four banks of oars project from below the boat, although perhaps these are meant to represent legs, giving the boat a theriomorphic form – again foreshadowing the later role of Seth's backbone as the keel of the boat that ferries the deceased to the otherworld.

Taken alongside the numerous other examples of the boat image on pre-dynastic grave goods, Naqada was clearly a source, arguably the source, of many central and celebrated elements of middle Egyptian iconography. The Boat,especially, is the vehicle that carries the 'soul' to the other world at death, often ferried by Nemty, a form of Seth. Petrie himself mentions finding an offering tray, of a kind that was to become such a characteristic artefact of the Pharaonic culture and the Osirian faith.

Living in Nubt

The cemeteries found by Petrie at Naqada were so large that they represented a land of the dead, foreshadowing the western lands of Egyptian mythology.[4]

Like many of his contemporaries, it never occurred to Petrie that the sex of the inhabitants of the graves might be significant.

Subsequent studies show that many of the best quality burials were in fact female. This led one later scholar of Egypt's prehistory to speculate that the people of Seth's town may have been matriarchal.[5]

'Tombs of women were larger and contained objects of greater interest than the graves of men. This strengthens an opinion which I have published in the second volume of my *Cultures*, namely that this ancient society may have been matriarchal and that perhaps even the nsw.t (king) may originally have been a woman. That the princes buried in the predynastic cemetery at Naqada were known by the title of *nesewet* is reasonable to assume. Badarian cemeteries also exhibited this bias towards larger female graves' Baumgartel (1970 : 124).

The red crown of Northern Egypt, with which this title is linked, appears for the first time on a sherd of the Naqada I period, and thus 400 miles south of Cairo. Was it an import or does it belong here?[6]

Saying this is bound to raise the spectre of the old controversy about the historical matriarchy and, for some, the discredited theories of Frazer, Murray, Graves, Gimbutas et al. Baumgartel was in fact Murray's successor at UCL, although given that Murray resented being forced to retire at the tender age of 72, the relationship between the two women was hardly warm. Murray was also criticised for the destruction of Petrie's field notes.

'The effect [of the 'Murrayite' fall from grace] upon professional prehistorians was to make most return, quietly and without controversy to that careful agnosticism as to the nature of the ancient religion which most has preserved since the 1940s. There had been no disproof of the veneration of a Great Goddess, only a demonstration that the evidence concerned admitted of alternative explanations.' (Hutton: 1999).

The evidence stemming from Egypt of the raised status of women in prehistoric times is therefore worth dwelling upon. In rejecting the presuppositions of Murray *et al*, we need to be careful not to throw the baby out with the bathwater. There are many other roles a woman may fill, apart from, as focus for a fertility cult or 'great goddess'. At Ombos, despite Seth's redneck reputation, woman are very visible, perhaps even running the show. Its maybe premature to say Ombos was a laid back place to live, but neither was it squaddie heaven. Recent research at Kerma in ancient Nubia has also exposed high status female burials.

Life at Nubt was good. The inhabitants were well nourished, many were very tall, often over six feet. Petrie found very few fractures in the remaining bones, from which he deduces that Nubt was by ancient standards, not a violent place. 'These people were not quarrelsome'.[7] Petrie may have erred in his overall thesis of a new race of immigrants; this does not vitiate many of his other interesting observations.

Many common household activities were organised on a communal basis.[8] For example grain parchers, used to roast low grade cereal before grinding or brewing, were communal and this seems to have been a feature of predynastic life. An ancient grain parcher was excavated in the lowest levels of the Temple of Sety I at Abydos. The city had a low outer wall of approximately five foot with houses built either side. At a comparable site on the south side of Abydos, all the domestic heaths were also communal. Baumgartel[9] thought this rather a remarkable arrangement coming as it does at the very beginning of urban life. Urbanisation being defined by fixed villages with aligned streets, communal or individual grain silos, threshing floors and livestock enclosures.

Baumgartel even went as far as to characterise Naqadan society as 'primitive communism'. There was she tells us 'No private property in the soil' because of the insuperable problem of establishing permanent boundaries in a land famous for its annual flood.[10] A male or perhaps female chieftain or king had responsibility for division of surplus and offerings on behalf of the clan which may well be the origin of the famous offering formula 'hetep di nesew - an offering which the king gives' – i.e. this standard offering formula is used by anyone making an offering, alluding to the idea that the king does this on behalf of the commonweal. This may

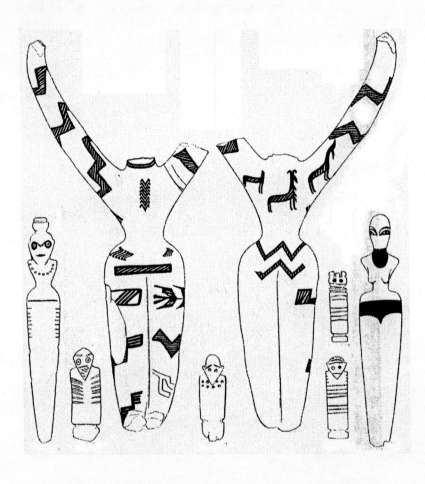

The 'Red Goddess of Naqada'. This artefact was sold to Petrie during the dig, its lack of provenance leading to some scepticism about its antiquity. The appearance of further examples of the 'Red Goddess of Naqada' has lessoned the controversy. Could the gesture represent the horns of a cow?

also be echoed in the biblical stories of Jacob and his son Joseph, where the ancient kingly duty was to store and distribute grain. Or was it, as some have suggested, to store water?

The varieties of ancient social organisation are very relevant to the modern world. It shows that there is nothing inevitable about the development of kingly elites. There are other variable models of social organisation, of co-rulership, even proto democracy. These mercantile, communitarian communities later mutated into the Egyptian form of kingship. That which survived was not necessarily the most fitting or efficient for the task. Weapons in predynastic graves are rare. Kingship was not wholly based on warriorship. The famous Narmer palette (see illustration) is indeed very martial in character, but is this a function of its dedication in a warlike Horus temple and not a tomb?

The inhabitants of Ombos were predominantly right handed. They tended to hunt by maiming their prey rather than outright killing – so perhaps they domesticated the beast, or it was an attempt to keep the skin undamaged.

They venerated Seth, Hathor and several other gods which may be reflected in several canine burials, one in particular a whole pack. They liked the colours red, yellow, green, black and white. The tattoo patterns shown on the so called 'Goddess of Naqada' are closely like those of the Libyans shown in the tomb of Sety I. This statue has no provenance and was bought by Petrie from a local dealer. One might well doubt its authenticity if not for the occurrence of similar examples, all with the distinctive sinuous, perhaps bovine pose? The Brooklyn museum has another fine example dated 3500-3400BC.[11]

Men and women wore their hair long, sometimes braided. Men were beardless and both are short by modern standards, although Petrie thought they were tall. The graves were looted in ancient times perhaps by other Naqadans.

All this points to an interesting dynamic between men and women, and indeed female and male gods. Could the goddess of Naqada, whose sinuous body seems to evoke some kind of cow goddess, be Seth's original consort? If so, perhaps it was of its time, similar rapprochements between human female and the horned cow goddess have been associated with neolithic sites such as Avebury in Wiltshire.[12] Furthermore, these associated with the square enclosures that in Egypt were connected with the constellation Ursa Major, or in its original Egyptian name Meshketyu – the Bull's Leg. It's a tantalising parallel.

Is the name of the goddess of Naqada really Nephthys – Seth's unfaithful wife of pharaonic times? Or, as I suggested earlier, could

Seth have had an original consort, whose nature is more in keeping with his own? I suggest that a strong candidate for such a consort is the goddess known in later times as Hathor (House of Horus) but whose original name was Bat.

Tomb robbery

'Another hallmark of later, ancient Egyptian civilization that first appears in Badarian times is tomb robbery. The practice is linked intimately to mortuary practices that required substantial offerings be interred with the dead . . . for nearly 5000 years [until time of Christ] piety and pragmatism survived side by side within the context of Egyptian Predynastic and Pharaonic culture, much like the two heads of the same coin, the one ideological the other economic.'[13]

Notes
1.   Hoffman: (1984 : 57).
2.   Baumgartel (1970 : 147).
3.   Welsby & Anderson (2004).
4.   Hoffman (1984 : 109).
5.   Baumgartel (1970).
6.   The object was found in grave 1610. For a continuation of this discussion see Hoffman (1984); Wainwright (1923); Baumgartel (1970).
7.   Petrie (1897: 32).
8.   Baumgartel (1970 : 134).
9.   Baumgartel (1970).

10.   Baumgartel (1970 : 142).
11.   Exhibit 07-447-505.
12.   Dames (1996).
13.   Hoffman (1987 : 143).

Part II
Magick

The force that through the green fuse drives the flower
Drives my green age; that blasts the roots of trees
Is my destroyer.
And I am dumb to tell the crooked rose
My youth is bent by the same wintry fever.

Dylan Thomas

A privileged moment from the 21st dynasty Papyrus B of Her-Uben in the Cairo museum. She was a chantress of Amon-Ra and second prophetess of Mut. Most women served as priestesses in such a cult. This short pictorial papyrus presents the key scenes she must witness in her post mortem journey. Here she sees the boat of Ra steered to safety thanks to Seth's spearing of Apophis the demon of 'non-being' (Piankoff 1954). The original is 2m long, ¼m wide, painted in black, red, white, green and brown.

15 Heka & Hekau

The Egyptian word usually translated, as 'magick' is Hekau (hereafter given in anglicised form). It can be difficult to work out whether the action involves gods, men or both. This above ambiguity arises from the failure of Egyptian scribes to use an appropriate determinative, when writing about Hekau. Perhaps this omission was deliberate? It is clear that Hekau has three connotations:

A quality something might possess

A rite to be performed.

words or spells to be spoken aloud (ah)–

These rites are seldom confined to words but require actions and substances – for example the burning of bryony to overcome Apophis. Internal repetition of words is seldom enough.

Thoughout this chapter, we will make good use of the *Setna* cycle of stories. You will find a complete version of both stories in the appendix. This series of interlocking stories was popular in Ptolemaic times when Egypt was ruled by the Greek successors to Alexander the Great. The first tale concerns the quest of Setna for the legendary magical *Book of Thoth*. The second tale is a sequel set when Setna has settled down to raise a family of his own. But his first child is wise beyond his years and turns out to be the reincarnation of a famous sorcerer from Egypt's past, who has returned to defend Egypt from one of its traditional enemies, the sorcerers of Nubia. Nubia, modern day Sudan, is one of Egypt's ancient enemies. Although set in 1200BC the stories are actually composed around 200BC.

In the second story, Setna provides a classic example of the efficacy of *spoken* spells. The narrator tells how one of the protagonists Panishi, '*uttered the words* of a spell and a flood of water appeared from the south, and put out the flame in an instant'.[1]

Practitioners of magick are called *ḥeka*; the same word as the god *Ḥeka*, which we can distinguish in English by the use of a capital letter, no such facility exists in the Egyptian language. The word *ḥeka* survived into the Coptic period and language as HIK. It occurs in chapter eight of the Coptic version of *New Testament*,

'Acts of the Apostles', in an account of the sorceries of Simon Magus. There is probably a connection between the word Heka and Ka, the essence of a human being, especially at the birth of the king. Heka as the magician is one of 14 Ka(s) of the king, just as the magician is one of the seven Ba(s) or external manifestations of Ra. Could *Heka* be one of the secret names in the *Litany of Ra*?

There is even some indication that at least some Egyptians saw Seth as the counterpart of Ra. Te Velde says this conflation of *order* and *chaos* had only one known example. Even so the contemporary Temple of Seth have amplified the idea with their archetype of Kephra. Rather confusingly they render this *Xeper*, the 'X' being the Greek letter 'kh', a distinction perhaps lost of most readers.

One possible meaning of *Hekau* is derived from Ahau or *akhu* meaning 'to shine'.

'So Setna went to the Necropolis of Memphis with Inaros, his foster brother. They spent three days and three nights searching among the tombs of the Necroplis of Memphis, reading the inscriptions on the stones and deciphering the formulae carved on the doors of the tombs. At last, on the third day, he found the place where Nanefer lay. When he had made certain that it was, indeed his tomb, Setna was able to descend into the place where the mysterious book [of Thoth] was kept, it was as light as though in full sunshine, because the radiance coming from the book lit up the surroundings' (Divin 1969: 106).

Setna Khemwaset uses magick to break into Nanefer's tomb in search of the legendary book, which in turn radiates its own light. Setna then uses the book to light his way out.[2] The story doesn't end there, Nanefer vows to hunt Setna down: 'Let your heart not grieve, I will make him bring that book back here, with a forked stick in his hand and a lighted brazier on his head'.[3] The forked stick or *stang* is a sign of Setna's repentance.

The purpose of Egyptian magick

> 'Ten measures of magic have come into the world. Egypt received nine of these, the rest of the world one measure.'   Talmud b. Qid 49b (quoted by Ritner)

The above quotation neatly encapsulates the ancient world's attitude to Egyptian prowess in magick. But what is the purpose of Egyptian magick? Bodily resurrection would on the face of it, appear to be one major aim. But I contend there is an older, perhaps in some way more profound magical aim. That aim is good rebirth. That reincarnation is a central belief of the Egyptians is well illustrated by the second tale of Setna Khemwaset. Composed around 200BC it is roughly contemporary with Indian discussion of the doctrine

as evidenced in texts such as the *Caraka Samhita*. It is clear that the
doctrine of reincarnation is extremely old and pervasive. It makes
sense of much of the literature before that time. Pharaonic funeral
rites, although supposedly based on the cult of Osiris and the ideal
of bodily resurrection. Actually they contain a heck of a lot of
birth imagery. That is to say *new birth* rather than *resurrection* of the
old body. This feature is often hidden from view or overlaid by the
much more showy aspects of the funeral.

It leads me to consider the difference between underworld
and stellar deities. We perhaps all want to 'come forth by day', to be
in the sun, but after that, you maybe have a choice between a starry
Otherworld and the caverns of the night accompanied by the doll-
like Osiris. I say this not out of rudeness, but merely as an
observation on the two dimensional nature of the Osirian archetype.
The passive nature of Osiris is pretty much all we see of him, for
example in the famous ritual drama of Abydos (see Appendix V).
Whereas all the other parts are played by actors, the role of Osiris
is literally a puppet or manikin. Osiris may rule in the caverns of
the night, but when the sun god Ra passes through on his nightly
journey, the gods that remain behind with Osiris groan when Ra
departs.

Lucky are those gods, such as 'The Elder Magician', who along with Isis are the two major exponents of magick in Egyptian religion. They get to accompany and guard Ra on his journey. Men of earth may also perform the magick and stay with Ra until the birth of a new day. The magician's quest for good rebirth is achieved by accompanying the sun god Ra in his solar barque. Their presence there was dependent on knowledge rather than faith.

Religious texts such as *Amduat* and *Book of Gates* show Heka, the god of magick, in the divine barque of Ra as one of the personifications of his power. In the *Amduat* he appears even before Hu (logos) hence his title as the 'Elder Magician'. The great scholar of this mythology, Herman Te Velde, thinks the 'Elder Magician' is another synonym for *Heka* . Heka was perhaps one of those primordial seven shamans who pray the universe into life. Heka is perhaps interchangeable with Shu, Atum's eldest son, the first of all offspring. Heka was the local god of the fourteenth Upper Egyptian nome, although nothing remains of ancient Qis/Kusai, near modern el-Qusiya.

There is a very close association between the Egyptian god Seth and Egyptian magick. Another distinguished scholar Hornung thought this 'elder magician' was in fact Seth. Hornung was the commentator on the *Book of Gates*, the same text inscribed on the

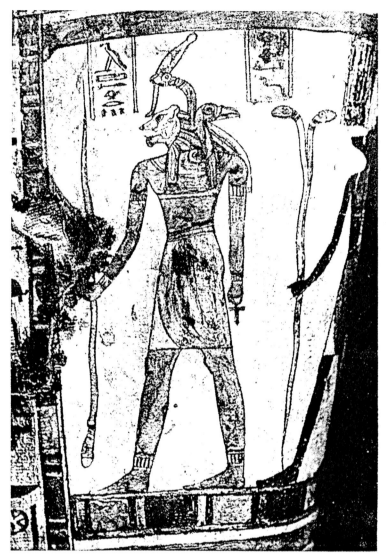

The god 'Ash' from a mummy-case in Brighton Museum (JEA, II 1925, 78f). He appears on sealings of Peribsen and Khasekhemui and thus is associated with Seth (Mercer 1949: 189). The *Book of the Dead* has a spell 'I am the Terrible One in the Thunderstorm. I am refreshed by this "Ash" ' (BD xcv). By the 26th dynasty, he has three heads - lion, snake and vulture. Margaret Murray discusses the possibility of the continuation of his worship as a medieval Frankish demon/deity 'Ash' consulted by King Marcomir. The latter also has three heads - lion, toad and eagle (See Murray 1973: 223).

alabaster coffin of Sety I. If Hornung is correct that this 'elder magician' is in truth another form of Seth, he is seen here as the helmsman of the solar barque. Seth's role as ferryman continues in the guise of Nemty, the ferryman god in the *Contendings of Horus and Seth*, discussed above. Heka's name is unusually written with a hieroglyph that represents the hinder parts of a lion or leopard. The leopard is yet another beast with strong Sethian associations by reason of its spots, said to be marks of branding. The hind legs of a leopard or lion are its powerhouse, hence magick or Heka signifies 'physical strength, sexual or creative power'!

Perhaps what is obvious from all this, is that magick is an activity of the Gods. The title *ah hekau* meaning 'great of magic' being one of the most common adjectives used of the gods, more so than men. Humanity must, if anything, assimilate to the magic-working gods in order to copy them. Ritner thought this was a strong indication of how much magick is seen as a part of nature.[4] According to Te Velde, the power of magick is especially necessary during the seventh hour of the night, a crucial moment just after midnight.

If you think about the above, you might see how it disposes of those theories that see magick as evidence of decline from religion. All of these activities are 'performed by priests as the

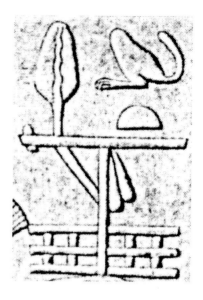

Left: The god Heka from the Papyrus of Khonsu-Renep in the Cairo museum. He was a scribe as well as one of the 21st dynasty clergy of Amon-Ra (Piankoff 1954). **Right:** The hieroglyph of the God Heka seen here (upper right) in ensign of the 14th Upper Egyptian Nome (Qis/Kusai), from the second courtyard scene of the Temple of Sety I at Abydos, drawn by Amice Calverley (1933).

techniques of religion, Egyptian 'magic' cannot be opposed to religion and the western dichotomy of 'religion vs. magic' is thus inappropriate when describing Egyptian practice.'[5] The same point was made by Sir Alan Gardiner back in 1915. It has taken a long time for the message to get through:

> 'That magic should have been regarded as an attribute of a deity and a fortiori as itself a deity, destroys at one blow the theories of those who discern a fundamental distinction between what is religion and what is magical.'
>
> Gardiner (1915) p 262 quoted in Ritner (1993).

It has to be said that Egyptian magick has not been well served by extant theories of magick (who has?), i.e. Frazer, Malinowski and Evan-Pritchard, all of which crumble as theories, when used outside of their original locus and are confronted by Egyptian material. R K Ritner adopts what is a new approach in Egyptology, by focussing on magical *activity* rather than some western definitions of magick such as 'obtaining a goal outside of the natural laws of cause and effect' etc, etc.[6] This emphasis on magical *activity*, rather than the futile quest for an essential *definition* of magick, is one used in the study of Hinduism. It's one I've used myself in this area, which I in turn learnt from the works of Gupta, Hoens, & Goudriaan T, *Hindu tantrism*.[7]

'The practical mechanics of magic may provide a focus not

only for the pertinent materials (magical essences) and attendant spells (magic words) of any magical procedure but also for the fundamental meaning of the procedure itself. It is in the rite – and not the spell – that the essence of Egyptian magic is to be sought.' (Ritner 1993: 67).

This is not to minimise the importance of the words spoken in a ritual. It's just that many other important lessons can be missed if you ignore the mechanics of a rite. The 'importance of ritual yields new knowledge of cultures, although the rubrics were often omitted by earlier scholars.'[8] Ritner is referred to the fact that papyri with *too much* practical information were often ignored or censored by earlier scholars. *The Papyrus Salt*, source of the 'Abydos Arrangement' being a prime example.

By 'magical activity', Ritner means, circumambulations, spitting, blowing, licking, swallowing, use of images, superposition, trampling, binding, use of red, breaking, use of sand, burning, numerological symbolism, piercing, decapitation, reversal, burial, use of the dead and oracular consultation. Wouldn't you agree that it would be strange to omit these from any presentation of magick, but this is how it once was?

Notes
1.   Divin 1969 : 140.
2.   Lichtheim 1980 : 133.
3.   Lichtheim 1980 : 135.

4.   Te Velde 1973 : 8.
5.   Ritner 1993 : 2.
6.   Ritner 1993 :1.
7.   Gupta, Hoens, & Goudriaan, 1979.
8   Ritner 1993 : 67.

16 Magical activities

'To ascribe feelings to nature as in "The Cruel Sea" is only a
fallacy to those who do not understand the power of metaphor.'

The Book of Shu

Words and speech (words spoken out loud)

Earlier I described the seven creative utterances that are hypostasized

as the seven sages or shamans of the primordial cow, those who

utter the seven creative words or spells that bring the world into

being. This also provides us with a key axiom of ancient magical

praxis — magick revolves around the power of the word that must

be uttered or spoken to be effective.

The ancient hieroglyph particularly connected with this activity

is, not surprisingly, a picture of the human mouth -

- vocalised as 'er' - quite a primal sound. This is fully expressed in

the archaic 'voice' offering alluded to in the famous Egyptian formula: *peret kheru* - 'a voice offering' which can be appended to the votive *bread* and *beer,* or stand alone as a word offering or song.

In the *Contendings of Horus & Seth,* Isis uses verbal magick to take the form of a beautiful young girl, and thus disguises herself from Seth. Apart from these chthonic sounds – as language developed, spells were constructed by a play on words, that can only occur if the words are spoken aloud. So for example the construction of an amulet often relies upon a word play, such as where the name of a semi-precious green stone (*wadj*), which coincidentally also means 'to flourish' (*wadj*) . Both words may be written differently but sound the same. This principle applies to all languages, so you might want to compile your own list of useful synonyms, for example a prolific synonym such as *rose.*

Take this a stage further, and we reach the kind of intimate relationship between medicine and magic – where the word *pechart* – is used for both. Taken even further, it leads to the use of certain medicaments, for example, a head wound is treated by an ostrich egg compress, because of its apparent similarity (pun) to the human skull. Now it might be objected that this kind of word play is hardly likely to be the basis of a very effective medicine. I've argued elsewhere[1] that many effective medicaments have in fact found their way into the pharmacopoeia via this strange route. In European medicine, a related doctrine of 'signatures' led some early physicians to experiment with aconite for eye disease, purely on the basis of the eye like flowers of the mature plant – a visual pun. They did in fact discover an effective medicine via this intuitive method. Incidentally, the ostrich is not even a native of this part of the Nile valley. This highly valued substance was transported to Ombos from the Africa motherland.

To sum up, speech and sound provide us with one of the primary means of working magick. Sound and vibration provide the matrix from which the entire cosmos is made. This doctrine is comparable to the sophisticated speculations of Tantrism, where sound is also seen as the primary material, and is manipulated by an archaic proto-language known as mantra yoga. In Egypt, especially in later times, any speech whatever by Thoth is *ipso facto* a vocal spell.[2] I mentioned earlier the vibration of the rune *Uroz* in the invocation of Seth. This highly effective technique grew out of the kind of word play alluded to above. Coming right up to date it is worth exploring Surrealist word games such as the *Exquisite Corpse*.

Texts

Where you have the spoken word, the next step is the text. Most of the surviving examples of texts with recognisable magical intent fall into the category of execration i.e. texts intended to do harm to an enemy. There are at least a thousand extant examples of execration texts. The text is again in the form of a picture – as indeed are all of the earliest hieroglyphs. Arguable one of the oldest such hieroglyphs is the image of a bound figure, representing one's enemy. Even in more literary constructions of later times, the proto image survives as a grammatical component of the text – the bound figure either becomes a so-called 'determinative' - i.e. a sign that determines the meaning of the foregoing sound signs and to define their meaning in a general way. Or the bound figure becomes the object on which the rest of the text is written. Next time you look at an Egyptian freeze, try not to see it as a text with a large incidentally illustration. Remember that an image, however large, is actually part of the text. To take an example that is familiar to some Thelemites – the otherwise undistinguished *Stele of Revealing*, has a winged disk at the top. In the Egyptian language, this is rendered 'Horus Behadit' – the winged solar disk Horus of Edfu (Behadit). Crowley misheard the translation and wrote this as Hadit – thus are new gods born everyday.

Curse objects are most often made of pottery. Here too the substance is no accident but a choice deliberate for magick; the god Khnum, is the divine potter who forms the foetus from clay. Lead, a Sethian metal is also widely used.

In later times it is Seth who become the prototype for this bound figure. That is to say, the characteristic posture and features of this motif stem from the mythology of Seth. The following images illustrate this point. Furthermore thirteen pins or miniature flint or iron knives pierce the object. Leave aside whether the number thirteen has lunar connotations, which I think is also a Sethian feature. Knapped flint power objects are amongst some of the very oldest human artefacts. They are a very distinctive feature of Ombos and the cult of Seth. They never loose this heavy ritual significance. Iron, as has already been noted, is another extremely significant magical substance. Before the so-called age of iron, it was only known from meteorites and was strongly, perhaps exclusively, associated with Seth. Now there is still a mystery here concerning how the cult practices of ancient times, that would have only positive connotations, are later used in negative way against *those same people*?? What do you think – is it a kind of perverse compliment?? Perhaps the conflict of ancient times was never as total as in the modern mind. My teacher once told me that the notion of total war, as in for example nuclear destruction, was actually quite alien to the ancient mind.

Figurine found by archaeologists, together with a lead tablet containing an inscription *nearly* identical to the 'love spell' discussed in section on *Image Magick* below. See S. Kambitsis, "Une nouvelle tablette magique d'Egypte, Musée du Louvre, Inv. E 27145, 3C/4C siecle," BIFAO 76 (1976): 213-23 and plates.

Encircling

The third major component of ancient Egyptian magick is to *encircle*. One modern commentator suggested that the word 'sorcery' might contain a similar notion. In Egypt, a common word used in this context is *pechart*, whose root is a hieroglyph[3] meaning 'to go around or encircle'. The image is a representation of the intestines. In one account, the god Osiris is encircled by goats, which in the Ramessium papyrus are the traditional enemies of Osiris and are sacrificed in the Temple of Seth at Sepermeru. On a micro level the practice features in the writing of a king's name, the so called cartouche, nothing more than a symbolic double encircling of the critical name, by a rope like line of ink. The practice is so old; it is not possible to say when it began. This form of magical activity is said to be coeval with Egyptian civilization. The circumambulation of mastaba or tomb is a feature of the earliest funeral rites. Later we find examples of encircling in first of Setna, when the hero eventually get his hands on the *Book of Thoth*, and is able to repeat one of the spells:

> 'He put the book into my hand and I read aloud the first formula which was written. I [circled] the skies, the earth, the world of the night, the mountains and the waters: I understood clearly what birds were saying, as well as fish and the four-footed beasts. Then I read aloud the second formula that was written, and I saw the sun appear with its escort of gods. I saw

the moon at its rising and all the stars of the sky in their places. (see Lichtheim 1980: 128-131).

After this reading of the second formulae, the magician joins the sun god Ra at the centre of a circling universe. What may have begun in the remote past as a funeral spell or rite, is reused for the benefit of the living? This leads us to yet another important feature of magick, the centrality of funeral rites in its activities.

Spitting/Ejaculating, Licking and Swallowing

Now we come to three related magical processes. Spit as magical substance, survives in modern folk attitudes from all over the world. We say 'spitting image' or in French 'c'est son père tout craché' – Spit is also a common euphemism for semen. In ancient physiology, both spit and semen were thought to originate in the bone marrow.[4]

> ' I have appeased Suty with the spittle of the earth and blood from Geb's marrow.' (BD spell 96§5).

The spitting mouth[5] is a common grammatical determinative as opposed to image of a pot to designate washing or purifying.

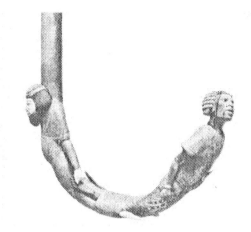

Above: Nubian and Asiatic prisoners bound on King Tutankhamun's walking stick. Nubian, Asian, Libyan and Egyptian were the four 'races' acknowledged in ancient Egyptian 'anthropology'. **Below**: a version of the 'Mehen' game found in one of the Ombos graves, a version of which survives in modern Sudan. Mehen is the serpent who guards the boat of Ra on his journey through the caverns of the night. This ancient game had mysterious funerary significance. Its fall from favour coincides with the decline of the cult of Seth. The slots that 'cut' the serpent perhaps added to the unlucky association. One version of the game found by Petrie had 545 divisions. I have an intuition this might be a 'bead game', for example guessing the permutation of glass beads in the opponent's hand, the lion shaped pieces used on the board to keep score. For more information see Decker 1992.

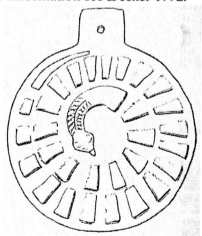

Spittle can thus be seen as a form of excrement, hence detoxification is a dominant component of Egyptian medicine.

In one of the most important Egyptian creation myths, spit and semen are interchangeable. Here we are again at the beginning of an exceptionally rich vein of magical ideas. From these foundations are built the entire edifice of tantrik body magick. In the myth, the mysterious demiurge Atum or Amun-Ra creates the first pair of beings from either spittle or more commonly by an act of masturbation or autogenesis. The results are the cosmological deities Shu (atmosphere, space) and Tefnut (moisture). Here is the divine precedent that is evoked in a great deal of later magick, the so-called 'histeriola' or divine precedent for a spell.

For example, the *Legend of Isis and the Secret Name of Ra* appears as the 'histeriola' for a spell designed to heal scorpion stings. The story of how Isis extracts Ra's secret name by the use of her bodily fluids, is recounted in greater detail in several places including my own *Tankhem*.[6]

Spittle or semen also plays a part in the otherwise miraculous birth of both Seth and Apophis. Hence the demotic proverb 'He who spits at heaven'. Even the oceans are said to be salty because of the accumulation of Seth's spit.[7]

The use of the substance is an activity with mythic elements, that go right to the core of Egyptian theology, and is far from being *small tradition* stuff. Spittle is a substance that never loses its malign and indeed curative power. See for example, how in later times it is used by the New Testament magician Jesus to accomplish many famous miracles.[8]

Licking

The power of spitting is part of a complex of magical techniques that stem from the occult qualities ascribed to human bodily fluids. This includes sexual fluids, sweat, blood, saliva and even the breath. All these things were often considered taboo, which is perhaps part of their power. But we need not view this as the whole story. It is an important occult doctrine, that human beings are able to imbue things with magical power, perhaps because bodily fluids contain hidden or microscopic qualities. Later, I will explore one of the key magical techniques, by which these taboo substances are used for magical ends. Following on from the above discussion of spitting, is the lick – a physical practice magically sanctioned by the Egyptian love goddess Hathor and her obvious cow-like qualities. Thus:

> 'I kiss your head, I lick your limbs with the pleasant tongue which has come forth from my mouth, you being born daily

from the head of your father Amon'

Sethe 1930 p.238 II 1-4 quoted in (Ritner 1993: 93).

In later erotic texts, licking in the relaxed manner of a cow is recommend for acts of cunnilingus. Licking something has a dual role of activating it by the power of the spittle. Also it is an important way in which we investigate our world, sensing things via the sense of taste, also absorbing things into our own bodies. The Egyptian magical technique associated with this sense combines it with the power of the hieroglyphic language. A picture representing the person's desire is painted in henna or red ochre and licked each day, enabling it to transition to the otherworld where it can do its work of change. In my contacts with the god Seth, he actually suggested the following technique, which combines licking with sexual magick. I found myself desirous of protection from persons or person unknown. My partner and I painted the appropriate hieroglyph on our bodies, using red ochre. The sign we choose for the protective component of the rite, was coincidentally that of Hathor in the form of the horned mirror. This is an excellent way to reflect back any bad vibes.

Incidentally, painting the hieroglyph of a particular deity on the shoulder, chest or forehead, was also the way in which ancient magicians did what is known in modern parlance as 'assume the god-form'. In Crowley's *Liber Al*, Nuit enjoins her companions, to come before her in a single robe, wearing a rich headdress. I think this may also be accomplished by the above painting technique, as an alternative to the more literal interpretations utilising a nemys (or bath towel and headband). Suitable attired my partner and I performed our ritual, which culminated in a bit of play of the love god. By the close of the ritual, all of the signs painted on our bodies had disappeared, either licked off or otherwise erased. The effects were very dramatic, revealing the culprits and giving them a very uncomfortable night!

If you do some investigation of your own you will soon find many other examples of licking spells from diverse magical traditions. Why not try one of the magical techniques used by the Bard Taliesin and known as Imbas Forosna. See the works of Jan Fries for much more background to Celtic licking spells. Not surprisingly the canine god Anubis has many spells of healing that involve the licking of wounds. And the classical *Mithras Liturgy* contains an important licking spell:

> 'Now the encounter with the great god is like this: Having obtained the above mentioned herb (*kentritis*), at the conjunction of [of the sun and the moon] occurring in the Lion [FN says this is the new moon] take the juice and, after mixing it with honey and myrrh, write on a leaf of the persea tree the eight-lettered name, as given below . And having kept yourself pure for 3 days in advance, come at morning to face

the sunrise; / lick off the leaf while you show it to the sun, and then he [the sun god] will listen to you intentively. Begin to prepare [the scarab] on the new moon in the lion, according to the god's [reckoning].[9]

Now this is the name: "I EE OO IAI" Lick this up, so that you may be protected; and rolling up the leaf/, throw it into the rose oil. Many times have I used the spell and have wondered greatly.' (Betz 1986: 53).

Sleep magick

'We reason on our dreams the way primitive man did when awake'   Carl Jung

Rituals to send a dream, whether to oneself or *to another*, were a common feature of ancient magick. If waking consciousness fails you in a task, for example, that of devising some further variations on the above techniques of eating magick, then I suggest you use sleep magick. Ask the gods to send you a dream with an application of the technique. Mark the appropriate sign on your body before going to sleep. If you have absorbed some of the information in *Tankhem*, you may already know that one of the core practice of the tradition, asks you to visualise the first journey through the Temple of Sety I to the shrine of Amon-Ra. The night time retiring of the magician to an astral temple is something I first encountered in the esoteric novels of Dion Fortune. When you go to bed, you fall asleep and your spirit spends the night safely tucked up in your astral temple. You will no doubt be rewarded with a visionary dream containing a variation of your own upon this technique.

Ancient dream manuals tell us that Seth is the source of evil sleep i.e. nightmares. The riding of the 'dreamy night air' is especially appropriate for the hidden god Seth, who has many associations with dream control. Dream control of one sort or another was a common element of ancient magick. As a counterpart to this there are manuals, many dating from quite early times, to help one interpret such dreams when they come. An example in Webb has:

'The god in him is Seth ... he is a man of the people ... He is one dissolute of heart on the day of judgement – discontent in his heart. If he drinks a beer, he drinks it to engender strife and turmoil. The redness of the white of his eye is this god. He is one who drinks what he detests. He is beloved of women through the greatness [a lacunae in which you might like to add you own bit] the greatness of his loving them, though he is a royal kinsman, he has the personality of a man of the people . . . he would not descend unto the west, but is placed in the desert as a prey to rapacious birds . . . he drinks beer so as to engender turmoil and disputes . . . he will take up weapons of warfare . . . he will not distinguish the married woman from ... As to any man who opposed him ... massacres arise in him and he is pleased in the Netherworld.'

(Webb says it's a 19th dynasty dream manual – from Papyrus Chester Beatty c1800BC).

Swallowing

The next stage takes in swallowing or eating, which by extension could be said to include cannibalism. Cannibalism is perhaps divisible into two kinds – what we might call the *elective* consumption of the corpse, either in whole or part by one's surviving relatives. The other, much less common variety is compulsory, the involuntary consumption by an enemy.

This is as good a point as any to introduce a discussion of so-called 'occult' crime. As I write this, a self-styled 'satanist' is in the news at the conclusion of his trial for the slaying his girlfriend. It is unlikely to be the last time such as crime is in the headlines.[10] Psychopaths exist in all societies. Restricting the discussion of taboo issues such as sacrifice and cannibalism will not, in my opinion make the world a safer place. Afterall we've had the way of restriction for a long while now and the results are every where to be seen. So called 'occult' crime has its own causes, one of them being ignorance. That's why I'm particularly keen to discuss this material in an informed way. The stream of thought we are about to follow leads to the contemporary magical conclusion that there is no need for *violent* sacrifice. The most powerful of all magical sacraments is freely given and does not involve harm to the donor.

But before revealing that, we need to look at the origin of cannibalism. Once again we find a religious precedent for both these practices. It comes from one of the oldest religious texts ever discovered, so far at least, those carved onto the walls of 5th dynasty pyramids, and therefore known as the pyramid texts, circa 2500BC. One of these texts is known as the *Cannibal Hymn* :

'The King is one who eats men and lives on the Gods. . .
The King eats their magick, swallows their spirits.'
Pyramid Texts 273-74

The so called 'Cippi' (no pun intended) of Horus use this technique. This child god is sometimes called Shed - who appears to be a later form of Horus as saviour. *Cippi* are clay plaques depicting the triumph of Horus over the Crocodiles and other desert beasts. This particular incident occurs during the sojourn of Horus and his mother Isis in the delta, hiding from Seth during the infancy of the future divine king. Drinking water passed over such images, that depict the above scene was then drunk as a prophylactic.

Another fine example comes from the first story of Setna.

'He put the book into my hand and I read aloud the first

formula which was written. I encircled the skies, the earth, and the world of the night, the mountains and the waters: I understood clearly what birds were saying, as well as fish and the four-footed beasts. Then I read aloud the second formula that was written, and I saw the sun appear with its escort of gods. I saw the moon at its rising and all the stars of the sky in their places.

I wanted to absorb these marvellous formulae, and as I did not know how to write, I had to reply on Nenofer, my brother and my husband, who was a skilled scribe and a very learned man. He sent for a piece of papyrus, and on it he carefully copied all the words that were in the book. Then he moistened the papyrus with beer (see glossary) and dissolved it all in water. When he was certain that it had melted, he drank, and in this way contained within himself all that was in the book. And then he did it all again for me.' (Divin 1969: 114)

Key incidents in the 'sethian' *Tale of Two Brothers* also involve magick connected with the drinking of water:

'And this is what shall come to pass, that I shall draw out my soul, and I shall put it upon the top of the flowers of the acacia, and when the acacia is cut down, and it falls to the ground, and thou comest to seek for it, if thou searchest for it seven years do not let thy heart be wearied. For thou wilt find it, and thou must put it in a cup of cold water, and expect that I shall live again, that I may make answer to what has been done wrong.' (Petrie)

So the eating of something is an ancient method by which magical substance is passed back into the body to make it powerful. In the examples given so far, what is eaten has been water, ink, maybe paper, but the precedent is a form of cannibalism, in the sense that either your own or another's bodily fluids are eaten. Could it be that the elective funeral cannibalism practiced by our Neolithic ancestors, was where they first learnt the technique? There is some contemporary research that indicates that memories can be passed from one organism to another by this eating process. Now you may well have heard that eating your own relatives can be a dangerous practice – in the modern world, it it said to be the cause of brain disease. Well in the Neolithic the person would be long dead before such a disease could manifest. There are even some, who say that the phenomenal human brain is some sort of mutation brought about by the cannibal habits of our ape ancestors. Perhaps things are not as simple as they at first appear.

Returning to the topic of eating spells, the Egyptian technique seems to have passed lock, stock and barrel into the Hebrew holy books. One of those obscure passages rarely mentioned by Sunday school teachers reads as follows:

Adultery curse from Bible, Number 5: 23-24

'Then the priest shall write these curses in a book and wash them off into the water of bitterness; and he shall make a woman drink the water of bitterness that brings the curse, and the water that brings the curse shall enter into her and cause bitter pain.

And the priest shall take the cereal offering of jealously out of the woman's hand and shall wave the *cereal offering* [my emphasis] before the Lord and bring it to the altar; and the priest shall take a handful of the cereal offering, as its memorial portion and burn it upon the altar, and afterward shall make the woman drink the water.

And when he has made her drink the water, then, if she has defiled herself and has acted unfaithfully against her husband, the water that brings the curse shall enter her body and cause bitter pain, and her body shall swell, and her thigh shall fall away, and the woman shall become an execration among her people. But if the woman has not defiled herself and is clean, then, she shall be free and shall conceive children.'

It goes without saying, that had such a passage been found in *any other* literature, it would be sufficient for scholars to dismiss the *entire* text as superstitious magick. But if you think about it, it is yet another example of how magick and religion are two sides of the same coin. The above passage may even have entered into the transmission of the third chapter of the *Book of the Law*, the moment

'Edible Astarte', with horns - used to create some form of *shew* bread - or cake of light - offered in her rites. Original height 8ins. Found at Nahariya, now in Israel National Museum. Reproduced courtesy of the Israel Antiquities Authority. (see Patai 1978: 65).

at which a very powerful 'new' technique of magick re-entered our

tradition. I'm talking about the famous *Cakes of Light* ritual. As is

well known, Crowley was very familiar with the Bible. Could it be

that in the process of channelling a mystical Egyptian text, he also

released an obscure cell of memory?

Notes
1.   Morgan (1999) *Medicine of the Gods*, Mandrake of Oxford.
2.   Ritner (1993: 67).
3.   F46 in Gardiner's sign list.
4.   Ritner (1993: 80).
5.   D26 in Gardiner's sign list.
6.   Morgan (2005).
7.   Ritner (1993: 101).
8.   Ritner (1993: 76).
9.   Betz (1986: 53fn) says this 'new moon of god' means
      'according to the heavens', whereas 'new moon of man', is
      'according to the calendar'.
10.   See for example *The Guardian*, UK 22.1.5.

17 Cakes of Light

The following is a modern ritual technique, that nevertheless manages to key into an extremely old form of 'eating magick'. Dare I say it, there is even an element of *elective* cannibalism, that ultimately derives from the nameless aeons of the Neolithic. The baking of a magical cake or loaves we might call *eucharist* magick. Archaeologists have found many clay bread moulds from all over the Middle East especially Palestine. They produce a bite-sized image of the ancient goddess Astarte for consumption by the celebrant. It is perhaps another of those well kept secrets of the ancient Hebrew religion, that there was in fact an image of this goddess, who was worshiped alongside Yahweh in the Solomonic temple.[1] To explore this issue in more depth, I recommend *The Hebrew Goddess* by Raphael Patai or Othmar Keel and Christoph

Uehlinger's, *Gods, Goddesses and Images of God in Ancient Israel.* It seems
likely that the Christian eucharist (literally: thanksgiving) stems from
this same tradition.

I am indebted for the following analysis to the work of Alex
Bennett, whose fuller document on *Eucharist Magick* can be viewed
on line at dowhatthouwilt.com. The *locus classicus* for this technique
is the third chapter of the *Book of the Law*, usually considered the
most difficult and controversial of this entire holy and *prophetic* text:

Liber Al , Chapter III vs 23-25

23. For perfume mix meal and honey & thick leavings of red
wine: then oil of Abramelin and olive oil, and afterward soften
& smooth down with rich fresh blood.

24. The best blood is of the moon, monthly: then the fresh
blood of a child, or droppings from the host of heaven; then
of enemies; then of the priest or the worshippers; last of some
beast, no matter what.

25. This burn: of this make cakes & eat unto me. This hath
also another use; let it be laid before me, and kept thick with
perfumes of your orison: it shall become full of beetles as it
were and creeping things sacred unto me.

If you want to work with this, you are going to need some
Abramelin oil. It is possible to buy this from various suppliers, but

the quality varies radically. You might find that the only alternative is make your own blend of the oil, something that is difficult, but does have its own rewards. I have been fortunate in knowing several good blenders over the years, so I'm never short of a good supply. I was also fortunate enough to be able to obtain supplies from *Id Aromatics* in Leeds, and when that went, from *Amphora Aromatics* in Bristol. Both shops are said to have connections with Chaos magick, who did much to widen interest in the use of good essential oils and incenses, long before the mainstream commercialisation of the art. If you do intend to do it yourself the recipe can be found in several books, including David Rankine's *Becoming Magick*.

The Abramelin oil and incense are essential to the modern Cakes of Light ritual. Its presence it not merely as a highly evocative magical fragrance, but equally as importantly as a preservative, allowing the cakes to be consumed over many weeks, perhaps even years. They can therefore be stored and used in the several rituals as you have need of them.

But the other important ingredient is the blood. This is perhaps one of the most misunderstood passages in magical literature. Aiwass, Crowley's spirit guide, gives the entire doctrine, warts and all. The spirit begins by emphasising how the best blood does not involve any permanent harm. It is funny how the blood that causes the very least harm, is freely given, is also in many cultures the most taboo. It tells you quite a lot about mainstream values. Even amongst Neo-Vampires – there can be some acceptance of drinking of a partner's venous blood – but consider for a moment how you'd feel drinking the menstrual variety? Do you detect a mental knot there?

Aleister Crowley is often accused of feeding the media frenzy over human sacrifice. This is the old 'blood libel.' levelled against all religions at some time in their development – the false accusation that they are stealing children to eat in their secret rituals. The Old Testament stories of Abraham preparing to sacrifice his son Isaac are usually seen as the moment at which, Judaism moved away from the older blood rites in favour of animal sacrifice. The *Book of the Law* continues a tradition whereby, even animal sacrifice is downgraded, as it was more than a century before in the occult tradition, when Francis Barrett proposed fumigations of incense, as an alternative to the sacrifice of a chicken.

Blood, so say the experts, should be fresh, for this is still a sacrifice. 'It is no good preparing this ingredient before making the Cake of Light. Every type of blood no matter what, must come directly from its source. The other ingredients should be prepared before making the sacrifice.'

The blood types in descending order of strength are:

1. Blood of the moon, monthly (menstrual blood). I have already mentioned how taboo, and also how progressive a notion is enshrined in the type of blood.

2. The 'fresh blood of a child' is usually said to be placental blood. Again very taboo, although in the modern world it is increasingly popular for the placenta to be used by the parents, perhaps in the form of pate consumed at the child's naming ceremony as a powerful protection rite.

3. Droppings from the host of heaven are taken to mean semen. Again freely given, it can be viewed as a type of blood.

4. Of enemies – this speaks for itself. It would be a bit po-faced to suppose that mortal enemies are not part of your possible universe. Personally I would have no moral qualms about using blood magick against an evil despot like Adolf Hitler etc. The use of magick against the Third Reich during WWII. is part of the *foundation myth* of modern witchcraft.

5. Of the priest or of the worshippers, i.e. blood taken from the veins, as self sacrifice either from you or other celebrants.

6. Of some beast, no matter what i.e. blood taken from any animal whether it be from the veins, menstruation or semen. It is possible to envisage such a usage, that does not involve the physical

death of the animal. It would be rash to deny the power of this kind of sacrifice, but in the new covenant, it is placed at the bottom of the scale in terms of efficacy.

The blood, Abramelin oil, etc, are blended together and cooked as a Cake of Light. This is then used in a future ritual; one is burnt on the altar, whilst an additional Cake is eaten by each of the participants to the rite. In the *Book of the Law*, the purpose of the rite is to hasten the development of the Aeon of Horus. But there is no principle reason why the Cakes should not be used in other rituals of your choice. It is also common practice for the Cakes to contain the blood of two (or perhaps more) participants in their making. I'm talking about tankhem or tantrik rites here, where two lovers contribute their bodily fluids to the creation of these very powerful magical talismans, otherwise known as Cakes of Light. I would remind you that a close reading of the *Contendings of Horus & Seth* (see appendix IV), reveals not an act of anal sex, but in fact more eating magick! When viewed through the Osirian lens, Seth's intentions seem abusive. But what actually happens, is an act of frottage which, leads to Seth eating the semen of Horus. Seth then gives birth to the golden moon god Thoth. There is an older technique hidden in this late version of the myth. It concerns the mysteries of 'dolphin sex' not to be written of in this place.

Image magick

The most famous of all Egyptian magical techniques, we might call image magick, which is in reality a more graphic extension of things discussed above. It is known in modern versions as the 'voodoo doll' or 'wax image spell'. Incidentally the term 'voodoo doll' is highly misleading, as voodoo is one religion from which the practice is unknown. Furthermore the surviving Egyptian examples use clay rather than beeswax, although there is some indication of wax in the Mirgissa deposit discussed below. In examining these kinds of thing one should not overlook the symbolic importance of the clay, mythologically considered the substance from which the god Khnum fashioned human beings. The doll must have hands bound and be pierced with thirteen needles. Binding has very negative associations in Egypt.

This spell is probably as old as Egyptian civilization itself. This image harkens back to the so-called 'bound prisoner' motif – an image always found in religious contexts in ancient Egypt and which, therefore cannot be dismissed as simple militarism. The second story of Setna provides another good example. In it an older Setna visits the underworld in the company of his precocious and otherworldly son, and he is shown the fate of the wealthy 'sinner' in 'hell'. Bound in the traditional manner, his eye socket provides the pivot for one of hell's many doors! This highly evocative and gruesome image might well be called to mind with one of your own enemies!

This mindset is expressed so well in the *Book of the Law:*

> . . . Trample down the Heathen;
> be upon them, o warrior, I will give you of their flesh to eat!
> (AL III:11)

Trampling down one's enemies was a fairly ubiquitous Egyptian activity. Amongst the grave goods of King Tutankhamum, were slippers whose soles were decorated with the image of nine bows. The 'nine bows' represent the nine tribes of Nubia, one of Egyptian's most feared ancient enemies. This image later becoming a cipher for any of Egypt's foreign enemies.[2] Once on the lookout, this type of image magick is everywhere. The so-called 'Golden Horus' name is a hieroglyph that depicts Horus as a falcon perched on a golden necklace (see illustration). For various reasons, it is quite likely that the golden necklace was understood by the ancient Egyptians to represent Seth – 'He of Nubt' literally the 'City of Gold'. From Egyptian prehistoric times, this town was probably a central point of access to the gold fields of the Eastern desert and Nubia. As with so many things, it is always Seth that provides the archetype for bound power.

The following text, extraordinary in so many ways, comes from the masterful anthology of the *Greek Magical Papyri* edited by Hans Dieter Betz.[3] Their discovery is itself rather a good story, which at the risk of boring you I shall repeat:

'We know from literary sources that a large number of magical books in which spells were collected existed in antiquity. Most of them, however, have disappeared as the result of systematic suppression and destruction. . But not everything was lost. At the end of antiquity, some philosophers and theologians, astrologers and alchemists collected magical books and spells that were still available.'

Buried in clay pots and tombs, these secret caches remained hidden until the nineteenth century when they fell into the hands of a diplomat 'at the court in Alexandria a man who called himself Jean d'Anastasi (1780?-1857). Believed to be Armenian by birth, he ingratiated himself enough with the Pasha to become the consular representative of Sweden. It was a time when diplomats and military men often were passionate collectors of antiquities, and M. d'Anastasi happened to be at the right place at the right time. He succeeded in bringing together large collections of papyri from Egypt, among them sizable magical books, some of which he said he had obtained in Thebes. These collections he shipped to Europe, where they were auctioned off and bought by various libraries.'

'Unfortunately, we know almost nothing about the circumstances of the actual findings. But it is highly likely that many of the papyri from the Anastasi collection came from the same place, perhaps a tomb or a temple library. If this assumption is correct, about half a dozen of the best-preserved and largest extant papyri may have come from the collection of one man in Thebes. He is of course unknown to us, but we may suppose that he collected the magical material for his own use. Perhaps he was more than a magician. We may attribute his almost systematic collections of *magica* to a man who was also a scholar, probably philosophically inclined, as well as a bibliophile and archivist concerned about the preservation of this material.' (Betz 1986: xii-xiii)

The term 'magick', is Persian in origin, and was used by the xenophobic Romans with a pejorative sense.[4] The Egyptian tongue has no word for either superstition or indeed religion. Whatever the Romans did not like they ascribed to foreigners. Magick was banned in the empire by various edicts from Augustus to Theodosius. Rigid classification with Latin words like 'religion' and 'magic' is really alien to the Egyptian point of view.[5] Other magicians make the best guides, as in for example Giordano Bruno, centuries ahead of his time, had the 'revolutionary' idea of interpreting magick in its own terms. In modern anthropological parlance, Bruno took an *Emic* rather than an *Etic* approach.

As the public religion was driven underground, the use of cipher become more common.[6] Some techniques such as bowl magick, scrying into a bowl of burning herbs, were still conducted in private by cautious Egyptian priests; Heryheb or Lector priest the most likely agent. One famous account of such an episode is found in Porphyry's *Life of Plotinus*.[7] Plotinus (AD 205-270) was a Neoplatonic philosopher, born in Egypt at Lycopolis:

'An Egyptian priest who had arrived in Rome and, through some friend, had presented himself to the philosopher, became desirous of displaying his powers to him, and offered to evoke a visible manifestation of Plotinus' presiding spirit. Plotinus readily consented and the evocation was made in the Temple of Isis, the only place, they say, which the Egyptian could find pure in Rome.

At the summons a Divinity appeared, not a being of the spirit-ranks, and the Egyptian exclaimed: "You are singularly graced; the guiding spirit within you is none of the lower degree but a God." It was not possible, however, to interrogate or even to contemplate this God any further, for the priest's assistant, who had been holding the birds to prevent them flying away, strangled them, whether through jealousy or in terror.'

Itinerant magicians probably didn't exist in ancient Egypt, even a humble scorpion charmer probably schooled in *House of Life*.

Priests would be called out to extending an index finger, *mudra* like, to protect the people from crocodiles during a canal crossing.[8]

Amongst the *magica* is the following papyrus:

'PGM.IV. 296-466

Wondrous spell for binding a lover: Take wax [or clay] from a potter's wheel and make two figures, a male and a female. Make the male in the form of Ares fully armed, holding a sword / in his left hand and threatening to plunge it into the right side of her neck. And make hers with her arms behind her back and down on her knees. And you are to fasten the magical material on her head or neck.' (Betz 1986: 44).

The god Ares, can be viewed as a substitute for Horus. The posture of the female figure is a clear derivative from Egyptian originals in which the victim is Seth. This spell was written at the end of the classical era (circa 2nd century BC to 5th century AD), when in many ways, the original prototypes were forgotten hence Seth's significant change of gender. Like a great deal of later 'sethian' magick, the tone is abusive. It's amazing to think that the purpose of this elaborate spell is to attract a woman! Compulsion is a strong characteristic of the ancient mind - and this is extended to the object of desire as well as the gods themselves. The magical relationship of the ancients to their gods seems alien to the modern mind.

After some instructions on magical names to be written on the head, right ear, left ear, face, right and left eye, right and left shoulder, right and left arm, the hands, the breast, heart, lower belly, pudenda, buttocks, sole of the right and of the left foot. This division of the body again plays upon the notion of dismemberment, a motif that can be traced backwards to prehistory, the forwards through the cult of Osiris. We might boldly follow this notion to its eventual home in the erotic speculation of Hindu tantrism, whereby the body is divided into erogenous zones through which, the hidden inner moon moves throughout the month.

The spell continues:

'Take thirteen copper[9] needles and stick 1 in the brain while saying, "I am piercing your brain, NN"; and stick 2 in the ears and 2 in the eyes and 1 in the mouth and 2 / in the midriff and 1 in the hands and 2 in the pudenda and 2 in the soles, saying each time, "I am piercing such and such a member of her, . . . so that she may remember no one but me." From elsewhere in the rubric it can be seen that these are thirteen points of connection that are the object of his desire 'head to head . . . lip to lip . . . belly to belly . . .thigh to thigh and fit black to black [?], and let her . . .carry out her own sex acts / with me

And take a lead tablet and write the same / spell and recite it. And tie the lead leaf to the figures with thread from the loom after making 365 knots while saving as you have learned,

"ABRASAX, hold her fast!" You place it, as the sun is setting, beside the grave of one who has died untimely or violently, placing beside it also the seasonal flowers.'

The above is yet another clear example of how funeral rites are reused in this 'binding spell' for the benefit of the living. The operant beseeching the 'chthonic gods' PERSEPHONE ERESCHIGAL etc, and ANUBIS who, by this stage in his history is said to 'hold the keys to Hades, to infernal gods and daimons, to men and women who have died untimely deaths, to youths and maidens, from year to year, month to month, day to day, / hour to hour. I adjure all daimons in this place to stand as assistants beside this daimon. And arouse yourself for me, whoever you are, whether male or female, and go to every place and into every quarter and to every house, and attract / and bind her.'

The spells continues at great length in this tone: 'Let her be in love with me, . . . Let her not be had in a promiscuous way, let her not be had in her ass, nor let her do anything with another man for pleasure, just with me alone, etc, etc etc. And finally there is a prayer to be recited at sunset, while holding the magical material from the tomb, saying:

'Borne on the breezes of the wandr'ing winds,

Golden-haired Helios, who wield the flame's

Unresting fire, who turn in lofty paths

Around the great pole, who create all things

Yourself which you again reduce to nothing,

From whom, indeed, all elements have been

Arranged to suit your laws which nourish all

The world with its four yearly turning points.

Hear, blessed one, for I call you who rule

Heaven and Earth. Chaos and Hades, where

Men's daimons dwell who once gazed on the light,

And even now I beg you, blessed one,

Unfailing one, the master of the world,

If you go to the depths of earth and search

The regions of the dead, send this daimon,

From whose body I hold this remnant in my hands,

To her, NN, at midnight hours,

To move by night to orders 'neath your force,

That all I want within my heart he may

Perform for me; and send him gentle, gracious

And pondering no hostile thoughts toward me,

And be not angry at my potent chants,

Female figure showing the changing location of erotic passion in
women starting with right big toe on the first day of the moon's
bright fortnight. Based on an 18th century Rajasthani miniature
(after Douglas & Slinger).

For you yourself arranged these things among

Mankind for them to learn about the threads

Of the Moirai, and this with your advice. /

I call your name, Horus, 72 which is in number

Equivalent to those of the Moirai,

ACHAIPHO THOTHO I'HIACHAAIE EIA IAE EIA THOTHO PHIACHA.

Be kind to me, forefather, scion of

The world, self-gendered, fire-bringer, aglow

Like gold, shining on mortals, master of

The world, / daimon of restless fire, unfailing,

With gold disk, sending earth pure light in beams.

Translation by:E.N.O'Neil in (Betz 1986).

Reproduced courtesy of University of Chicago Press

As if to prove that this spell was probably fairly common currency in the classical world, the picture above is actually of a *similar* figurine found by archaeologists, together with a lead tablet containing an inscription *nearly* identical to the above.[10]

The use of image magick is extended to the vivifications of divine statues (splendours) by what is known technically as *pheneter.*

Under the patronage of the god of magick Heka, the now sentient image could be used for sorcery or oracular consultation.

Notes

1. Patai (1978 : 65).
2. Ritner (1993·: 123).
3. Betz (1986).
4. Cheke: 2004.
5. Ritner (1993 : 241).
6. Ritner (1993 : 218).
7. Mackenna (1917: 11).
8. Ritner (1993 : 227).
9. A metal associated with Venus, Isis and perhaps Hathor.
10. See S. Kambitsis (1976).

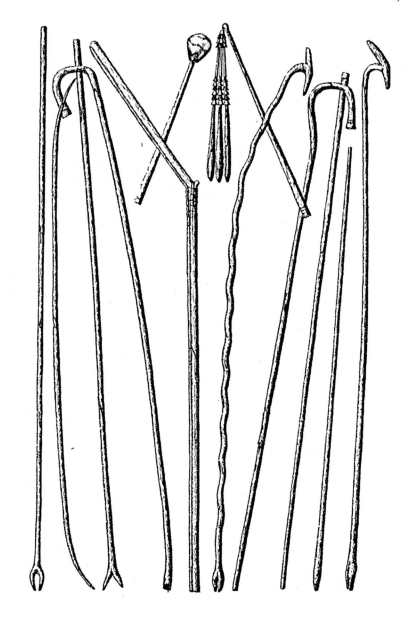

A selection of wands deposited in the pyramid of Senwosret I at Lisht. The *Was* and *Djaam* scepters are first and fifth from the left respectively (Gautier 1902: 76). There is no consistant distinction as to use, both bestow 'well being' on the bearer, both are seen holding up vault of heaven.

18 Magick as use and misuse of the funeral rite

Several times now I have alluded to the fact that, a great deal of Egyptian magick is essentially derived from funeral spells used for the benefit of the living. There is any number of options here:

Performance of your own funeral as a kind of dry run. This provides the more 'gnostic' side to magick - not so much bound up with mundane results, but more about the preparation of the Self for the journey across the abyss. It also links in with those magical techniques, such as *Liber Samech* whereby one seeks contact with beings of the 'inner planes' as a means to higher knowledge.

Performance of someone else's funeral for their benefit or indeed as a way of getting rid of them.

Performance of the funeral rites of a particular ethnic or national group as a way of deriding Egypt's troublesome enemies.

Performance of 'outmoded' versions of the funeral rite as a way of harming or controlling others.

Performance of the funeral rites of the past, in a deliberately distorted, reversed or contradictory manner as a way of harming or controlling others.

All these things and more are features of Egyptian magick, and indeed occur in many other subsequent cultures. Now you might be asking yourself – whose funeral? If it's not already obvious, the rubric for all of the above practices is provided by the ancient and indeed the normal Sethian way of death. All magick, especially that with a negative purpose, implicates Seth. It is therefore a way, by deconstruction, of viewing the original Sethian cult that lies behind it, albeit in distorted form. Is this an affront to Seth, or does it go with his territory? The difficulty of resolving this question, is perhaps the reason why Seth is sometimes said to be a hazard to the unwary - a demonic initiator.

The Mirgissa Deposite & Human sacrifice

Mirgissa is a 12th dynasty (c 2000BC) fortress situated on Egypt's southern frontier, above the second cataract of the Nile. The time leading up to the so-called second intermediate period, was one of political instability, when many external enemies seriously threatened Egypt's existence. Most powerful amongst these, was the coalition of nine Nubian tribes, represented by the hieroglyphs of the bow, hence the phrase 'nine bows' to designate Egypt's enemies. Much of this ancient territory falls within modern day Sudan. Complex societies have existed in Sudan for at least as long as they have in Egypt. The high culture of Sudan is roughly contemporaneous with that of Egypt, although this is a recent discovery, and for most of the last four thousand years, this has been hidden from history.

Amongst the neglected remains of Mirgissa, archaeologists found a virtually intact execration burial. Unlike normal burials, this is an elaborate ritual assemblage whose purpose, seems to be to ward off enemies on this dangerous frontier. The Mirgissa deposit provides the first indisputable evidence of human sacrifice in classical Egypt.

Curiously it resembles one of the burials from Ombos as described in detail above. Although it was once the normal mode of burial for the ancient Ombites, the practice was discontinued by the time this so-called execration burial was unearthed. It also has many similarities with the burial practices of Egypt's Nubian enemy. Indeed it might well be, that the people of Ombos, were once migrants from Nubia.

This deposit contains the remains of a human sacrifice, which not surprisingly turns out to be one of the Nubian enemies, probably a captive. The skull and skeleton are found in different locations, and when the possibility of disturbance is ruled out, human sacrifice seems the most likely explanation. The head and jaw were removed from the skeleton, and deliberately buried with the rest of the assemblage in what seems to be a reversed position. The upper jaw of the inverted skull is flush with surface.

Near the skull were found remains of the ritual that accompanied these actions, included a melted beeswax figurine dyed with red ochre – providing yet another example of the quintessentially Sethian wax image spell discussed above. In fact, everything about this burial brings together all of the Sethian magical techniques discussed before. Even the burial in sand should be seen as a ritual substance, symbolic of the desert necropolis. Sand is associated with Seth – placing something under sand is significant – and probably represents the image magick of *separation* of the two parts during burial.[1] Mention of sand may also bring to mind geomancy – divination by marks in sand. Examples of the crooked hippopotamus tusk wand, shows signs of wear from repeated use to draw signs or sigils, probably in prepared sand. Could the phrase 'vision in the feet', sometimes applied to Seth, be a reference to a geomantic practice, whereby footprints in sand were interpreted as an oracle?

The burial also includes incineration, figurines, word magick, broken pottery, invariably in multiples of seven. Noticeable too is the use of flint knives, which is traditional for ritual slaughter. Traces of similar rites have been found in other parts of Egypt, and indeed Nubia, modern Sudan. It is plain from the above rubrik, that the ethnicity, real or symbolic, of the victim, can be changed depending on the intention of the magician.

Flint Knives

'My nails like knives of flint are against the faces of them that do these (things) against thee.'   BD spell 172

The preparation of flint artefacts, along with the collection of red ochre, is one of humanity's oldest activities. Amongst all of the many flint power objects found at ancient Ombos, the flint knife was plainly the most treasured. Such a knife may have a talismanic function. The contemporary 'throwing knives' of Southern Sudan play a similar role, the blade and handle representing the two domains of the bearer's world.

Next consider the fishtail knife that Seth, in canide form, wears strapped to his tail! The examples found at Ombos by Petrie are amongst the very finest knapped flint weapons ever devised. These objects were the Ombite's innovation. This one was bought from a local dealer at Abydos by Petrie.

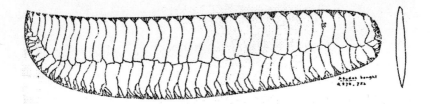

The possession of such a magical weapon was something no Ombite could abjure. It was the *must have* thing, even when superseded by more modern materials such as bronze. The flint knife was the weapon of choice for acts of magick, ritual slaughter etc. The confusion in contemporary magical practice, between the knife and the wand is relieved by meditating on the original sacrificial function of the knife. It is said to provide the precedent for the later practice of *bisecting* of *harmful* hieroglyphs. Images such as a hieroglyph have a latent power, that needs to be treated with care. Therefore a hieroglyph of a dangerous beast needs to be neutralised by bisection. At Ombos, the ubiquitous flint knives are almost always found broken in burials, and this is probably a deliberate magical act. This is the precedent for those examples of symbolic breaking of text and images in the pyramid texts. Despite the extreme antiquity of the Pyramid texts (c3500BC), it happened first at Ombos. Flint continued in agricultural use even to the present day – providing a cheap blade for sickles and scrapers.

In pharaonic culture, images of Seth were routinely neutralised in this manner. In a sense, Seth was stabbed with his own flint knife. Miniature flint knives in the form of nails or pins were used as an obvious substitute. The thirteen pins used in the 'wax image spell are a classical example of the practice. As the practice was internalised, Isis and Horus used copper against Seth. Contemporary magicians consider copper to be a 'venusian' metal. Cast your mind back to the 'love spell' discussed earlier, and you may recall that the thirteen pins were also of copper. Seth had his own metal, iron or lead, with which to ward off his old enemy Apophis, the demon of non-being.

Decapitation and reversal

The integrity of the corpse was something that became a taboo, for the later Egyptian followers of Osiris. Hence, the two greatly feared punishments of the Coffin texts were decapitation and reversal or otherwise jumbling, of the body parts. 'Coffin Texts' is a term reserved for those spells which are peculiar to the early coffins, and do not recur later, not at least until the Saite period, when some of them were sporadically revived. These Coffin Texts contain excerpts from the earliest Pyramid Texts, usurped by the nobility of the IX-XI dynasties for their own benefit.[2]

In some ways, we might see this fear of dismemberment after death as irrational. The whole process of mummification necessitates, what is essentially an elaborate dismemberment and then re-assembly. The integrity of the finished product must in many ways, be in the eye of the beholder. Egyptian sacred texts express a fear of the going down or reversal of bodily functions. This is linked with other disruptions to the normal order of things, such as, the eating of excrement and urine, something normally only reserved for the damned in *hell*. This taboo seems to have continued unabated even into the early modern and modern era. In his innovative study of the *Archaeology of Magick and Ritual*, Ralph Merrifield describes the incidence of deliberate reversals of such things as 'witch bottles'.[3] The rite of Mirgissa is pretty much identical with that prescribed for enemies of Horus in the Amduat . In late period texts such as *Papyrus Jumilhac*, such fate is reserved for Seth. And again, we must point out the odd paradox here: reversal and decapitation may have been part of the funeral rites of the original pre-dynastic Egyptians, the residents of Ombos, the people of Seth.

Burning sand

Fire is universally considered a threshold between one realm and another. We find the fullest development of this important idea in Hinduism. Fire of various varieties, the physical fire of the cremation or cooking pyre, or the internal fire of the stomach, is the main nexus of transition from one state to another. For the Egyptians, the burial in sand, a Sethian substance, was a practice loaded with meaning and therefore power. In the Mirgissa deposite, burning and burial were final acts of an elaborate execration rite. The burial was especially effective, if done in an existing necropolis otherwise, the burial was *de facto* a creation of same. Ritner maintains that this sends the object or talisman to realm of the dead - the underworld. The sandy pit is the equivalent of the abyss. Canopic jars or glass coffins, made ultimately from sand, provide an alternative. The *Papyrus Salt* has a parallel rite to protect the 'House of Life' or temple scriptorium. That rite forms the basis of what I call the 'Abydos arrangement'. The canopic jar is another form of *encirclement*. Later spells amplify the Sethian component, written defixiones or spells for benefit of the living are actually placed in the mouth of the corpse.[4]

Breaking the Red Pots

'Hail [Osiris NN] this is the Eye of Horus. Take it so that you
may be strong and that he may be terrified of you – break the
red pots.' PT spell 244, 249

To continue with this necromantic theme, we come to one of the
most common magical techniques of the ancient Egyptian world.
The breaking of the red pots was associated with the funerary
offering meal.[5] Once again Seth is involved. Cast your mind back
to the descriptions of the burial practices at Ombos, the Citadel of
Seth. A distinctive feature of the Sethian mode of death was a vast
funeral feast. To give some idea of possible scale, in nearby Nubia,
which had similar burial practices, one assemblage had the remains
of 5000 cattle, presumably slaughtered for the funeral feast. It is
quite likely, that communal feasting was the method by which,
surplus wealth was redistributed amongst the more communitarian
people of the Neolithic. Some of these practices continue in
changed form right into dynastic Egypt. The culture has moved
away from what Dr Jude Currivan calls its 'shamanic' roots, to the
more familiar 'geomantic' culture of the King and his followers.[6]
Hence the beautiful red pots associated with archaic Sethian worship,
become objects to be broken releasing their great magical power.
This practice is reinforced in the Coffin Texts. The timing is circa

2000BC, just after the first intermediate period, notable again as a time of crisis and civil war.

In Osirian religion, the breaking occurs simultaneously with the slaughtering of a bull in the temple slaughterhouse. The bull and the pot are substitute figures for the repulsed enemy i.e. Seth. The bulls, the pot, the colour red, the clay, all possess well-known and ancient Sethian associations. The breaking pot ritual is extended by the priests, to breaking of hieroglyphs in order to counteract their power. In the twilight of Egyptian culture, the Coptic Christians turned the same technique against Egyptian religion. Before desecrating and looting the great shrines of Abydos and

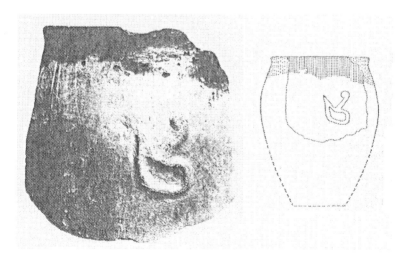

This same example was reproduced above in connection with proto Egyptian kingship. This pot is also a good example of Naqada's black top redware much favoured in the later rite of 'breaking the red pots.' Its fragmentary state may show the 'Sethians' use of the same type of magick.

elsewhere, they were careful to nullify the power of the images by breaking – hacking the faces and hands from the stone.

I guess if you've read this far, you have some sympathy with the archaic Sethian point of view. I don't know about you, but for me just the thought of breaking a pot already carries quite a lot of charge. Try visualizing it, start by imagining a ceramic pot with the most pleasing shape and decoration. Try to make it one you would really like to own. Perhaps you see one you already do own and treasure. Or maybe call to mind a favourite exhibit in an art gallery or museum. Imagine the process of manufacture or creation, either with slabs of clay or on a wheel.

The use of pots still plays an important role in modern sorcery. My friend, the cunning man Jack Daw, has fired many a 'clay virgin', in a simple outdoor kiln made from discarded house bricks. For fuel, he uses a packing of sawdust, which most sawmills are glad to give away. Having moulded the pot without a wheel, he fires it in a simple brick kiln. By controlling the airflow, the sawdust once lit smoulders for several days. Although not as hot as a professional kiln, the results are impressive. It's quite possible for the average person to make quite a fine pot. You might find you are even more attached to those you make for yourself. You can use your emotional connection. (see www.cornishwitchcraft).

The breaking of the red pots, may appear to you as a deliberate act of desecration, practiced only by the followers of Osiris. Although that is a tempting mindset, it is probably not really justified by the evidence. In truth, all of these practices are so old there is no way of knowing when they began. All that's needed is a pot, and the Sethians made many innovations in pottery design and creation. It is just as likely that, in some circumstances, the Sethians also broke the red pots as a magical act. Their emotional attachment makes the activity even more redolent with magical power. There is no taboo against the postmodern Sethian taking advantage of the same magical act. The breaking of such a beautiful object, specially crafted for the event, is indeed a very acceptable form of sacrifice.

The breaking of green faience in the *Book of the Dead* (125C) re-enacts the destruction of Osiris by Seth. This may also influence the choice of a broken potsherd for a written spell.

Letters to the dead

> Then Thoth said to the Master of the Universe: Cause a letter to be sent to Osiris, that he may pronounce judgement upon the two youths.
>
> *Contending of Horus and Seth*

Writing to the dead was a magical act used by the Egyptians, almost as soon as they discovered hieroglyphs. Precedent for this can be taken from the above letter to Osiris, lord of the dead. This was often combined with the kind of magick described earlier in the section on breaking the red pots. Examples of specially made and consecrated bowls can be viewed in various museums, including the 'Oxford Bowl' now in the Pitt Rivers.[7] Broken pieces of pottery, known as ostracae, are also much favoured for this kind of work. I'd remind you that, the red clay from which they are made, is a substance with strong sethian associations, as indeed is the breaking and burial. Their substance and condition remind us of the realm of the earthy underworld. The inclusion of a large number of valuable pots interred with the deceased, is a practice as old as the potter's art. It is very likely that these always functioned as 'letters to the dead', or contained coded messages to the ancestors. Is it also a kind of prayer? You might think prayer is the technique favoured by many of the enemies of magick. I would suggest to you that, it is a useful magical technique worthy of reclamation. It is another example of how, the illustrious dead can still work on behalf of the living. What could be simpler than taking a piece of broken red pot, scratching a message or sigil addressed to an ancestor, thereafter burying that in a grave, preferably their grave or if that isn't possible, a recently made one, on the principle that the newly dead will deliver the message for you.

The Harem Conspiracy

You might be wondering how effective was Egyptian magick? To answer that, it is probably worth a look at the so-called Harem Conspiracy.[8] The conspiracy took place during the reign of Ramesses III (c1182-1151BC). His failure to nominate an heir from his many children (and wives) fuelled a conspiracy led by the formidable royal wife Tiye. The attempted coup d'état involved several dozen key individuals including an army commander, the royal prince Pentawere, the overseer of the priests of Sekhmet (specialists in medicine), a magican called 'Prekamenef' and scribes in the temple library. What was once a single book roll, subsequently broken up by antiquities dealers into six manuscripts, is the only surviving ancient record, of the conspirators trial for sorcery. The magician, known only by the deliberately 'mutilated' name Prekamanef (Ra blinds him), was charged to 'prepare magical texts for the purpose of confusing and disturbing. And to make waxen (figures) of some gods, and some potions for disabling the limbs of the people'.[9] He also began 'a ritual of consulting the divine oracle (pekh-neter) so to delude people. He reached the side of the harem of that other great expansive place, and he began to use the inscribed wax figures in order that they be taken inside by the inspector Adi-ran'.[10] Magick was used to pacify and spellbind the guards, so that messages could be taken in and out .

The wax figures are of precisely the kind discussed earlier. The 'harem' was the secure residence of the many wives of the King. The ultimate aim was, to coordinate an assassination attempt on the king using magick, with a coup d'état by supporters of Queen Tiye's son Pentawere. Ramesses III was indeed murdered, although the coup d'état failed and the succession passed to another prince, who became Ramesses IV and, presumably organised the trial of the conspirators. Which shows the truth of the old saying 'he who wields the knife cannot wear the crown.' Here then is clear evidence of the practice of lethal magick in the ancient world. Many of the magical techniques already described were used. The records show that magick was perfectly legal, although attempting to kill the king was obviously not. This sorcerous act against the king is what is condemned, not the act of sorcery. The conspirators, including the hapless guards were variously exiled, mutilated, executed, or forced to commit suicide.

Notes
1. Ritner (1993: 167).
2. Gardiner (1927:13).
3. Merrifield (1987 : 168).
4. Ritner (1993 : 179).
5. Ritner (1993 :145).

6.   Lecture, Pagan Federation Convention, 27th Nov 2004.
7.   Gardiner (1928).
8.   Redford (2002).
9.   Translation Redford (2002: 18).
10   Translation Redford (2002: 19).

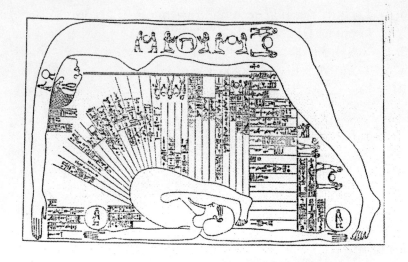

Nuit and Geb in a 'yoga' position from temple of Hathor at
Dendara. There are many elements of Egyptian body magick
that suggest parallels with Hindu yoga. Some modern
practitioners have been inspired to create breathing exercises
based on the fusion of Seth & Hathor.

19 Re-emergence of the Hidden God

'the 47th spirit Uvall, or Vual or Voval. He is a Duke, Great Mighty and Strong; and appeareth in the form of a Mighty Dromedary at the first, but after a while at the command of the Exorcist he putteth on Human Shape, and speaketh the Egyptian tongue, but not perfectly.' (The editor adds the humourus note to the effect that this spirit now converses in colloquial Coptic.)

Goetia L W de Laurence (1916 : 37).[1]

Throughout, I've aimed to introduce some interesting aspects of the mythology and magick of Seth the 'Bull of Ombos'. He is a mysterious, archaic entity, whose has a demonised cult, but isn't all demon. Seth represents the way of initiation and magick. Seth's constellation is *Ursa Major,* although one of his early *consorts* was associated with Sothis. Seth and Hathor make an interesting, more sensual pairing than the usual suspects.

As in my earlier book *Tankhem,* I wanted to draw attention to the lunar aspects of his magick, and the powerful doctrine of the *kalas* and associated body magick. About 93% of modern magick derives from the so-called Hermetic tradition of Egypt. With the disastrous and devastating rise of Christianity, this current was forgotten. It lay dormant and dreaming beneath the sands of the desert, and also in its new home in Hindu Tantrism. The priests of Koptos took it there, as they fled across the desert to the Red Sea, where they took sail to South India. For an exploration of this theme see my *Isis In India*. For the last 100 years, the magick of the Hidden God has reawakened after 2000 years of 'stony sleep'.

There is no obvious beginning to the cult of Seth the 'Hidden God'; neither is there a complete explanation of his character. Perhaps, that is what makes him such an interesting archetype with which to work. He is a powerful spirit, that despite his outwardly frightening form, teaches initiation and liberation.

Crowley states that we, the *mystoi*, should be one pointed and focussed on one overarching aim – in the words of our holy books, 'one star in sight'. That star represents the inner abiding spirit or genius that, according to occult theory, is within each of us: 'every man and every woman is a star'.

In Crowley's tarot deck, his *Book of Thoth*, one card above all others seems to stand out. It is even the subject of a special message - 'Tzaddhi is 'Nuit' the Star'. This card shows the constellations known by the ancient Egyptians as 'the imperishable stars'. One in particular stands out as the 'Son of Nuit' - The Plough, Ursa Major, the star of Seth. Hence the prayer from the Pyramid texts where Nuit stretches herself over the gods:[2]

' Oh my mother Nuit,

spread yourself over me,

so that I may become one

of the imperishable stars

that are in thee,

and I shall not die.'

It is the first axiom of *Tankhem* magick that, such a star or group of stars, *points the way*, just as the constellation known variously as Ursa Major, The Starry Plough, Big Dipper points the way to the centre of the universe, our own centre. The first step in opening the door to the Hidden God, is to go out under the stars and draw down the plough.

In the oldest Egyptian magico-religious texts, this constellation was known, as Meshketyu or Khepesh (Meshkhet = Bull's Leg).[3] From the time of the Egyptians, this image of the Bull's Leg recurs time and again, in many diverse religions. It finds its way into Mithraism and even into the final book of the Christian *New Testament*. I hazard a guess that, there is no religious or magical current where this image does not play a role. It is said that this constellation contains the soul of the Stellar god Seth. And hence whatever the religion, the Hidden God is there, if you know his signs.

This information comes from the so-called Pyramid texts, sacred writings carved onto the walls of the very first pyramids and therefore approximately four and half thousand years old. But even as they were copied they contain their own internal evidence of being much older, of being copied from very ancient originals indeed.[4]

Mercer[5] tells us that Seth was the 'indigenous god', i.e. the first whose worship was general among the indigenous people of ancient Egypt. Red is the primary colour of Seth and any deity with Sethian affiliations. See for example his estranged consort Nephthys, who retains an underworld connection, and appears in a spell to enable a man (or perhaps a woman) to attract to himself a lover.[6]

Like all classical and ancient magick, the mindset is quite different to our own. There is an element of compulsion, both of the God and indeed of the object of desire. The piety of the ancient Egyptian magicians, was maybe more sanguine than our own. They were unafraid of compelling their deities to do their work – and in return, those deities seem to accept the bargain? Once such spell involves the use of 'the red veil of Nephthys'. This is probably a strip of fabric once used to clothe the image of the deity in a local temple, subsequently sold as a relic. Such a cloth could function as a gateway to further understanding of the lost mysteries of Nephthys. In Middle Egyptian times, Nephthys was the consort of Seth. I have argued elsewhere, that she may not have been his original choice or Nephthys her original name. Like many of the later goddess names, it really addresses her as a piece of temple furniture. Nephthys is enticed away to become the lover of Osiris. This must have some relevance to the way the spell works.[7] Seth often occurs in love spells of this kind.

Seth, the Egyptian god of ambiguity was associated with foreign lands, and the adversary of the god Osiris. Seth was usually depicted in human form with a head of indeterminate origin. He had a curved snout, erect square-tipped ears, and a long forked tail. Sometimes he was represented in entirely animal form, with a body similar to that of a greyhound. He was said to be the son either of Nuit and Geb, or of Nuit and Ra, and therefore brother of Isis, Osiris and Nephthys. Nephthys was sometimes given as his consort, although he is more commonly associated with the foreign, Semitic goddesses Astarte and Anat.

Egyptian religion is completely permeated by sex and sexual magick, to an extent that is often suppressed in earlier studies. There are strong parallels between the Egyptian worldview and that of Hindu Tantrism. Ancient Egyptian society is also surprisingly like our own – they drank beer (Egyptian for beer is Hnkt, perhaps pronounced Heineken),[8] they used contraception and they practiced sexual magick. The sexual and sensual aspect of ancient Egyptian religion, is something that took a while to filter through to modern books.

Seth, who is a great lover of men and women, was very jealous of Isis's new addition to the holy family. Isis believed Seth meant to harm her child, so she fled to the Nile delta and gave birth to Horus at Chemmis near Buto. With the assistance of other deities, such as the goddesses Hathor and Selket, Isis raised Horus until he was old enough to challenge Seth and claim his royal inheritance.[9]

If Seth represents the Indigenous God, i.e. one of the gods known of in Egypt before the cult of Osiris came to the fore, and before the followers of Horus came on the scene. You can see why, some feel that Seth represents an original or indigenous spirituality, that was demonised by later incomers.

Many in the modern world see initiation and individualism as the new evil. The nature of the good, so we are told, is the collective good. In modern politics, the collective is subsumed under the category of the state. So Sethian qualities are seen as all things opposed to the state, and opposed to collective religion. The ancient opposition between Seth & Horus/Osiris is essentially the same – it's the individual versus the new religion of Statism.

It is these two gods in particular – Horus and Seth, along with their associated family and consorts, that appear to be re-manifesting in the modern magical realm. You might think that what I've so far said is only relevant to a very small group of dedicated occultists. But it is possible to show that, what I've called 'The Cult of the Hidden God' is the secret force behind many, if not all magical currents of the new age. In that, I include Wicca and Witchcraft, Tantrism, even the Northern tradition.[10]

It's worth considering this issue of the guardian spirit for a while. Occult theory maintains that individuals have a guardian spirit allocated to them at birth. We find this idea in many differing cultures of the ancient world.

Most people don't know of the existence of this guardian spirit until near or after death. Some important magical rituals, deriving from ancient Egypt, were able to activate this knowledge whilst the person was still living. The Egyptian god form Seth was often connected with such operations.

It's the often-levelled critique of Seth, that he wants his own way. And this is seen as a very human failing, we want our own way. So it's another example of how, Egyptian Seth is a very important piece in the puzzle of the human psyche. Flowers says that 'Seth represents the individual will, in contradistinction to the collective will of the Egyptian state.[11] Like many powerful 'night-side' spirits, Seth clearly has a beneficent side. His ferocious side may be a mask, that tests our true desire for initiation.

Myths of dismemberment

I discussed the most ancient burial customs in Egypt, the dismembering of the body, especially the head or burning. Then some kind of reassembly, wrapping in a leather bag or exposure as carrion. The 'Osirians' ,who *may* have been immigrants into the Nile valley, preferred their bodies to remain whole and indeed one of the spells in the 'Book of the Dead' is designed to prevent decapitation in the afterlife.[12] This later taboo about decapitation is an obvious bone of contention between the followers of Seth and Horus (defender of Osirian faith). Seth's companions, the *smaiut n seth*, are punished by decapitation, and Seth is often called the 'headless demon'.[13]

There is also said to be a secret method by which, the phases of the moon are somehow 'controlled' or predicted by Seth's northern constellation Ursa Major. But the primary lunar reference comes from the fact that in myth, Seth dismembers the first king Osiris into fourteen pieces. The Egyptians, when talking about the inner nature of a person, use this lunar number fourteen. We too talk of someone as divided into various parts: mind, body, spirit, soul, ego, consciousness, memory etc. All peoples seem to have done such a thing. Just exactly how the ancient Egyptian did this is a bit sketchy, as there is no surviving work of what you might call Egyptian anthropology. In ancient Egypt, the individual is said to be a conglomeration of *seven* parts Viz: Heart, Sekhem (power), Ka, Ba etc.[14] The Ka, is some kind of childlike double, that takes hold of the person at birth. An individual can have anything up to 14 Kas of doubles attached.[15]

The Egyptians celebrated a bewildering number of festivals. One of the commonest was the celebrations for the new and full moons – the moon was called Yael, represented as the latest Egyptological opinion, is that what the Egyptians called the 'half-moon festival' is the full moon - written as a five pointed star with half moon:

Pronounced either as *semedet*, or more recently in a reading based around the number fifteen *mededint*.[16] The fifteenth day of the moon was known as the 'day of rams', when the moon begins to wane and thus loses its virile powers – it was on this day that the ritual of filling the eye was performed.

In Babylonian astronomy, the cycle of the moon is divided into two halfs of 14 days each – so it seems likely that what we are seeing here is a very ancient system of correspondences between the parts of the moon and the human body.[23] I've argued elsewhere that the contention found in several authors, including Kenneth Grant's of some kind of parallel between the Tantrik doctrine of the Kalas or lunar phases, and its earlier Egyptian model, is essentially correct. In fact, it seems highly likely that many of the secret body magick techniques of the ancient Egyptians were transferred or certainly only survive in India, after the systematic destruction of the Egyptian religion and sacred technologies by Roman Christianity.

The term 'kala' as found in the works of Kenneth Grant, is a Sanskrit term meaning part or digit. There is a maxim in Hinduism that 'Man is a microcosm of the universe– as above so below'. Sound familiar? This is pretty much identical with the Hermetic doctrine of the so-called Emerald Tablet. The physical moon can be described as have twenty-eight different parts or phases throughout the month, 14 waxing, 14 waning.[24] These parts are also reflected in the subtle anatomy of every human being.[25]

These twenty-eight parts are most noticeable in the doctrine of erogenous zones (chandrakala)– zones of sensitivity that migrate around the body through the course of a month. We might also compare this with the thirteen 'puncture' points used in the wax image spell. Throughout the above I've aimed to introduce some interesting aspects of the mythology and magick of Seth. I wanted to draw attention to the lunar aspects of his magick and the powerful doctrine of the Kalas and its associated body magick. About 93% of modern magick derives from the so-called Hermetic tradition of Egypt. With the disastrous and devastating rise of Christianity, this current lay dormant and forgotten. It laid dormant and dreaming beneath the sands of the desert, and also in its new home in Hindu Tantrism. The priests of Koptos took it there, as they fled across the desert to the Red Sea, where they took sail to South India. For the last 100 years, the magick of the Hidden God has reawakened, after 2000 years of 'stony sleep'. Seth is this 'Hidden God'. There is no obvious beginning to his cult, neither is there a complete explanation of his character – perhaps that's what makes him such an interesting archetype with which to work. He is a powerful spirit that despite his outwardly frightening form, teaches initiation and liberation.

Notes
1.   quoted in Ritner (1993).
2.   Pyramid Text 777a, b.
3.   The phoneme ms (msh) is an apron of foxes skins – meaning uncertain but may have some connection with birth rites.
4   See Budge BOTG, xxxiii for example. Also Edwards Pyramids of Egypt.
5.   Mercer (1949: 48sq).
6.   PDM lxi 100-105: The Red Cloth of Nephthys: "Pre arose; he sent for the Seket boat (morning boat of Re) of heaven; the water under the bark of Pre has dried up. The gods and the two crowns (of the south and the north) complain until NN is brought to NN. If not doing it is what will be done, the gods whose names I said will bend down so that they fall into the fire . . . I am the one who said it, she will repeat it 'Be destroyed, impious one!' She is the one who said it; / she is the one who heard it [and][repeated it." [It is] very good when he says it. (Betz p. 289).
7.   PDM Lxi 100-105 is a spell of compelling that contains much Sethian imagery. Quoted in Betz p. 289.
8.   See 'Beer' in glossary.
9.   Edited from Anthony C. DiPaolo, M.S. (internet).

10   See for example the eightfold festivals and miracle play of
      Abydos.

11.   Flowers (1995 : 75).

12.   Budge (1901 : xxviii)

13.   See Crowley's *Liber Samech*.

14   Is the ordinal seven (sefekh) linguistically connected with
      Seth. His name may mean 'to cut' or 'pierce' and begins
      with same consonant (O34) bolt. This sound may originally
      have been distinguished from (S29) which Budge says in
      his dictionary entry is same consonant as Hebrew Shin. The
      Heart (ib) The name (ren) – axiom of magick being that
      knowing the name gives one power over something.
      Linked with sound – a spell must be spoken ie via
      mouth. The power (sekhem)/The magical power Khu/
      Heka /The Double (ka)/'soul' or 'life force'(Ba) ,
      personified as a bird, agent of sexual activity in afterlife./
      The Shadow (Khaibit). Three parts of (from Flowers)
      social self/physical self/psychic / spiritual self (sahu). See
      Mailer (1983) for interesting realization of all this).

15.   Mercer (1949 : 43).

16.   Collier & Manley (1998:76).

17   Fourteen in the 'Solar' zodiac, the observation of the more
      abstract 'Lunar' zodiac of 16 lunar days (tithis) may have
      been beyond most people's powers of observation.
      Classical magick made a distinction between a 'new moon
      of god' ie. 'according to the heavens', and 'new moon of
      man', 'according to the calendar' Betz (1986: 53fn).

18   See for example the Picatrix where its Indian origin is
      acknowledged. see Chapter 4 p19sq. Ghayat Al-Hakim,
      Picatrix: Goal of the Wise, vol 1, Oroboros Press 2002.

19   The system appears in some but by no means all grimoires.
      One of the earliest is the *Sworn Book of Honorius the
      Magician* in which it appears as a mere listing of the angels
      of the mansions of the moon. It also appears more fully in
      the work of Cornelius Agrippa. Another important
      instance is Barrett's *Magus* in which the system broadly
      derives from Agrippa. See book ii p.165.

Appendix I

Setna and The Magic Book

This story, translated here by Flinders Petrie and illustrated by Tristram Ellis is set in the XIXTH dynasty (c.1100BCE) among the High Priests of Thebes. It survives in two Ptolemaic manuscripts, which naturally enough contain some Greek concepts.

The mighty King Ramesses the Great had a son named Setna Khaemwast who was a great scribe, and very learned in all the ancient writings. And he heard that the magic Book of Thoth, by which a man may enchant heaven and earth, and know the language of all birds and beasts, was buried in the cemetery of Memphis. And he went to search for it with his brother Anhehoreru; and when they found the tomb of the king's son, Nanefer, son of the king of Upper and Lower Egypt, Merneptah, Setna opened it and went in.

Now in the tomb was Nanefer, and with him was the ka of his wife Ahura, for though she was buried at Koptos, her ka dwelt at Memphis with her husband, whom she loved. And Setna saw them seated before their offerings, and the book lay between them. And Nanefer said to Setna 'who are you that break into my tomb in this way?' To which he replied 'I am Setna, son of the great King Ramesses, living for ever, and I come for that book that I see between you.' And Nanefer said 'You cannot have it' 'Then' said Setna, 'I will take it by force.'

Then Ahura said to Setna, 'Do not take this book; for it will bring trouble on you, as it did to us. Listen to what we have suffered on account of it.'

Ahura's Tale

We were the two children of the King Merneptah, and he loved us very much, for he had no others; and Nanefer was in his palace as heir over all the land. And when we were grown, the king said to the queen, 'I will marry Nanefer to the daughter of a general, and Ahura to the son of another general.'

And the queen said, 'No, he is the heir, let him marry his sister, like the heir of a king, none other is fit for him.'
And the king said, 'That is not right.'

And the queen said, 'It is you who are not dealing rightly with me.'

And the king answered, 'If I have no more than these two children, is it right that they should marry one another? I will marry Nanefer to the daughter of an officer, and Ahura to the son of another officer. It has often been done so in our family.'

And at a time when there was a great feast before the king, they came to fetch me. And I was very troubled, and did not behave as I used to do. And the king said to me, 'Ahura, are you troubled that you shall not be married to your brother?'

I said to him, 'Well, let me marry the son of an officer, and he marry the daughter of another officer, as it often happens so in our family.'

I laughed, and the king laughed. And the king told the steward of the palace,' Let them take Ahura to the house of Nanefer tonight, and all kinds of good things with her.'

So they brought me as a wife to the house of Nanefer; and the king ordered them to give me presents of silver and gold, and things from the palace.

And Nanefer passed a happy time with me, and received all the presents from the palace; and we loved one another. And when I expected a child, they told the king, and he was most heartily glad; and he sent me many things, and a present of the best silver and gold and linen. And when the time came, I bore this little child that is before you. And they gave him the name of Merab, and registered him in the book of the 'House of Life.'

And when my brother Nanefer went to the cemetery of Memphis, he did nothing but read the writings that are in the catacombs of the kings and on the tablets of the 'House of Life,' and the inscriptions that are seen on the monuments. And there was a priest there called Nesiptah; and as Nanefer went into a temple to pray, it happened that he went behind this priest, and was reading the inscriptions that were on the chapels of the gods. And the priest mocked him and laughed. So Nanefer said to him, 'Why are you laughing at me?'

And he replied, 'I was not laughing at you, it was at your reading writings that are worthless. If you wish so much to read, come to me, and I will bring you to the place where the book is that Thoth himself wrote with his own hand, and which will bring you to the gods. When you read but two pages, you will encircle the heaven, the earth, the abyss, the mountains, and the sea; you shall know what the birds of the sky and the crawling things are saying; you shall see the fishes of the deep, for a divine power is there to bring them up out of the depth. And when you read the second page, if you are in the world of ghosts, you will become again in the shape you were in on earth. You will see the sun shining in the sky, with all the gods, and the full moon.'

And Nanefer said, 'By the life of the king! Tell me of anything you want done, and I'll do it for you, if you will only send me where this book is.'

And the priest answered Nanefer, 'If you want to go to the

place where the book is, you must give me a hundred pieces of silver for my funeral, and provide that they shall bury me as a rich priest.'

So Nanefer did as he wished. Then the priest said to Nanefer, 'This book is in the middle of the river at Koptos, in an iron box; in the iron box is a bronze box; in the bronze box is a sycamore box; in the sycamore box is an ivory and ebony box; in the ivory and ebony box is a silver box; in the silver box is a golden box; and in that is the book. It is twisted all round with snakes and scorpions and all the other crawling things around the box in is a deathless snake.'

And when the priest told Nanefer, he did not know where on earth he was, he was so much delighted. And when he came from the temple, he told me all that had happened to him. And he said, 'I shall go to Koptos, for I must fetch this book.'

And I said, 'Let me dissuade you, for you prepare sorrow and you will bring me into trouble in the Thebaid.' And I laid my hand on Nanefer, to keep him from going to Koptos, but he would not listen to me; and he went to the king, and told the king all that the priest had said.

The king asked him, 'What is it that you want?'

And he replied, 'Give me the royal boat with its belongings, for I will go to the south with Ahura and her little boy Merab, and fetch this book without delay.'

So we went with him to the haven, and sailed from there up to Koptos. Then the priests of Isis of Koptos, and the high priest of Isis, came down to meet Nanefer, and their wives also came to me. We went into the temple of Isis and Harpokrates; and Nanefer brought an ox, a goose, and some wine, and made a burnt offering and a drink offering before Isis of Koptos and Harpokrates. They brought us to a very fine house, with all good things; and Nanefer spent four days there and feasted with the priests of Isis of Koptos, and the wives of the priests of Isis also made holiday with me.

And the morning of the fifth day came; and Nanefer called a priest to him, and made a magic cabin that was full of men and tackle. He put the spell upon it and put life into it, and gave them breath, and sank it in the water. He filled the royal boat with

sand, and took leave of me, and sailed from the haven: and I sat
by the river at Koptos that I might see what would become of
him.'

And they toiled by night and by day; and reached it in three
days. He threw the sand out and made a shoal in the river. And
then he found on it entwined serpents and scorpions, and all
kinds of crawling things around the box in which the book was;
and around it he found a deathless snake. And he laid the spell
upon the entwined serpents and scorpions and all kinds of
crawling things which were around the box, that they would not
come out. And he went to the deathless snake, and fought with
him, and killed him; but he came to life again, and took a new
form. He then fought again with him a second time; but he came
to life again, and took a third form. He then cut him in two parts,
and put sand between the parts, that he should not appear again.

Nanefer then went to the box. He uncovered a box of iron,
and opened it; he found then a box of bronze, and opened that;
then he found a box of sycamore wood, and opened that; again
he found a box of ivory and ebony, and opened that; yet, he
found a box of silver, and opened that; and then he found a box
of gold; he opened that, and found the book in it. He took the
book from the golden box, and read a page of spells from it. He
enchanted the heaven and the earth, the abyss, the mountains,
and the sea; he knew what the birds of the sky, the fish of the
deep, and the beasts of the hills all said. He read another page of
the spells, and saw the sun shining in the sky, with all the gods,
the full moon, and the stars in their shapes; he saw the fishes of
the deep, for a divine power was present that brought them up
from the water. He then read the spell upon the workmen, 'Work
for me, back to the place from which I came.'

And they toiled night and day, and so he came back to the
place where I sat by the river of Koptos; I had not drunk nor
eaten anything, and had done nothing but sat like one who is
dead.

I then told Nanefer that I wished to see this book, for which
we had taken so much trouble. He gave the book into my hands;
and when I read a page of the spells in it, I also enchanted
heaven and earth, the abyss, the mountains, and the sea; I also

knew what the birds of the sky, the fishes of the deep, and the beasts of the hills all said. I read another page of the spells, and I saw the sun shining in the sky with all the gods, the full moon, and the stars in their shapes; I saw the fishes of the deep, for a divine power was present that brought them up from the water.

As I could not write, I asked Nanefer, who was a good writer and a very learned one; he called for a new piece of papyrus, and wrote on it all that was in the book. He dipped it in beer, and washed it off in the liquid; for he knew that if it were washed off, and he drank it, he would know all that there was in the writing.

We went back to Koptos the same day, and made a feast before Isis of Koptos and Harpokrates. We then went to the haven and sailed north. And as we went on, Thoth discovered all that Nanefer had done with the book; and Thoth hastened to tell Ra, and said, 'My book and my revelation are with Nanefer, son of the King Merenptah. He has forced himself into my place, and robbed it, and seized my box with the writings, and killed my guards.'

And Ra replied to him, 'Take him and all his kin.'

He sent a power from heaven with the command, 'Do not let Nanefer return safe to Memphis with all his kin.'

And after this hour, the little boy Merab, going out from the awning of the royal boat, fell into the river: he called on Ra, and everybody who was on the bank raised a cry. Nanefer went out of the cabin, and read the spell over him; he brought the body up to the surface. He read another spell over him, and made him tell of all that happened to him, and of what Thoth had said before Ra. We turned back with him to Koptos. We brought him to the Good House, where he was embalmed; and we buried him in his coffin in the cemetery of Koptos like a great and noble person.

And Nanefer, my brother, said, 'Let us go without delay, for the king has not yet heard of what has happened, and his heart will be sad about it.'

So we went to the haven and we set sail. When we came to the place where the little boy Merab had fallen into the water, I went out from the awning of the royal boat, and I fell into the river. They called Nanefer, and he came out from the cabin of the royal boat. He read a spell over me, and brought my body up to the surface. He drew me out, and read the spell over me, and made me tell him of all that had happened, and of what Thoth had said before Ra. Then he returned with me to Koptos, he brought me to the Good House, where I was embalmed and laid in the tomb where Merab my young child was.

He turned to the haven, and again set sail. When he came to the place where we had fallen into the river, he said to his heart, 'Shall I not better turn back again to Koptos, that I may lie by them? For if not, when I go down to Memphis, and the king asks after his children, what shall I say to him? Can I tell him, 'I have taken your children to the Thebaid and killed them, while I remained alive, and I have come to Memphis still alive?'

Then he made them bring him a linen cloth of striped byssus; he made a band, and bound the book firmly, and tied it to his body. Nanefer then went out of the awning of the royal boat and fell into the river. He cried on Ra; and all those who were on the bank made an outcry, saying, 'Great woe! Sad woe! Is he lost, that good scribe and able man that has no equal?'

The royal boat went on without any one on earth knowing where Nanefer was. It went on to Memphis, and they told all this to the king. Then the king went down to the royal boat in mourning, and all the soldiers and high priests and priests of Ptah were in mourning, and all the officials and courtiers. And when he saw Nanefer, who was in the inner cabin of the royal boat he lifted him up. And they saw the book by him; and the king said, 'Hide this book that is with him.'

And the king had him laid in his Good House til the sixteenth day, and then had him wrapped to the thirty-fifth day, and on the seventieth day, they put him in his grave.

I have now told you the sorrow which has come upon us because of this book for which you ask, saying, "Let it be given to me." You have no claim to it; and indeed, for the sake of it, we have given up our life on earth.

And Setna said to Ahura, 'Give me the book which I see between you and Nanefer; or I will take it by force.' Then Nanefer rose from his seat and said, 'Can you take this book by your skill? If, indeed, you can play games with me, let us play a game.'

And Setna said, ' I am ready,' and the board and its pieces were put before him. And Nanefer won the first game; and he put the spell upon him, and struck him with the board, and knocked Setna into the ground up to his ankles.   He did the same at the second game, sunking him into the ground to his waist. He did the same at the third game, and made him sink into the ground up to his ears. Then Setna struck Nanefer a great blow with his fist. And Setna called his-brother Anhehoreru and said to him, 'Make haste and and tell the king all that has happened to me, and bring me the talisman of my father Ptah, and my magic books.'

And he hurried up to the surface and told the king all that had happened. The king said, 'Bring him the talismans of his father Ptah, and his magic books' And Anhehoreru hurried down into the tomb; he laid the talismans on Setna, and immediately he sprang up again.

And then Setna grabbed the book. And Setna ran from the tomb—there went a light before him, and darkness behind him.

And Ahura wept, and said 'Glory to the King of Darkness!
Hail to the King of Light! all power is gone from the tomb. 'But
Nanefer said to Ahura, 'Do not let your heart be sad; I will make
him bring back this book, with a forked stick in his hand, and a
fire-pan on his head.' But Setna would not listen; instead he
unrolled the book, oblivious to everthing but to read it to
everybody.

Petrie does paraphrases the next section - as like a great deal
of Victorian scholarship some things were thought best left unsaid
- believing it not creditable to Egyptian society, seems to be intended
for one of the vivid dreams which the credulous readily accept as
half realities.

After these things, Setna was walking in the temple of Ptah
when he saw an exceedingly beautiful woman. Not only was she
beautiful but extremely rich, with many ornaments of gold,
female attendants and a household full of servants. When Setna
saw her he was lost. He called to his own servant saying, 'Go
immediately to the place where this woman is and find out
everything about her.'

He went without delay to speak to her handmaid saying, 'Who
is she?'

She replied, 'She is Tabubue, the daughter of the prophet of
Bast, mistress of Ankh-Tawi; and she has come here to pray to
Ptah the great God.'

The slave returned to Setna, he told him everything.

And Setna said, 'Go and speak to the slave girl saying, "Setna
Khamwas, the son of Pharaoh Ramesses, has sent me saying, I
will give your mistress ten pieces of gold, or anything else she
may desire, if she will spend one hour alone with me.'

The slave returned to Tabubue and gave her the message.

Furious at this, Tabubue, said, 'Go speak to Setna saying, 'I
am a priestess, not some cheap tart. If you really want me come
to my home as the Chez-Bast.'

The slave returned to Setna, and related before him
everything. Said he, 'That is excellent.' which scandalized every
man that was about Setne.

Setna set sail for Chez-Bast, which was west of the Qemy. He
found a house exceeding high, with an enclosure wall around
about it and a garden on the north, with a diwan in front.

Setna went inside, and waiting in anxious anticipation in the garden. Tabubue soon joined him, taking his hand she said: 'Prosperity of the house of Bast. Come with me.'

Setna ascended the steps of the house with Tabubue. The upper story of the house was clean and fragrant, the floor inlayed with true lapis lazuli and turquoise. The many couches were furnished with royal linen, and upon the dresser were several golden cups.

She filled one of those cups with wine and gave it to Setna. She offered him food but he He said, 'I cannot eat.'

Incense was put on the censer, and unguents of the kind that Pharaoh useth were brought before him. Setna dallied with Tabubue, he had not ever seen her like before.

Setna said unto her, 'Let us get down to it.'

She said to him, 'I am a priestess, I am no cheap tart; if you want to have me, you must make a deed of maintenance and a sign over all your property to me.'

Bewitched, Setna immediated agreed.

Then someone said 'Your children are below.'

Setna asked for them to be brought up.

Tabubue arose, she put a garment of royal linen that left nothing to the imagination. Setna was mad with desire.

Setna said, 'Tabubue, I must have you!'

She said to him, 'I am a priestess, I am no cheap tart; if you want me you must make sure there is no future quarrel between mine and your children concerning your possessions.'

His children were brought in and signed the deed. He said to Tabubue, 'Now will you let me have you?'

But still she demured saying:

'First you must get rid of your children, they must be slain lest they will quarrel with my children.'

Setna said, 'Do to them whatever abomination you have in mind.'

And so she had his children slain before him, afterwards they were thrown from the window, their flesh to be picked over by the dogs and the cats. They ate their flesh, he hearing them, while he drank with Tabubue.

Setna said, 'Tabubue, let us accomplish that for which we came hither. Everything that thou hast said I have done for thee, all.'

At last Tabubue said unto him, 'Come with me to my boudoir.' And Setna went unto the chamber, he lay down upon a couch of ivory and ebony.

Tabubue lay down by his side; but when he tried to touch her, she opened her mouth wide in a great cry. Setna awoke in a burning fever, naked, his phallus swollen and still erect.

Just at that moment a noble person rode by in a litter, many men running at his side, like a Pharaoh. And Setna was about to get up, but for shame he could not because he was naked.

The Pharaoh said, 'Setna, what are you up to, lying about in this sorry state?'

He replied, 'Indeed I'm in a sorry state, I've a feeling Nanefer is to blame!'

The Pharaoh said, 'Go thou to Memphis; your children are safe and asking for you there.'

Setna said, 'My great lord the King, may you live long and prosper! But how can I go to Memphis, naked as the day I was born?

The Pharaoh called to a slave and ordered him to give clothing to Setna. Then the Pharaoh said, 'Setna, go now. Your children are waiting.'

So Setna went to Memphis, and embraced his children. And the king said to him, 'Were you not drunk to do so?' Then Setna told all things that had happened with Tabubue and Nanefer.

And the king said, 'Setna, I warned you before, "you will die if you do not take back the book." But you did not listen. Now, then, take the book to Nanefer, with a forked stick in your hand, and a fire-pan on your head.'

So Setna did as he was told. He went down to the tomb of Nanefer. And Ahura said to him, 'It is Ptah, the great god, that has brought you back.'

Nanefer laughed, and said, 'This is justice.' And when Setna had praised Nanefer, he , found, as the proverb says, 'The sun was in the whole tomb'

And Setna said, 'Nanefer, is it anything I can do to make

amends??'

To which Nanefer said, 'Setna, you know that Ahura and Merab, her child, are buired in Koptos; bring them here into this tomb.'

Setna then went to the king, and told him everything.

The king said, 'Setna, go to Koptos and bring back Ahura and Merab'

And they gave him the royal boat and its belongings, and he left the haven, and sailed; without stopping till he came to Koptos. And they made this known to the priests of Isis at Koptos and to the high priest of Isis. He entered into the temple of Isis of Koptos and of Harpokrates. He offer an ox, a goose, and some wine, and he made a burnt-offering and a drink-offering. Then he went to the cemetery of Koptos with the priests. They dug about for three days and three nights, they searched all the catacombs; they turned over the steles of the scribes of the 'double house of life' and read the inscriptions. But they could not find the resting place of Ahura and Merab.

Now Nanefer perceived that they could not find the resting-place of Ahura and her child Merab. So he raised himself up as a venerable old man and appeared to Setna. The old man said to Setna, 'It was told by the father of the father of my father to the father of my father, and the father of my father has told it to my father; the resting-place of Ahura and of her child Merab is in a mound south of the town.'

But Setna said to him 'Perhaps we will do too much damage to the houses of the town?'

The old man replied, 'Listens to me, and no harm will come. If you do not find Ahura and her child Merab under the south corner of their town may I be disgraced.'

And sure enough they found the resting-place of Ahura and her child Merab under the south corner of the town. Setna laid them in the royal boat to bring them as honoured persons, and restored the town of Pehemato as it originally was. And Nanefer let Setna know who he was.

So Setna left the haven in the royal boat, and sailed without stopping, reached Memphis safely. And the king he came down to meet the royal boat. He took them as honoured persons escorted to the catacombs, in which Nanefer was, and smoothed down the ground over them.

This is the completed writing of the tale of Setna Khaemwast and NaneferkaPtah and his wife Ahura and their child Merab, It was written in the 35th year the month Tybi.

Appendix II

The second story of Khamuas:
Prince Khamuas and SaOsiris

The second story of Setna is found only in a fragmentary manuscript
of the Roman period. I'm not going to show every lacunae in the
text, if you are interested take a look at Llewellyn Griffith's original
edition. We are thrown directly into the story some time after the
events of Setna I, when the hero is married but childless. His wife
has spent the night in the temple of Ptah in order to incubate a
curative dream. The story begins with the details of Ptah's remedy.

She dreamt they were speaking to her saying: Are you
Mehwesekht the wife of Setna, who lies in vain seeking healing?
Tomorrow morning go to the place your husband Setna passes
water. You will find a melon vine growing there. Wind it with its
gourds, and put it back. Later you shall make it into medicine
and you shall conceive.

Mehwesekht awoke from the dream. She acted according to
everything that she had been told: she lay down by the side of
Setna, her husband, and she conceived. Setna made the
announcement of it before Pharaoh. His heart was exceedingly
glad because of it. He gave her an amulets, he read to her. One
night Setna also received a message in a dream: The child should
be named SaOsiris. Numerous are the marvels that he shall do in
the land of Egypt.

Setna awoke from the dream. His heart was exceedingly glad.
In due course she bore a male child. He named him SaOsiris,
according with what had been said in the dream.

After the months of pregnancy, they nurtured him. When the child SaOsiris was one year old, people might have said he was two. When he was two years old, they might have said he was three. Setna never passed an hour without looking at SaOsiris. The love that he had for him was very great. He grew big and strong, and was sent to school.

Soon he rivalled the scribe appointed to give him instruction. The child SaOsiris grew and he began to learn magic with the scribes of the House of Life in the temple of Ptah. He was soon considered a prodigy and Setna loved the fact the King requested he be brought to his banquet and presented to all the guests.

And on a certain day Setna was purifying himself and his son SaOsiris before going to the banquet. Setna heard the sound of a wailing near his house; the funeral of a rich man whom they were carrying out to the desert. The wailing was very loud as was in keeping with the dignity of such a great man.

He looked again and saw a poor man being carried out from Memphis to the cemetery. He was wrapped in a mat and there were no mourners. Said Setna: By Ptah, the great God, how much better it shall be in Amenti for the great men whom they glorify with loud wailing compared to poor man whom they take to the desert without the glory of a funeral.[1]

But SaOsiris said: You shall be treated in Amenti like this poor man. That which shall be done to this rich man in Amenti shall not be done to you. Thus father shall you go into Amenti.

The heart of Setna was much grieved on account of what he had heard. But the child SaOsiris responded with the question: Father would you like to see what really happens to both these men in the otherworld? Setna replied that he would. Thus by magical means SaOsiris took his father into the seven chambers of the underworld.

When they entered the fourth hall Setna saw some men were plaiting ropes while donkeys were chewing them up. Their provision, water and bread, was hung over them. When they ran to take them down, others were digging pits at their feet to prevent them from reaching.

They entered the fifth hall and behold! Setna saw noble spirits, standing in their positions, those who were accused of violence,

were standing at the entrance praying. The hinge of the door of
the fifth hall being fixed in the right eye of a man, who was
praying and uttering loud lamentation.

They went into the sixth hall, and Setna saw the gods of
Amenti standing in their order making a proclamation.

They went into the seventh hall, and Setna saw the figure of
the great god Osiris. He was seated upon his throne of gold,
crowned with the Atef, the great god Anubis on his left, the great
god Thoth on his right, the gods of the council of Amenti
standing to the left and right of him. The balance was set in the
middle before them. They were weighing the evil deeds against
the good. The great god Thoth writing, Anubis giving the word
to his colleague.

The law was that he who was found to have done more evil
deeds than good ones was thrown to Ama of the Lord of
Amenti, who destroyed his soul and body and did not allow him
to breathe ever again.

He who had committed more good deeds than evil was taken
to the gods of the council of the Lord of Amenti, and his soul
went to heaven with the noble spirits.

He who was found to have committed as many good deeds as
evil, was taken amongst the excellent spirits that serve Sokari-
Osiris.

And Setna saw a great man clothed in fine linen who was near
the place where Osiris was. His position was elevated. Setna
marvelled at the things that he saw in Amenti.

SaOsiris walked out in front of him and said: My father Setna,
don't you see this great man, who is clothed in fine linen and is
near the place where Osiris is? That poor man whom you saw
being carried out from Memphis and not a man walking after
him, was wrapped in a mat. They brought him to the Tê, they
weighed his good deeds that he had done upon earth. They
found his good deeds had been more numerous than his evil,
according to the measure of his term of life that Thoth
determined, according to the measure of his greatness of eye
upon earth. It was commanded before Osiris that the burial
outfit of that rich man whom you saw being carried out from
Memphis, the praise that was made of him being great, be given

to this poor man, and that they should take him amongst the
noble spirits as a man of God who follows Sokaris Osiris, he
being near to the place in which is Osiris.

That great man whom you saw, they took him to the Tê, they
weighed his evil deeds against his good deeds. They found that
his evil deeds were more numerous than the good that he did
upon earth. It was commanded to imprison him in Amenti. He is
that man that you saw with the hinge of the gate of Amenti
being fixed on his right eye. They were shutting and opening on
his eye, his mouth was open in loud lamentation.

By the great god Osiris, Lord of Amenti, behold! I say to you
upon earth: There shall be done to you just as is done to this
poor man.

Said Setna: My son SaOsiris, many are the marvels that I have
seen in Amenti. In the course of time tell me what has happened
to those other men.

Said Si-Osiris: These men whom you saw at the useless task
of braiding ropes merely to see them eaten by donkeys. They are
under the curse of the god. They work night and day for their
livelihood, their women rob them, they find no bread to eat.
They came to Amenti again. They found their evil deeds to be
more numerous than their good. What had become of them on
earth, they became in Amenti.

Concerning those other men whom you saw, whose food,
water and bread is hung over them. They came to Amenti. Their
deeds on earth have caught up with them. Behold! They received
their soul in the Tê. He who is good upon the earth, they are
good to him in Amenti, while he who is evil, they are evil.

These matters are established, they shall never be changed.
The things that you see in the Tê in Memphis happen in those 42
nomes in which are the assessors of the great god Osiris; who
dwells in Abydos, the place of the oracle, the dwelling of princes
and in Philae.

They went into the desert of Memphis, his father Setna
embracing him. Setna asked: My son SaOsiris, separate is the
place down there where we are going, separate is the place from
which we have come up.

Setna marvelled at the words that he had heard, saying: He

will be able to become like the noble spirits as a man of God.
'This is my son.' Setna intoned spells from the book of
exorcising demons. He marvelled at the things he had seen in
Amenti which weighed upon him heavily since he was not able to
reveal them to any man on earth.

Twelve years passed, and there was no good scribe or learned
man who rivalled the boy SaOsiris in Memphis.

One day Pharaoh Ramesses went to his house in Memphis.
The council, the princes, the generals, the great men of Egypt
were standing according to their rank at court. A courtier said:
There is a chieftain of Nubia[2] carrying a sealed letter.

He was brought to the court and prayed: Is there someone
who can read this letter which I have brought to Egypt before
Pharaoh without spoiling its seal, who will read the writing in it
without opening it? Should there be none such good scribe and
learned man in Egypt who is able to read it without opening it, I
will take news of Egypt's humiliation back to the land of Nubia,
my country.

When Pharaoh heard these words with his princes he was
much dismayed: Summoned Setna Khamwast my son.

They ran and brought him. He bowed to the ground. He
saluted Pharaoh. He raised himself.

Pharaoh said to him: My son Setna, have you heard the words
of this chieftain[3] of Nubia: Is there a good scribe or learned man
in Egypt who shall be able to read this letter that is in my hand
without breaking its seal, and shall know what is written in it
without opening it?

When Setna heard these words he did not know what to do?
Give me ten days of delay that I may see what I shall be able to
do, to prevent the humiliation of Egypt being reported in the
land of Nubia, the country of gum eaters.

Apartments were given to Setna. Pharaoh rose from court, his
heart heavy with grief. He lay down without drinking and eating.
Setna went to his apartments not really knowing what to do.

His wife Mehwesekht was informed. She came to the place
where Setna was. She reached inside his clothes and did not find

any warmth. He lay quiet in his clothes. She said to him: 'My brother Setna, there is no warmth in your lap, illness, and sadness of heart.

He said to her: Do not bother me, my sister Mehwesekht, the matter on account of which my heart is grieved is not a thing that it is right to reveal to a woman.

The child SaOsiris came in. He stood over Setna his father and said to him: My father Setna, what are you lying here with a sad heart?

He said: Don't bother me my son. You are young, look after yourself.

SaOsiris said: Tell me so I may lighten your heart.

Setna told him the whole story

When SaOsiris heard these words he laughed for a long time.

Setna said to him: Why are you laughing?

He answered: I am laughing because I shall be able to read the letter that was brought to Egypt without opening it and to know what is written in it without breaking its seal.

When Setna heard these words he got up at once and said: how do I know you can really do that?

He said to him: My father Setna, go to the apartments on the ground floor. With every book you take out of the case I will tell you what book it is, and I will read it without seeing it.

Setna got up and stood on his feet. He did everything that SaOsiris had said to him. When Setna returned his joy was boundless. He hurried to the Pharaoh, telling him everything that the child SaOsiris had said.

The morning of the next day came. Pharaoh ordered the chieftain of Nubia to be fetched. He stood in the middle of the court. The child SaOsiris advanced to the centre and stood near him. He spoke against him: Woe! Wicked one of Nubia, may Amen, smite you! The inspiration of your god Amen is cast on thee. The words that I shall narrate are written in this letter. Listen, you shall confirm the truth of what I say!

SaOsiris began as follows:

Once upon a time the Pharaoh Menkhpare ruled as the beneficent king of the whole land, Egypt was overflowing with everything, he financed abundant work in the great temples of

Egypt. Till one day, the ruler of Nubia heard the voice of three
chieftains: I would cast my magic up to Egypt that I might cause
the people of Egypt to pass three days and three nights without
seeing light except an oil lamp.

Said the other of them: I would cast my magic up to Egypt
that I might cause the Pharaoh of Egypt to be brought to the
land of Nubia, and cause him to be beaten with 500 blows
before the Viceroy, and cause him to be brought back up to
Egypt in six hours.

When the viceroy heard this, he ordered them to be brought
before him. He said to them: Who of you is he that said, 'I will
cast my magic up to Egypt, I will not allow them to see light in
three days and three nights?'

They replied: It is Hor, the son of the Sow.

Said he: Who is he that said, 'I will cast my magic up to Egypt,
I will bring Pharaoh to the land of Nubia, I will cause him to be
beaten with a scourging of 500 blows before the Viceroy, I will
cause him to be taken back to Egypt in six hours?'

They said: It is Hor, the son of the Negress.

The Viceroy said: Do your feat of magic in writing. By the life
of Amen, the bull of Meroe my god, if sucessful, I will shower
you with wealth.

Hor, the son of the Negress, made of wax a group of four
runners, he read some writing to them, he gave them the breath
of life. He commanded them: 'Go up to Egypt and bring
Pharaoh of Egypt to the Viceroy is. He shall be beaten 500
blows, and then you will take him back up to Egypt in six hours.'

The sorceries of the Nubian proceeded to Egypt by night,
they overpowered Pharaoh Menkhpare, they took him to the land
of Nubia, to the Viceroy. And he was indeed beaten and
returned to Egypt.

SaOsiris finished narrating the story before Pharaoh and his
princes. He said: Are the words I have recounted those that are
written in the letter which is in your hand?

The sorcerer of Nubia said: Continue reading! Every word
you have said is true.

SaOsiris said to Pharaoh: After these things had happened,
Pharaoh Menkhpare lay down in the shrine of Horus, his hind

parts hurting from the cruel beating. The morning of the next day arrived. Pharaoh said to his courtiers: What has happened in Egypt when I was made to depart from it?

Shame on the words of the courtiers who said: Probably Pharaoh has lost his mind.

They said: You are well, you are well, O Pharaoh, our great lord. The great goddess Isis will stop your troubles. What is the meaning of the words that you have said before us? You were lying down in the shrine of Horus, the gods protect you.

Pharaoh got up, showed them his back which had been beaten exceedingly.

When they saw the hind parts of Pharaoh they made a great noise. Menkhpare had a librarian who was called Hor, son of Paneshe, who was a highly learned man. He came to the palace where Pharaoh was and he exclaimed: My lord, these were the sorceries of the Nubians. I will order them to be thrown into your house of torment and execution.

The pharaoh said to him: Come quickly to me! Don't let me be taken another night.

The librarian, Hor, son of Paneshe, came at once. He took his books and amulets to the place where Pharaoh was. He read spells to him and fastened an amulet on him to prevent the sorceries of the Nubians from getting power over him. He left Pharaoh, taking his offerings and libations, and went on board a boat and sailed to Khmun without delay. He went into the temple of Khmun, and made offerings and libations before Thoth the great great great great great great great great, the lord of Khmun. He said a prayer: Look upon me favourably, my lord Thoth. Let not the Nubians report the humiliation of Egypt in their land. It is you who make magic spells, you suspended the heaven, established the earth, the underworld, and placed the gods among the stars. Let me know how to save Pharaoh from the sorceries of the Nubians.

Hor, son of Paneshe, lay down in the temple. He dreamed a dream that night in which the great god Thoth spoke to him: When the morning comes, go to the library of the temple of Khmun. You shall find a shrine which is closed and sealed. Open it. You shall find a box in that shrine. There is a roll of papyrus in it, which I wrote with my own hand. Bring it up, make a copy of it, and return it to its place. Its name is 'The Book of Thoth'. It protected me from the impious, it shall protect Pharaoh, that he may be saved from the sorceries of the Nubians.

Hor, son of Paneshe, awoke from the dream. It was in the hand of the god. He did everything according to what he had been told in his dream. He hurried to the place where Pharaoh was. He made for him an amulet against sorceries in writing. The next day arrived.

The sorceries of Hor, the son of the Negress, returned to Egypt by night, to the place where Pharaoh was. They could not get power over Pharaoh because of the amulets. The morning of the next day arrived.

Pharaoh told the librarian Hor, son of Paneshe. Horus, son of Paneshe, ordered pure and abundant wax brought to him. He made a group of four bearers. He pronounced spells over them. He gave them the breath of life. He made them come alive. He commanded them: Go to the land of Nubia tonight. Bring the Viceroy to Egypt, to the place where Pharaoh is. After he has been beaten with 500 blows of the stick before Pharaoh, you shall return him in six hours.

The sorceries of Hor, son of Paneshe, travelled under the clouds of heaven, they hurried to the land of Nubia by night. They overpowered the Viceroy. They brought him up to Egypt, he was beaten with 500 blows of the stick before Pharaoh. They returned him in six hours.

SaOsiris narrated this story before Pharaoh and his nobles, the people of Egypt heard his voice, saying: The power of your god Amen is cast upon you, O wicked one from Nubia. The words I have spoken, are they written in this letter?

The Nubian, his head turned to the ground, said: Continue reading! Every word you have spoken is written in this letter.

SaOsiris said: After all these events had happened, after they had brought back the Viceroy to the land of Nubia in six hours, they put him in his place, he lay down.

He rose in the morning, badly beaten by the blows that had been given him above in Egypt. He turned his back towards the princes, they uttered loud lamentations. The Viceroy ordered them to go after Hor, son of the Negress. He said: May Amen curse you, the bull of Meroe, my god! You went to the men of Egypt, consider and let me see the method with which you will save me from the hand of Hor, son of Paneshe.

He made his sorceries and bound them on the Viceroy to save him from the sorceries of Hor, son of Paneshe. The night of the next day came. The sorceries of Hor, son of Paneshe, travelled to the land of Nubia. They carried the Viceroy up to Egypt. He was beaten with 500 blows of the stick before Pharaoh. He was taken back in six hours.

This happened to the Viceroy for three days, the sorceries of the Nubians were not able to save the Viceroy from the hand of Hor, son of Paneshe.

The Viceroy was in deepest anguish. He ordered Hor, the son of the Negress, to be brought to him. He said to him: Woe, you enemy from Nubia, you have caused me to be humiliated by hand of the men of Egypt. You could not save me from their hands. By the life of Amen, the bull of Meroe my god, should it be that you should not be able to save me. I will order them to put you to an evil death.

He said: My master, the Viceroy, send me to Egypt that I may meet him who does magic among them, that I may strive against him, that I may let him see the scorn that is in my heart

Hor, the son of the Negress, was sent away. He came to the place where his mother the Negress was: You are going to Egypt to do sorcery there, beware of the men of Egypt. You will not be able to contend with them. Don't let yourself be caught by their hands, or you will never return.

He said: I shall not be able to avoid going up to Egypt in order to cast my magic on it.

The Negress his mother said to him: Should it happen that you do go to Egypt, let us agree on some signs between me and you: Should you fail I will come to you in order to see whether I can save you.

He said to her: Should I be overcome then, the water before you will turn the colour of blood, the food that are before you will turn the colour of flesh, the sky shall turn the colour of blood.

Hor, the son of the Negress, having set the signs between himself and his mother, went to Egypt, crammed with magic. He traversed as far as Memphis, to the place where Pharaoh was, hunting after him who was doing magic in Egypt.

He came to the court, stood before Pharaoh and spoke in a loud voice: Ho! you who do magic against me in the court of Pharaoh, you, scribe of the House of Life, who casts magic spells on the Viceroy.

As he was speaking these words, Hor, son of Paneshe was standing in the court before Pharaoh. He said: Ho! Enemy from Nubia, are you not Hor, son of the Negress, whom I saved in the reeds of Re, with your companion from Nubia who accompanied you, you were drowning in the water, you were cast down from the hill on the east of On? Did you not repent? You have come up to Egypt, asking: 'Is he who does magic against me, here?' By the life of Atum, lord of On, the gods of Egypt have brought you here for punishment.

When Hor, son of the Negress, heard the words he answered him: Is it he to whom I taught jackal-language who does sorcery against me?

The man of Nubia made an effort to cast a written spell: he caused fire to break out in the court. Pharaoh with the princes of Egypt uttered a loud cry: Hasten to our side, librarian Hor, son of Paneshe!

Hor, son of Paneshe, cast a written spell. He caused the sky to open up with southern rain over the flame. It was extinguished in an instant.

The Nubian made another effort of magic in writing. He created a great covering over the court. No one could see his brother or his companion. Hor, son of Paneshe, read a spell to the sky. He caused it to cease. It cleared from the evil wind.

Hor, the son of the Negress, made another effort of written magic. He caused a great vault of stone, 200 cubits in length by 50 cubits of width, to appear above Pharaoh and his princes, with the intention to leave Egypt without a king. Pharaoh looked at the sky, he saw the vault of stone above him. He opened his mouth and uttered a loud cry, together with the people that were in court. Hor, son of Paneshe, pronounced a magic formula: He caused an air-boat of papyrus to appear. Behold! It flew with it forward to the Mighty Pool, the great water of Egypt.

The man of Nubia knew that he was not able to defeat the Egyptian. He made an effort to cast a written spell to make himself invisible. Hor, son of Paneshe, pronounced a spell causing the sorceries of the Nubian to be revealed. He was in the form of a bad fox-gander and was about to depart. Hor, son of Paneshe, pronounced a spell causing him to turn back, and there was a fowler standing over him, his piercing knife in his hand.

After all these things had happened, the signs which Hor, son of the Negress, had set between himself and his mother, they all happened in front of her eyes. She immediately went up to Egypt, taking on the form of a fox-goose. She stood over the palace of Pharaoh bewailing her son with her voice, while he was in the form of an evil fox-gander and the fowler was standing over him.

Hor, son of Paneshe, looked at the sky. He pronounced a spell causing her to be turned on her back with a fowler standing over her about to kill her with his knife.

She changed from the form in which she was, she took on the guise of an Nubian woman, praying: Do not make an end to us, Hor, son of Paneshe, let go for us this occasion of failure. Should you give us an aerial boat, we will not return to Egypt.

Horus, son of Paneshe, swore an oath by Pharaoh and the gods of Egypt, saying: I will not remove my spell, until you have sworn an oath never to return to Egypt.

The Negress raised her hand and swore for all eternity. Hor, the son of the Negress, swore an oath, saying: I will not come up to Egypt for 1500 years.

Hor, son of Paneshe withdrew his hand from his written spell. He gave an aerial boat to Hor, the son of the Negress, and the Negress, his mother. They returned to their city.

SaOsiris finished his narration. The head of the man from Nubia was facing the ground. SaOsiris said: By the life of your face, my great lord, this man who is standing before you, is Hor, the son of the Negress. This man, whose words I am relating, who has not repented of those things that he did long ago, has come up to Egypt at the end of 1500 years to cast the sorceries here.

By the life of Osiris, great good lord of Amenti, before whom I rest, I am Hor, son of Paneshe, this man who stands before Pharaoh, found this out, that the wicked one of Nubia would cast his sorceries up into it and there would be no good scribe and learned man in Egypt at the time able to contend with him.

I prayed before Osiris in Amenti to let me come forth to the world again, to prevent reporting the humiliation of Egypt to the land of Nubia. Osiris commanded to bring me out into the world. I awoke. I flew to the crown of the head to find Setna, the son of Pharaoh, upon the gebel of Memphis. I grew as this vine with the intent of returning to the body again, that I might be born to the world to do magic against this enemy from Nubia who stands in court.

Hor, son of Paneshe, in the shape of SaOsiris, then cast a spell on the man of Nubia. He caused the fire to surround him, it consumed him in the middle of the court. Pharaoh saw him together with the nobles and the people of Egypt.

SaOsiris passed away as a shadow from the company of Pharaoh and Setna, his father. They did not see him again. Pharaoh marvelled with his great men at the things they had seen in the court and they said: There is no good scribe and learned man like Hor, son of Paneshe. There will not be his like ever.

Setna opened his mouth and shouted loudly when SaOsiris had passed away as a shadow. Pharaoh rose from court, anger in his heart at the things that he had seen.

When evening fell Setna went to his apartments, his heart exceedingly sad. Mehwesekht lay at his side. She conceived from him that night. She gave birth to a male child, who was given the name of Wesymenthor. Setna never forgot his son and regularly made offerings and libations before the genius of Hor, son of Paneshe.

The end

Source: Griffith, F. Ll, *Stories of the High Priests of Memphis, The Sethon of Herodotus* and *The Demotic Tales of Khamuas*.

Notes

1. The distinction between both funerals mirrors that between the archaic followers of Seth and the later Osirian mode of death.
2. Griffith translates *Nehes* as Ethiopia - but most subsequent authorities have this as Nubia.
3. Griffith was uncertain of the meaning of *ate*, thinking it might be a kind of sorcerer, which certainly fits the context. Later authorities translate it as chieftain.

Appendix III

The Tale of the Two Brothers
Anubis and Bata

Once there were two brothers, of one mother and one father; Anpu was the name of the elder, and Bata was the name of the younger. Now, as for Anpu he had a house, and he had a wife. But his little brother was to him as if he were a son; he it was who made for him his clothes; he it was who followed behind his oxen to the fields; he it was who did the ploughing; he it was who

Bucrania or Ox skulls, invariably found in association with tombs, these two from the predynastic graves of Badari (See Brunton 1930). In Nubian they are invariable arranged in an arc at the southern side of graves, in alternate rows: cow & calf, bulls, then oxen (Welsby & Anderson 2004).

harvested the corn; he it was who did for him all the matters that were in the field. Behold, his younger brother grew to be an excellent worker, there was not his equal in the whole land; behold, the spirit of a god was in him.

Now after this the younger brother followed his oxen in his daily manner; and every evening he turned again to the house, laden with all the herbs of the field, with milk and with wood, and with all things of the field. And he put them down before his elder brother, who was sitting with his wife; and he drank and ate, and he lay down in his stable with the cattle. And at the dawn of day he took bread which he had baked, and laid it before his elder brother; and he took with him his bread to the field, and he drove his cattle to pasture in the fields. And as he walked behind his cattle, they said to him, 'Good is the herbage which is in that place;' and he listened to all that they said, and he took them to the good place which they desired. And the cattle which were before him became exceedingly excellent, and they multiplied greatly.

Now at the time of ploughing his elder brother said unto him, 'Let us make ready for ourselves a goodly yoke of oxen for ploughing, for the land has come out from the water, it is fit for ploughing. Moreover, do thou come to the field with corn, for we will begin the ploughing in the morrow morning.'

Thus said he to him; and his younger brother did all things as his elder brother had spoken unto him to do them.

And when the morn was come, they went to the fields with their things; and their hearts were pleased exceedingly with their task in the beginning of their work. And it came to pass after this that as they were in the field they stopped for corn, and he sent his younger brother, saying, 'Haste thou, bring to us corn from the farm.'

And the younger brother found the wife of his elder brother, as she was sitting fixing her hair. He said to her, 'Get up, and give to me corn, that I may run to the field, for my elder brother hastened me; do not delay.'

She said to him, 'Go, open the bin, and help yourself, I drop my locks if I come now.'

The youth went into the stable; he took a large measure, he

loaded it with wheat and barley; and he carried it out.

She said to him, 'Do you really need all that, how much have you got there on your shoulder?'

He replied, 'Three bushels of barley, and two of wheat, in all five.'

To which she replied 'There is great strength in thee.' And her heart knew him with the knowledge of youth. And she arose and came to him, and conversed with him, saying, 'Come, stay with me, and it shall be well for thee, and I will make for thee beautiful garments.'

Then the youth became like a panther of the south with fury; and she feared greatly. And he spoke to her, saying, 'You are to me as a mother, your husband as a father, for he is the elder. What is this wickedness that your are saying to me? Say it not again.'

And with that he lifted up his burden, and went to the field and came to his elder brother; and they took up their work in silence.

Now afterward, at evening, his elder brother returned to his house; and the younger brother followed after his oxen, and he loaded himself with all the things of the field; and he brought his oxen before him, to make them lie down in their stable. And the wife of the elder brother was afraid on account of what she had said. She took a parcel of fat, she became like one who is evilly beaten, saying to her husband, 'It is your younger brother who has done this wrong.'

Her husband found his wife ill of violence; she did not give him water upon his hands as he used to have, she did not make a light before him, the house was in darkness, and she was lying very sick. Her husband said to her, 'Who has done this to you?' She replied, 'None but your younger brother. When he came to take corn he found me sitting alone; he said to me, "Come, let us lie together, fix your hair." I did not listen 'Behold, am I not like a mother to you, is not your brother as a father?' And he feared, and he beat me to stop me from saying anything, and if you let him live I shall die. Behold he is coming.'

The elder brother became as a panther of the south; he

sharpened his knife; he took it in his hand; he stood behind the
door of his stable to slay his younger brother as he came in the
evening to bring in his cattle. The sun went down, and he loaded
himself with herbs in his daily manner. He came, and his
foremost cow entered the stable, and she said to her keeper,
'Behold your elder brother hiding before thee with his knife to
slay thee; flee!'

He heard what his first cow had said; and the next entering,
she also said likewise. He looked beneath the door of the stable;
he saw the feet of his elder brother; he was standing behind the
door, and his knife was in his hand. He cast down his load to the
ground, and fled; his elder brother pursueing him with his knife.
Then the younger brother cried out unto Ra-Harakhti, saying,
'My good Lord! Thou art he who divides the evil from the good.'

And Ra stood and heard all his cry; and he made a wide canal
between him and his elder brother, and it was full of crocodiles;
the elder brother struck himself twice in frustration. And the
younger brother called to the elder, saying, 'Stand still until the
dawn of day; and when Ra ariseth, I shall judge with thee before
Him. For I shall not stay with thee any more; I shall go to the
valley of the acacia.'

Now when the next day appeared, Ra-Harakhti arose, and one
looked unto the other. And the youth spake with his elder
brother, saying, 'Why do you want to kill me without first hearing
what I have to say? For I am your brother in truth, and thou art
to me as a father, and your wife even as a mother: is it not so?
Verily, when I was sent to bring for us corn, your wife said to me,
'Come, stay with me.'

And the Elder borther understood all that happened with his
wife. Then the youth took a knife, and cut off his phallus, and
cast it into the water, and the fish swallowed it. He became faint;
and his elder brother cursed his own heart greatly; he stood
weeping for him afar off; he knew not how to pass over to where
his younger brother was, because of the crocodiles. And the
younger brother called unto him, saying, 'Whereas thou hast
devised an evil thing, wilt thou not also devise a good thing, even
like that which I would do unto thee? When thou goest to your
house look to your cattle, for I shall not stay in this place; I am

going to the valley of the acacia. And this is what shall come to
pass, that I shall draw out my soul, and I shall put it upon the top
of the flowers of the acacia, and when the acacia is cut down,
and it falls to the ground, and thou comest to seek for it, if thou
searchest for it seven years do not let your heart be wearied. For
you will find it, and you must put it in a cup of cold water, and
expect that I shall live again, that I may make answer to what has
been done wrong. And you shall know that things are happening
to me, when one shall give to thee a cup of beer, and it shall be
troubled.'

And the youth went to the valley of the acacia; and his elder
brother went to his house; his hand was laid on his head, and he
cast dust on his head; and he slew his wife, he cast her to the
dogs, and he sat in mourning for his younger brother.

Now many days after these things, the younger brother was
alone in the valley of the acacia he spent his time in hunting the
beasts of the desert, and he came back in the evening to lie down
under the acacia, which bore his soul upon the topmost flower.
And after this he built himself a tower with his own hands, it was
full of all good things, that he might provide for himself a home.

And he went out from his tower, and he met the Company of
Nine Gods, who were walking forth to look upon the whole

land. The Nine Gods talked one with another, and they said unto
him, 'Ho! Bata, bull of the Nine Gods, are your always alone?
You have left your village for the wife of Anubis, your elder
brother. Behold his wife is slain. You have given him an answer
to all that was transgressed against thee.'

And their hearts were vexed for him. And Ra-Harakhti said to
Khnum, 'Behold, frame thou a woman for Bata, that he may not
remain alone.'

And Khnum made for him a mate.

She was more beautiful than any woman who is in the whole
land. The essence of every god was in her. The seven Hathors
came to see her: they prophesied with one mouth, 'She will die
by the knife.'

And Bata loved her exceedingly, and she dwelt in his house; he
passed his time in hunting the beasts of the desert, and laid them
before her. He said, 'Go not outside, lest the sea seize thee; for I
cannot rescue thee from it, for I am a woman like thee; my soul
is placed on the head of the flower of the acacia; and if another
find it, I must fight with him.'

And he opened unto her his heart in all its nature.

Now after these things Bata went to hunt in his daily manner. And the young girl went to walk under the acacia which was by the side of her house. Then the sea saw her, and cast its waves up after her. She betook herself to flee. She entered her house. And the sea called unto the acacia, saying, 'Oh, would that I could seize her!'

And the acacia brought a lock from her hair, and the sea carried it to Egypt, and dropped it in the place of the fullers of Pharaoh's linen. The smell of the lock of hair entered into the clothes of Pharaoh; and they were wroth with the fullers, saying, 'The smell of ointment is in the clothes of Pharaoh.'

And the people were rebuked but they knew not what they should do. And the chief fuller of Pharaoh walked by the bank, and his heart was very troubled after the daily quarrel. He stood still upon the sand opposite to the lock of hair, and he made one enter into the water and bring it to him; and there was found in it a smell, exceeding sweet. He took it to Pharaoh; and they brought the scribes and the wise men, and they said unto Pharaoh, 'This lock of hair belongs to a daughter of Ra-Harakhti: the essence of every god is in her, and it is a tribute to thee from another land. Let messengers go to seek her: go to the valley of the acacia, let many men go to bring her.'

Then said his majesty, 'Excellent idea.'

And many days after the people who were sent to strange lands came to give report to the king: but there came not those who went to the valley of the acacia, for Bata had slain them. His majesty sent many men and soldiers, as well as horsemen, to bring her back.

And his majesty loved her exceedingly, and raised her to high estate; and he spake unto her that she should tell him concerning her husband. And she said, 'Let the acacia be cut down, and chopped up.'

And they sent men and soldiers with their weapons to cut down the acacia; and they cut the flower upon which was the soul of Bata, and he fell dead.

And when the next day came, and the earth was lightened, the acacia was cut down. And Anubis, the elder brother of Bata, entered his house, and washed his hands; and one gave him a cup of beer, and it became troubled; and one gave him another of wine, and the smell of it was evil. Then he took his staff, and his sandals, and likewise his clothes, with his weapons of war; and he betook himself forth to the valley of the acacia. He entered the tower of his younger brother, and he found him lying upon his mat; he was dead. And he wept when he saw his younger brother lying dead. And he went out to seek the soul of his younger brother under the acacia tree.

He spent three years seeking for it, but found it not. And when he began the fourth year, he desired in his heart to return to Egypt; he said 'tomorrow I will go'.

Now when the next day appeared, he was walking under the acacia still seeking it. He found a seed. He returned with it. Behold this was the soul of his younger brother. He brought a cup of cold water, and he cast the seed into it. Now when the night came Bata's soul sucked up the water; he shuddered in all his limbs, and he looked on his elder brother. Then Anubis took the cup of cold water, in which the soul of his younger brother was; Bata drank it, his soul stood again in its place, and he became as he had been. They embraced each other, and they conversed together.

And Bata said to his elder brother, 'Behold I am to become a great bull which bears every good mark; no one knows its history, and you must sit upon my back. When the sun arises I shall be in the place where my wife is. For all good things shall be done for thee; for one shall load you with silver and gold, because you bring me to Pharaoh, for I become a great marvel, and they shall rejoice for me in all the land. And you shall return to your village.'

And when the next day appeared, Bata became the form which he had told to his elder brother. And Anubis sat upon his back. He came to the place where the king was; he saw him, and was exceeding joyful. He made for him great offerings, saying, 'This is a great wonder which has come to pass.'

There were rejoicings over him in the whole land. They presented to him silver and gold for his elder brother, who went and stayed in his village. They gave to the bull many men and many things, and Pharaoh loved him exceedingly above all that is in this land.

And after many days after these things, the bull entered the purified place; he stood in the place where the princess was; he began to speak with her, saying, 'Behold, I am alive.'

And she said to him, 'And, pray, who art thou?'

He said to her, 'I am Bata. I perceived when you had the acacia destroyed by Pharaoh, that I might not live. Behold, I am alive as an ox.'

Then the princess feared exceedingly for the words that her husband had spoken to her. And he went out from the purified place. And his majesty was sitting, making a good day with her. And she said to his majesty, 'Swear to me by God, saying, "What thou shalt say, I will obey it for your sake."'

'Let me eat of the liver of the ox, because he is fit for nought!' thus spake she to him. And the king was exceeding sad at her words. And on the next day, they proclaimed a great feast with offerings to the ox. And the king sent one of the chief butchers of his majesty, to sacrifice the ox. And when he was sacrificed, as he was upon the shoulders of the people, he shook his neck, and he threw two drops of blood over against the two doors of his majesty. The one fell upon the one side, on the great door of Pharaoh, and the other upon the other door. They grew as two great Persea trees, and each of them was excellent.

And one went to tell unto his majesty, 'Two great Persea trees have grown, as a great marvel of his majesty, in the night by the side of the great gate of his majesty.'

And there was rejoicing for them in all the land, and there were offerings made to them.

And when the days were multiplied after these things, his majesty was adorned with the blue crown, with garlands of flowers on his neck, and he was upon the chariot of pale gold, and he went out from the palace to behold the Persea trees: the princess also was going out with horses behind his majesty. And his majesty sat beneath one of the Persea trees, and it spake thus with his wife: 'Oh thou deceitful one, I am Bata, I am alive, though I have been evilly treated. I knew who caused the acacia to be cut down by Pharaoh at my dwelling. I then became an ox, and thou causedst that I should be killed.'

And many days after these things the princess stood at the table of Pharaoh, and the king was pleased with her. And she said to his majesty, 'Swear to me by God, saying, "That which the princess shall say to me I will obey it for her." '

And he hearkened unto all she said. And he commanded, 'Let these two Persea trees be cut down, and let them be made into planks.'

And he hearkened unto all she said. And after this his majesty sent skilful craftsmen, and they cut down the Persea trees of Pharaoh; and the princess, the royal wife, was standing looking on, and they did all that was in her heart unto the trees. But a chip flew up, and it entered into the mouth of the princess; she swallowed it, and after many days she bore a son. And one went to tell his majesty, 'There is born to thee a son.':

And they brought him, and gave to him a nurse and servants; and there were rejoicings in the whole land. And the king sat making a feast, as they were about the naming of him, and his majesty loved him exceedingly at that moment, and the king raised him to be the royal son of Kush.

Now after the days had multiplied after these things, his majesty made him heir of all the land. And many days after that, when he had fulfilled many years as heir, his majesty died. And the heir said, 'Let the great nobles of his majesty be brought before me, that I may tell them all that has happened to me.'

And they brought also his wife, and he judged her all and ordered that she be killed with a butcher's knife,. They brought to him his elder brother; he made him hereditary prince in all his land. He was thirty years king of Egypt, and he died, and his elder brother stood in his place on the day of burial.

Excellently finished in peace, for the ka of the scribe of the treasury Kagabu, of the treasury of Pharaoh, and for the scribe Hora, and the scribe Meremapt. Written by the scribe Anena, the owner of this roll. He who speaks against this roll, may Tahuti smite him.

.

W.M. Flinders Petrie, ed. *Egyptian Tales*, Translated from the Papyri,

Second Series, 18th to 19th dynasty.

Appendix IV

The Contending of Horus and Seth

This text has been translated several times, the most recent being Lichtheim (1973), and Wente (1972). My rendition owes most to Gardiner's original 1931 transcription. Gardiner (1931) Chester Beatty Papyrus I. This is a powerful piece of myth making which could well be a record of colonisation. The listener is invited to accept as fair, a judgement that gives both Upper and Lower Egyptian lands to one claimant. This is Horus, whose legitimacy is accepted despite his conception after the death of his father Osiris. His uncle/brother Seth is deprived of his birthright in a judgement eventually accepted by all as a fair one, including the audience. Not one god ever suggests a return to the archaic *status quo*, whereby the kingdom is divided equally between both brothers. The story should be read in conjunction with the *Tale of Two Brothers*, which seems to present some of the same events from the perspective of the ethnic 'sethians':

In the beginning[1] it happened there was a trial of Horus and

Seth, mysterious of form, great, mighty princes that ever came
into being. Thoth was presenting the Eye [to] the mighty prince
who is in Heliopolisin when a [little] child sat before the Master
of the Universe claiming the kingly office of his father Osiris,
him beautiful of appeariance, the son of Ptah, who enlighteneth
[the netherworld with] his comeliness.

Then spoke Shu, the son of Ra, before [Atum], the mighty
[prince] who is in Heliopolis: All justice is powerful; saying, Give
the kingly office to Horus.

Then spoke Thoth to the Divine Company of Heaven: Right,
a million times *right*!

And Isis uttered a great cry, and rejoiced exceedingly. And she
came and stood before the Master [of the] Universe, and she
said: North wind, go to the West, and bear the good tidings to
Osiris!

[Then] spoke Shu: [The] presenting of the Eye is the Justice
of the Company of Heaven!

Then said the Master of the Universe: How dare you take
such a decision without me!

But [the Company of Heaven] said: He hath taken the royal
cartouche of Horus, and they have [set] the White Crown upon
his head.

Then was the Master of the Universe silent a long while,
being angry with the Company of Heaven.

Thereupon Seth, the son of Nut, said: Let him be cast forth
with me, that I may defeat him before this Company of Heaven,
there is no other way to sort it out.

But Thoth spoke to him: We shall not be able to discern the
guilty one. Shall the office of Osiris be given to Seth, while [his]
son Horus is yet alive?

And Ra-Harakhti was exceeding angry, for it was the wish of
Ra to give the kingly office to Seth, great of strength, the son of
Nut. And Onuris uttered a great cry before the face of the
Company of Heaven, saying, What are we to do?

Thereupon Atum, the mighty prince who is in Heliopolis,
said: Let Banebdedet, the great god, the living, be summoned, in
order that he may pronounce judgement upon the two youthful
contenders.

So they brought Banebdjedet, the great god who dwelleth in Sehel, before Atum, together with Ptah-Tanen.

And Banebdjedet said: Let not us take action in our ignorance, but let us write a letter to Neith, the mighty, the god's mother. What she shall say, that will we do.

Thereupon the Company of Heaven cried: Judgement was made between them in the primeval time in the hall called 'All Truth's are One'.

And to Thoth they said: Make thou a letter to Neith, in the name of the Master of the Universe, the bull which dwells in Heliopolis.

Thoth said: I will do so, verily I will do so.

Thereupon he sat down to make the letter, and he said: The king of Upper and Lower Egypt, Ra-Atum, the beloved of Thoth, the lord of the two lands in Heliopolis, the sun which enlighteneth the two lands with his comeliness, the Nile mighty in taking possession, Ra-Harakhti (whilst Neith, the mighty, the god's mother, who enlightened the first face, still liveth, and is in health, and flourisheth), the living manifestation of the Master of the Universe, the bull in Heliopolis as the good king of Egypt, to this effect: thy servant spend the night in thought for Osiris, taking counsel with the two lands every day, while Sobek endures for ever. What are we to do to the two men who these eighty years past have been before the tribunal, and none knoweth how to pronounce judgement upon them? May you write to us what we shall do.

Then Neith, the mighty, the god's mother, replied to the Company of Heaven, saying: Give the office of Osiris to his son Horus, and do not do those great acts of wickedness which are illegal, else I shall be angry, and the heaven shall crash to the ground. And let it be spoken to the Master of the Universe, the bull which dwells in Heliopolis, double Seth in his possessions, and give to him Anat and Astarte your two daughters, and set Horus in the place of his father Osiris.

And the letter of Neith, reached the Company of Heaven as they sat in the hall called 'Horus-prominent-of-horns', and Thoth read it before the entire Company of Heaven. And they spoke with one mouth: his goddess is in the right.

Thereupon the Master of the Universe was angry with Horus, and he said to him: Thou art feeble in thy limbs, and this kingly office is too great for you, child, the taste of whose mouth is bad!

And Onuris was angry a million times, and so was the entire Company of Heaven, even the Thirty. And the god Bedon rose up, and he spoke to Ra-Harakhti, Your shrine is empty!

Ra-Harakhti was aggrieved at this taunt which had been spoken to him, and he laid himself down upon his back, and his heart was very troubled.

And the Company of Heaven went forth, and they cried aloud before the face of the god Bedon.And they said to him, Get thee forth, this crime that thou hast done is exceeding great. And they went to their tents.

And the great god passed a day alone. And after a long space Hathor, the lady of the southern sycamore, came and stood before her father, the Master of the Universe, and she uncovered her yoni in his face. And the great god laughed at her. Then he rose up, and he sat down with the great Company of Heaven, and he said to Horus and Seth, speak concerning yourselves.

Thereupon Seth, great of strength, the son of Nut, said: As for me, I am Seth, the greatest of virility among the Company of Heaven, and I slay [Apophis], the enemy of Ra daily, being in front of the Bark-of-Millions, and no other god is able to do. I am entitled to the office of Osiris.

Thereupon they said: Seth, the son of Nut, is in the right.

Then Onuris and Thoth cried aloud: Shall the office be given to a brother on the side of the mother, while a son of the body is yet alive?

Then spoke Banebdjedet: Shall the office be given to this child, while Seth, his elder brother, is yet alive?

Then the Company of Heaven cried aloud: Do not speak such abominable things?

Then Horus, the son of Isis spoke: Do not insult me in presence of the Company of Heaven!

And Isis was angry with them, and she made an oath to the God: As my mother, the goddess Neith, lives, and as Ptah-tanen, high of plumes, curber of the horns of the gods, lives, these words shall be placed before Atum, the mighty prince who is in Heliopolis, and before Khepra who dwells in the Bark.

The Company of Heaven said to her: Be not vexed, Hours will get what is rightly his.

But Seth, the son of Nut, when he heard these words to Isis, was angry with the Company of Heaven, and he said: I will take my sceptre of four thousand and five hundred pounds, and I will kill one of you each day. Seth made an oath to the Master of the Universe, saying: I will not contend in this tribunal whilst Isis is in it.

Then Ra-Harakhti spoke to them: Cross you over to the Island-in-the-Middle, and judge you between them, and say to Nemty, the ferryman, do not ferry let Isis cross.

So the Company of Heaven crossed over to the Island-in-the-middle, and they sat down and ate bread.

But Isis approached Nemty, the ferryman, as he sat near his ferryboat, and she had changed herself into an aged woman, and she went along all bowed wearing a little ring of gold on her finger. And she spoke to him, saying: Ferry me across to the Island-in-the-middle, for I have come with bowl of porridge for the child. He has been looking after some cattle on the island for five days and he is hungry.

But he said: I was told not to ferry across any woman. But she replied: that is only on account of Isis?

So he asked her: What will you give me, if I ferry you across to the Island-in-the-middle?

To which Isis replied: I will give you this loaf.

Thereupon he said: What's that to me, your loaf? Shall I ferry you across to the Island—when it has been said to me, Ferry no woman across—for the sake of a loaf?

Thereupon she said to him: I will give you this gold ring. To which he said: Give me the ring. And she gave it to him.

Thereupon he ferried her across to the Island-in-the-middle.

And while she was walking beneath the trees, she looked and she saw the Company of Heaven, as they sat and ate bread in presence of the Master of the Universe in his arbour. Seth looked and he saw her, as she was coming. Then she uttered an incantation, and changed herself into a maiden fair of limb, and there was not the like of her in the entire land. And he really lusted after her.

So Seth rose up from the picnic and he went to intercept her, for no one had seen her except him. He stood behind a sycamore and called to her: I am here with thee, fair maiden.

And she said to him: No, my lord! I was the wife of a herdsman of cattle, and bore to him a male child. But my husband died, and the child came to look after his father's cattle. Then a foreigner came, and he sat down in my byre, and spoke to my son: I will beat you, and I will take away the cattle of your father, and I will throw you out. I wish you would become his protector.

And Seth spoke to her: Shall the cattle be given to the foreigner, while the son of the good man is alive?

And Isis changed herself into a kite, and she flew, and she perched on the top of an acacia. And she called to Seth, and she said to him: Weep for yourself, it is your own mouth that has said it, it is your own cleverness which has judged thee!

And he stood weeping, and he went to the place where Ra-Harakhti was, and he wept. Thereupon Ra-Harakhti spoke to him: What ails thee now?

And Seth told him: I said to her this foreigner's face should be smitten with a rod and he should be evicted and your son put in his father's position.

And Ra-Harakhti said to him: You have judged yourself?

And Seth spoke to him: Let Nemty, the ferryman, be brought, and let a great punishment be inflicted upon him, saying: Why didst thou let her cross?

Thereupon Nemty, the ferryman, was brought before the Company of Heaven, and they removed the soles of his feet.

And Nemty forswore gold to this day in presence of the great Company of Heaven, saying, Gold hath been made to me into an abomination for my city.

Thereupon the Company of Heaven crossed over to the Western Tract, and they sat down upon the mountain. And when it was evening, Ra-Harakhti and Atum, the lord of the two lands in Heliopolis, sent for the Company of Heaven, saying: What are you doing, still sitting here? As for these two youths, you will cause them to end their lives in the tribunal! You shall set the White Crown upon the head of Horus, the son of Isis, and you shall promote him to the place of his father Osiris.

And Seth was very angry. And the Company of Heaven spoke to Seth: Why are you angry? Shall no one do as Atum, the lord of the two lands in Heliopolis, and Ra-Harakhti have said?

Thereupon they established the White Crown upon the head of Horus, the son of Isis. And Seth cried aloud before the face of the Company of Heaven, and he was vexed, and said: Shall the office be given to my little brother, while I, his elder brother, is yet alive?

Thereupon he made an oath, saying: They shall remove the White Crown from the head of Horus, the son of Isis, and they shall cast him into the water, that I may contend with him regarding the office of ruler.

Ra-Harakhti did accordingly.

And Seth spoke to Horus: Come, let us change ourselves into two hippopotamuses, and let us plunge into the waters of the great green sea. And whoso shall emerge within the period of three months, to him shall this office not be given.

Thereupon they both plunged in. And Isis sat weeping and said: Seth will kill my son Horus.

So she took a quantity of twine and made a rope, and she took a pound of copper, and melted it down into a harpoon, and she tied to it the rope, and threw it into the water. And the barb bit into the body of her son Horus. And he cried aloud, saying: Come to me, my mother Isis! Call to thy barb, that it loose from me, for I am Horus, your son!

And Isis cried aloud, and she said to the barb: Loose thou from him. And her barb loosed from him.

Thereupon she threw it again into the water, and it bit into the body of Seth. And Seth cried aloud, saying: What have I done against thee, my sister Isis? Call to thy barb that it loose from me, for I am your brother on the side of the mother. Then had she compassion upon him. And Seth called to her: Didst thou love the foreigner more than your brother? And Isis called to her barb, saying: Loose from him. Thereupon the barb loosed from him.

Then Horus was angry with his mother Isis, his face was savage like a panther of Upper Egypt, and his chopper of sixteen pounds was in his hand. And he removed the head of his mother Isis and ascended into the mountain. Thereupon Isis changed herself into a statue of flint which had no head.

And Ra-Harakhti spoke to Thoth: What is this female that is come, and hath no head?

And Thoth spoke to Ra-Harakhti: O my good lord, this is Isis, the mighty, the god's mother, and Horus her son hath removed her head. And Ra-Harakhti cried out aloud, and said to the Company of Heaven: Let us go and inflict a great punishment upon him. Thereupon the Company of Heaven ascended into the mountains in order to search for Horus, the son of Isis. Now as for Horus, he was lying under a Shenusha-tree in the Oasis country.

[Then Hathor, Mistress of the Southern Sycamore, set out and she found Horus lying weeping in the desert. She captured a gazelle and milked it. She said to Horus: Open your eyes so I may put this milk in them.][2]

Thereupon she went to speak to Ra-Harakhti: I found Horus, and Seth had deprived him of his eye. And so I raised him up again, and behold, he is come.

Thereupon the Company of Heaven said: Let Horus and Seth be summoned, in order that judgement may be made between them.

Then they were brought before the Company of Heaven. Then spoke the Master of the Universe before the great Company of Heaven to Horus and Seth: Go you, and let what I have said to you be listened to; eat you, and drink you, and let us be at peace, and cease you from wrangling thus every day.

Thereupon Seth spoke to Horus: Come, let us pass a happy day in my house. Thereupon Horus said to him: I will do so, verily, I will do so.

And when it was evening the bed was spread for them, and they both lay down. And in the night Seth's member became stiff, and he inserted it between the loins of Horus.

Then Horus put his two hands between his loins, and he caught the seed of Seth.

Thereupon Horus went to speak to his mother Isis: Come to me, O Isis, my mother! Come and see what Seth hath done to me! And he opened his hand, and he let her to see the seed of Seth. And she cried out aloud, and she seized her knife, and she cut off his hands, and cast them into the water. And she drew out for him hands of like worth.

Thereupon she took a dab of sweet and fragrant ointment, and put it upon the member of Horus, which made it become erect, he put it into a pot, and ejaculated.

Thereupon Isis went with the seed of Horus in the morning to the garden of Seth. And she spoke to his gardener: What herb is it that Seth eats here with thee?

And the gardener replied: He does not eat any herb except lettuces. And Isis put the seed of Horus upon them. And Seth came after his fashion of every day, and he ate the lettuces. And he arose pregnant with the seed of Horus.

And Seth went to speak to Horus: Come, let us go, in order that I may contend with thee in the tribunal. Thereupon Horus replied: I will do so, verily I will do so.

Thereupon they both went to the tribunal, and they stood before the great Company of Heaven.

Seth said: Let there be given to me the office of Ruler, for as to Horus, this same that standeth here, I have buggered him, as a warrior does to his vanquished foe.

Thereupon the Company of Heaven cried aloud, they belched and spat into the face of Horus. But Horus laughed at them, swearing to God: False is all that which Seth has said. Let the seed of Seth be summoned, that we may see where it is. And let mine own be summoned.

Thereupon Thoth, the lord of divine words, the scribe of truth of the Company of Heaven, placed his hand upon the arm of Horus, and he said: Come forth, thou seed of Seth. And it answered to him from the water in the fen.

Thereupon Thoth placed his hand upon the arm of Seth, and he said: Come forth, thou seed of Horus! Thereupon it spoke to him: Where shall I come forth?

Thereupon Thoth spoke to it: Come forth from his ear!

And it replied: Shall I come forth from his ear, I who am a divine effluence?

Thereupon Thoth said: Come forth from his forehead!

Then it came forth as a disk of gold upon the head of Seth.

Seth was exceedingly angry, and he stretched forth his hand to lay hold of the disk of gold. But Thoth took it away from him, and put it as an ornament upon his own head.

The Company of Heaven said: Horus is in the right, and Seth is in the wrong.

And Seth was exceeding angry, and made a great oath to God, saying: They shall not give the office to him, until he hath been cast forth with me. And we will fashion for ourselves some ships of stone, and we will sail around, we twain. And whoso shall prevail over his fellow, to him shall they give the office of Ruler.

Thereupon Horus fashioned for himself a ship of cedar, and he plastered it with gypsum, and he cast it upon the water at eventide, and no man who was in the entire land had seen it.

And Seth saw the ship of Horus, and he thought it was stone.[3] And he went to the mountain, and he cut off a mountain peak, and he fashioned for himself a ship of stone of one hundred and thirty and eight cubits.

Thereupon they went down into their ships in presence of the Company of Heaven. But the ship of Seth sank in the water.

And Seth changed himself into a hippopotamus, and caused to founder the ship of Horus.

Thereupon Horus took his barb, and he threw it at of Seth. But the Company of Heaven told him to stop.

Horus took his harpoons, and he placed them in his ship, and he fared down to Sais to speak to Neith, the mighty, the god's mother: Let judgement be pronounced upon me and Seth, forasmuch as these eighty years we have been in the tribunal, and none knows what to do. Yet hath he not been declared in the right against me, but for a thousand times before this have been in the right against him every day. Nor yet doth he regard aught that the Company of Heaven have said. I contended with him in the hall Way-of-Truths, and I was declared in the right against him. I contended with him in the hall Horus-prominent-of-horns, and I was declared in the right against him. I contended with him in the hall Field-of-reeds, and I was declared in the right against him. I contended with him in the hall The-field-pool, and I was declared in the right against him. And the Company of Heaven spoke to Shu, the son of Ra: Right in all that he hath said is Horus, the son of Isis.

Then Thoth said to the Master of the Universe: send a letter to Osiris, that he may pronounce judgement.

Thereupon Thoth sat down to complete a letter to Osiris, saying: The Bull, lion-that-hunteth-for-himself; the Two Goddesses, protecting-the-gods-curbing-the-two-lands; Horus of Gold, inventor-of-men-in-the-primeval-time; king of Upper and Lower Egypt, Bull-which-dwelleth-in-Heliopolis; son of Ptah, fertile-of-territory-who-arose-as-father-of-his-Company of Heaven-he-eateth-of-gold-and-all-manner-of-rare-gems—Mayst thou write to us that which we shall do to Horus and Seth, in order that we may not take action in our ignorance.

Osiris answered it very quickly: Wherefore shall my son Horus be defrauded, seeing that it is I who make you strong, and it is I who made the barley and the spelt to nourish the gods, and even so the living creatures after the gods, and no god nor any goddess found himself able to do it. And the letter of Osiris came to the place where Ra-Harakhti was, as he sat with the Company of Heaven at the bright moment in Xois. And Ra-Harakhti said: Answer thou for me this letter very quickly to Osiris, and speak to him in respect of this letter: Suppose thou hadst never come into existence, suppose thou hadst never been born, the barley and the spelt would still exist.

Thereupon he sent to Ra-Harakhti again, saying: Exceedingly good is all that thou hast done, thou inventor of the Company of Heaven in very truth, whilst Justice hath been suffered to sink within the nether world. But look thou at the matter thyself also! As for this land in which I am, it is full of savage-faced messengers, and they fear not any god nor (any) goddess. I will cause them to go forth and they shall fetch the heart of whosoever doeth evil deeds, and they shall be here with me.

Moreover, what signifieth it that I be resting here in the West, whilst you are without, all of you? Who is there among them stronger than I? But behold they have invented falsehood in very truth. Is it not so that when Ptah, the great, south of his wall, the lord of Ankh-tawi, made the sky, did he not speak to the stars which are in it: You shall go to rest in the West every night in the place where king Osiris is. And after the gods, nobles and plebeians shall go to rest also in the place where thou art—so said he not to me? And after (many days) following upon these things the letter of Osiris reached the place where the Master of the Universe was together with the Company of Heaven.

Thereupon Seth said: Let us be taken to the Island-in-the-midst in order that I may contend with him. Thereupon he went to the Island-in-the-midst, and Horus was declared in the right over him. Thereupon Atum, the lord of the two lands in Heliopolis, sent to Isis, saying: Bring thou Seth, he being made fast with bonds. Thereupon Isis brought Seth, he being made him a prisoner. Thereupon Atum spoke to him: Wherefore hast thou not allowed judgement to be pronounced upon you, but hast taken way for thyself the office of Horus?

Thereupon Seth spoke to him: Not so, my good lord! Let Horus, the son of Isis, be summoned, and let be given to him the office of his father Osiris. Thereupon they brought Horus, the son of Isis, and they set the White Crown upon his head, and he was set in the place of his father Osiris. And they spoke to him: Thou art the good king of Egypt, thou art the good lord of every land for ever and ever. And Isis cried aloud to her son Horus, saying: Thou art the good king, my heart is in joy that thou enlightenest the earth with thy comeliness.

Thereupon Ptah, the great, south of his wall, the lord of Ankh-tawi, said: What is that which shall be done to Seth, for now behold, Horus hath been set in the place of his father Osiris?

Thereupon Ra-Harakhti said: Let Seth, the son of Nut, be given to me, that he may dwell with me and be as my son, and he shall thunder in the sky, and men shall fear him. Thereupon they went to speak to Ra-Harakhti: Horus, the son of Isis, is arisen as Ruler. And Ra was in joy exceedingly, and he spoke to the Company of Heaven: Jubilate you! To the ground before Horus, the son of Isis!

Thereupon Isis said: Horus is arisen as Ruler, the Company of Heaven is in holiday, heaven is in joy! Then they took wreaths, when they saw Horus, the son of Isis, arisen as great Ruler of Egypt. The Company of Heaven, their hearts were content, the entire earth was in rejoicing, when they saw Horus, the son of Isis, the office of his father Osiris, the lord of Djedu, having been allotted to him.

IT HAS COME TO A HAPPY ENDING IN THEBES, THE PLACE OF TRUTH.

Notes

1. The first few characters of this manuscript are damaged although Gardiner transcribed them as 'Kephra'- meaning 'come to pass' or happen. In other texts the first line is always very significant, often a ritual expression such as 'once upon a time' - hense my rendering as 'in the beginning'.
2. This passage is missing in Gardiner's transcription, and is interpolated from a later translation.
3. 'Stone ships' may have some role in ancient shamanism. See Fries (2005 : 228).

Appendix V

The Wake of Osiris

Adapted from one of the oldest dramatic texts, the so-called

'Ramesseum Drama'. See Sethe (1910) and Gaster (1961). This

was tentatively proposed as a 'Lammas Ritual'.

Act I

Spoken as Seth and Nephthys

Nephthys:
Be not unaware of me O Seth
If you know me then I shall know you

Seth:
Be not unaware of me O Nephthys
If you know me then I shall know you

Nephthys:
Wandering amongst the fields of rushes
I searched for the corn king
and there found him
sinking beneath the water
where his brother Seth had left him,
when his jealous rage had gone
I raised him up as Osiris and he spoke thus:
The reed boats are set down for me
that I may cross on them to the horizon
The nurse canal is opened
and the winding waterway is flooded
the field of rushes filled with water
and I am ferried over them to the eastern side of the sky

to the place where the gods fashioned me
and where I was born, new and young
convey to Horus the Eye that by its power
This waterway may now be opened

Seth:
Behold I can endure and stand no more
Against Osiris who was nobler than I
Your brother Seth will chill your heart no more
Oh my mother Nuit, stretch yourself over him
And place him in the imperishable stars
which are in thee, so that he may not die.
Isis, utter the word and make it so
let Horus possess the Eye!
That I tore from him in our fight
Horus the son shall in his father's place arise
The prince shall now become the king

Act II

Nephthys and Seth:
Fish of the deep, fowl of the skies
Go seek Osiris where he lies!
[everyone joins in the chant]
Begin swaying and/or hyper ventilating

Seth:
Let an animal be sacrificed in his place
and a potion of Beer be drunk
a handfull of Grain I strew upon the floor
The soul of Osiris will never die
It is in the grain preserved.
And as this to the granary is conveyed,
so do I convey to you
the sacred sight
The eye of Horus,
that I took from him in our struggle

wrenching it from its socket.
Never shall it be lost again,
with sight in your feet
dance for joy

Nephthys :
With my sister Isis
widows of the corn king
Have made him anew
In the form of the Ankh
symbol of eternal life
Seth, as an oxen
shall raise him up
upon his back
then remembering
their quarrel
throw him down again
cutting him into fourteen pieces
like the moon
and the confederates of Seth
will eat of the bread of life
How noble, fair and beautiful he is
Seth struggles no longer

A loaf Ankh or Man shaped loaf of bread is presented. Each of the participants sees its fourteen parts, seven on the back and seven on the front. Focus on one particular part, and if it is the ankh, associate that with a particular part of your own body using techniques you know. When the priest says eat, all grab the loaf and tear into pieces and consume or otherwise burn that part, visualizing it going to the part of your own body you first thought of, that will make it strong.

Nephthys:
But there is a price to pay for such a sacrifice
Horus, the seed shall become the plant
as the son succeeds the father,
and receives the Eye of Power!

Behold confederates of Seth
[I will strike you as you struck my father}!
I command you: thrash him no more

Seth:
The thrashed grain is loaded on the ox's back
How sweet it smells
A barge is dressed in red paint
To carry him to the western lands
and I, as red devil, will guard him through the
darkest parts of the night
he shall never slip free
from me who is his clear equal

Eye paint is applied to all present - Hands are lifted and a ritual combat occurs

Seth:
Now Horus stands up and longs to fight with me
and the earth cries out for us to stop
By the sweet influence of this, your Eye
may protection be shed over us
striking and biting
striking and biting
The eye of Horus is split
he cries out, keep it away
Restore it, I pray you, to my face!
For Set is out of tune with us;
and alone disturbs the harmony of all our ways
restore to my face the eye
which, wine red, flows with blood
Never again take it from me!
Hand back my eye which was wounded
when you bit it, covering it with blood
See I have now retrieved the eye from you,
Which was blood red like a carnelian bead
turn your back, for lo, these eyes of mine

Now fix their fearsome gaze upon your face!
with green eye paint, I set a bright eye in my face
and with black may it sit sweetly in my face
and with brown, never may its luster be dulled
with frankincence, fragrance of the gods
This eye, which was plucked out, do I restore
and with this perfume scent my face
till it be fragrant!

Nephthys:
Now in the fight
Horus tears the thighbone from you - Seth
He flings it into the sky, as a permanent memorial

Now in the fight
Horus tears the thighbone from you - Seth
and makes of it a plough
to scrap the earth
and plant the seed of his father
and as a mummy cloth is bound around a corpse
so shall our enermies be bound
and I Great Nephthys, reunite his limbs!
And as a panther-cat destroy all evil

Now in the fight
Horus tears the thighbone from you - Seth
and opens his fathers mouth
so he may speak truly
Lord of the Upper and Lower worlds

Now in the fight
Horus tear the testicles from you - Seth!
And grafts them to his own body
Thereby increase still more his potency!

The oil of my eye that gleams so brightly against Seth
Now raise ye up your father who lies here!
We are all embalmers

masked, our faces those of wolves or monkeys
Our heads anointed with oil
we stoop and are bowed beneath the weight of him!
Now Nuit, raise us to heaven, for your back
A ladder is,
its vertibra the rungs.

My sister Isis
sing with me a final lamentation

Beautiful Youth,
Beautiful Youth
come, come to your house;
Beautiful Youth,
Beautiful Youth
come, come to your house;

Holy image of the earth,
essence of our time

Beautiful Youth,
Beautiful Youth
come, come to your house.

Bibliography

BIFAO: Bulletin de l'Institut Français dArchéologie Orientale.

EES: Egyptian Exploration Society.

JEOL: Jaarbericht van het Vooraziatrich Egyptisch Genootschap (Gezelschap) "Ex Orient Lux"

JEA: Journal of Egyptian Archaeology, 3 Doughty Mews, WC1N 2PG

Lexicon: Lexikon de Ägyptologie (six vols) ed. Wolfgang Helck, Eberhard Otto, and Wolfhart Westendorf (Wiesbaden: O. Harrassowitz, 1972), VI

Urk: Urkenden des ägyptischen Altertums; see Steindorff, G (1903)

Books

Adams, Barbara, (1986b) 'Egyptian Objects in the Victoria and Albert Museum', *Egyptology Today*, no. 3, Warminster, Aris and Phillips.

Archéo Nil No 13 (2003) 'Bibliography of Prehistoric and Early Dynastic Period'.

Assmann J, (1996) *The Mind of Egypt: history and meaning in the time of the Pharaohs*, Metropolitan NY.

Baines, J & Malek, J, (2000) *Cultural Atlas of Ancient Egypt*, Andromeda

Baumgartel, E J (1947) *Cultures of Prehistoric Egypt*, Vol 1 Griffith, Oxford.

Baumgartel, E J (1960) *Cultures of Prehistoric Egypt*, Vol 2 Griffith, Oxford.

Baumgartel, E J (1970) *Naqada Excavation*: A Supplement, Quaritch, London (331 R3 [fol])

Betz, H D (ed) (1986) *The Greek Magical Papyri in Translation*, Chicago.

Bika Reed, (1987) *Rebel in the Soul*: translation of Berlin Papyrus 3023, Vermont.

Blackman, A. M. and Fairman H. W. (1943) *The myth of Horus at Edfu* II, *JEA* 29.

Brugsch, H (1883) *Thesaurus Inscriptionum Aegyptiacarum*, 6 vols Leipzig.

Burgsch H (1891) *Die Aegyptolgie*, Leipzig.

Breasted, James H (1906) *Ancient Records of Egypt*, 5 vols, Chicago.

Brewer, Douglas & Friedman, R F (1989) *Fish and Fishing in Ancient Egypt*, Aris & Phillips, UK.

Budge, E A Wallis (1901) *The Book of the Dead*, Kegan Paul.

Budge, E A Wallis (1906) *Egyptian Heaven & Hell*, Vol II, 'Book of Gates'.

Butzer, K W. (1976) *Early Hydraulic Civilization in Egypt*, London & Chicago.

Calverley, A M. (1933) *The Temple of Sethos I at Abydos*, 4 vols, Chicago.

Collier Mark & Manley Bill (1998) *How to Read Egyptian Hieroglyphs*, BM London.

Clarke, John R (2003) *Roman Sex,* New York, Abrams.

Clagett, M (1995) *Ancient Egyptian Science II, Calendars, Clocks and Astronomy*, American Philosophical Society.

Michael, (1996) *The Avebury Cycle*, Thames & Hudson.

David, Antony E (1981) *A Guide to Religious Ritual at Abydos*, Aris & Phllips, Warminster.

David, Antony E & Rosalie (1992) *A Biographical Dictionary of Ancient Egypt*, London.

de Morgan, J (1897) *Recherches sur les origins de l'Egypte*, ii, p147-202, Paris.

Decker, W (1992) *Sports and Games of Ancient Egypt*, New Haven.

Divin, Marguerite (1969) *Stories From Ancient Egypt*, London.

Duell, Prentice (1938) *The Mastaba of Mereruka*, 2 Vols, Chicago.

Edwards, I E S (1947 & 1972), *Pyramids of Egypt*, London.

Emery, W B (1972) *Archaic Egypt*, Harmondsworth.

Evans, L (2001) *Kingdom of the Ark*, Simon & Schuster.

Faulkner, (1956) *JEA* 42, text of Berlin Pap 3024.

Flowers, Stephen (1995) *Hermetic Magick*, New York.

Forbes, D C (2005) 'Set, Lord of Chaos' *KMT*, Vol 15 No 4 pp 67-71

Fries, J (1992) *Visual Magick: A Handbook of Freestyle Shamanism*, Mandrake of Oxford.

Fries, J (2004) *Cauldron of the Gods: A Manual of Celtic Magick*, Mandrake of Oxford.

Fries, J (2005) *Helrunar: a Manual of Rune Magick*, Mandrake of Oxford.

Depuydt, L (1999) *Fundamentals of Egyptian Grammar*, Frog Publishing, Massachusetts.

Galvin, John (2005) 'Egypt's First Pharaohs', *KMT,* April pp 106-121.

Gardiner, A H & Sethe, K (1928) *Egyptian Letters to the Dead - mainly from the Middle Kingdom, copied, translated and edited*, EES.

Gardiner, A H (1931) *Chester Beatty Papyrus I*, Oxford Univerity Press.

Gardiner, A H (1941-48) *The Wilbour Papyrus*, 3 Vols, Oxford.

Gardiner, A H (1944) 'Horus the Behdetite' *JEA* 30 pp24ff.

Gardiner, A H (1947) *Ancient Egyptian Onomastica*.

Gardiner, AH (1950) 'The Baptism of Pharoah' *JEA* 36 pp3-12.

Gardiner, A H (1957) *Egyptian Grammar: being an introduction to the study of Hieroglyphs*, 3rd revised edition, Oxford.

Gasse, A (2004) 'Une Stèle d'horus sur les crocodiles à propos du <text C>' *Revue D'Égyptologie*, tome 55, pp23-44.

Gaster, Theodor H (1961) *Thespis: ritual, myth and drama in the ancient Near East*, New York.

Gautier J E & Jéquier, G (1902) *Fouilles de Licht*, L'Institute Français D'Archeologie Oriental, Vol 6.

Cheke, Aaron (2004)'Magic through the linguistic lenses of Greek mágos, Indo-European *mag(h)-*, Sanskrit *māyā* and Pharaonic Egyptian *Ḥeka*' in *Journal for the Academic Study of Magic II*, Mandrake of Oxford.

De Lubicz, Schwaller (1997) *The Temple of Man*, Inner Traditions, Vermont.

Gibbon, Edward (1977) *History of the Decline and Fall of the Roman Empire*, Penguin, London.

Griffiths, J G (1960) *The Conflict of Horus and Seth*, Liverpool.

Gupta, S, Hoens, D K & Goudriaan T (1979) *Hindu Tantrism*, Leiden.

Hayes, B William C. (1953) *The Scepter of Egypt: a background for the study of the Egyptian antiquities in the Metropolitan Museum of Art*, 2 Vols, Abrams, NY.

Hawkes, Jacquetta, (1973) *The First Great Civilizations: life in Mesopotamia, the Indus Valley and Egypt* London.

Hoffman, Michael A (1984) *Egypt before the Pharaohs* (Arkana).

Hutton, R (1999) *The Triumph of the Moon: a history of modern pagan witchcraft*, OUP.

Jacq, C, (1986) *Egyptian Magic*, Aris & Phillips, England.

Keel, Othmar (1988) and Uehlinger, Christoph, *Gods, Goddesses and Images of God in Ancient Israel*, Fortress Press, Minneapolis..

Katzeff, Paul (1990) *Moon Madness and other effects of the Full Moon*, Hale.

Kees, Herman (1923-4) *Horus and Seth als Götterpaar*.

Kees, Hermann (1977) *Ancient Egypt*, Chicago UP.

Kinnaer, Jacques, (1990) 'What is really known about the Narmer Palette: it may not document the unification of the two lands afterall', *KMT*, vol 15 no 1 pp 48-54.

Koefoed-Petersen, O, (1948) *Les Stèles Égyptiennes*, Copenhagen.

Lami, Lucy (1981) *Egyptian Mysteries: new light on anicent knowledge*, Thames & Hudson.

Lehner, Mark (1997) *The Complete Pyramids*, Thames & Hudson.

Lexikon de Ägyptologie (six vols) ed. Wolfgang Helck, Eberhard Otto, and Wolfhart Westendorf (Wiesbaden: O. Harrassowitz, 1972)

Lichtheim, Miriam (1980) *Ancient Egyptian Literature*, 3 vols, University of California Press.

Mackenna, Stephen (1917), *Plotinus: The Ethical Treatises*, London.

Mailer (1983) *Ancient Evenings*, London.

Mercer, S A B (1949) *The Religion of Ancient Egypt*, London, London, Luzac 1949).

Metcalf P & Huntington, W R (1979) *Celebrations of Death*, CUP NY

Morgan, M (2005) *Tankhem, Seth and Egyptian Magick*, Mandrake of Oxford.

Murray, M (1973) *The Splendour that was Egypt*, London.

Murray, M, 'The Astrological character of the Egyptian magical wnad' SCA Taylor PG Viii b112.

Nabarz, Payam (2005) *The Mysteries of Mithras: The Pagan Belief That Shaped the Christian World*, USA.

Newberry, P E, (1922) 'The Set Rebellion of the Second Dynasty', *Ancient Egypt*, pp 40-6.

Nicholson P T & Shaw I, (2000) *Ancient Egyptian Materials and Technology*, Cambridge.

Patai, Raphael (1978) *The Hebrew Goddess,* Wayne State University, Detroit.

Piankoff, Alexandre & Rambova, N, (1954) *Egyptian Religious Texts and Representations* - vol III - Mythological Papyri, Texts and Plates, Bollingen)

Papparis, Konstantinos (2002) *Abortion in the Ancient World*, Duckworth

Parker, Richard (1950) *The Calendars of Ancient Egypt*, Chicago.

Petrie, W M Flinders (1895) *Egyptian Tales,* Methuen, London.

Petrie, W M Flinders & Quibell, J E (1896a) Naqada and Ballas, Quaritch, London. (330 BSA fol)

Petrie, W M Flinders (1896b) *Koptos* (331 R1 [fol])

Petrie, W M Flinders (1901) *The Royal Tombs of the Earliest Dynasties*, vols, London.

Pinch, Geraldine (1994) *Magic in Ancient Egypt*, British Museum Press.

Plutarch, Isis and OsirisPorten B (1986) 'The Tale of the Son of Paweresh' p 16, *Select Aramaic Papyri from Ancient Egypt,* Institute for the Study of Aramaic Papyri, n.p.

Quibell, J E, (1900-2) *Hierakonpolis,* London.

Ramsay, G G (1918) *Satires of Juvenal,* Harvard UP.

Rankine, David (2004) *Becoming Magick,* Mandrake of Oxford.

Redford, Susan (2002) *The Harem Conspiracy: the Murder of Ramesses III,* Illinois.

Reeder, G (1999) 'Musing on the sexual nature of the human headed Ba bird', *KMT,* Autumn, p.72-78 .

Reeder, G (1999) 'Seti I, his reign and monuments' *KMT,* Autumn, pp.47-68 .

Reeder, G (2005) 'The Eunuch and the Wab Priest - another look at the mysterious Manchester Museum Mummies', *KMT* Vol 16, No1, pp54-65.

Reymond, E A E (1969) *The Mythological Origin of the Egyptian Temple,* Manchester University Press.

Ritner, R K (1993) *The Mechanics of Ancient Egyptian Magical Practice,* Chicago

Roth, Ann Macy (1992) 'The '*PSS-Kt* and the 'opening of the mouth' ceremony. A ritual of birth and rebirth' *JEA* vol 78 pp 113-147.

Roth, Anne May & Roehring, Catherin H (2002) 'Magical Bricks and the Bricks of Birth', *JEA* vol 88 2002 pp121-139.

Samuel D & Bolt P (1995) 'Rediscovering Ancient Egyptian Beer', *Brewer's Guardian UK,* December pp27-32.

Schumann, Ruth Antelme & Stéphanie Rossini (2001) *Sacred Sexuality in Ancient Egypt*, Inner Traditions. Formely 'Secrets de Hathor.'

Seligman, C G (1934) *Egypt and Negro Africa, a study of divine kingship*, Routledge.

Sethe, K (1928) *Dramatische Texte zu altaegyptischen Mysteriernspielen* I-II Leipzig.

Servajean, F (2004) 'Lune ou Soleil d'or un Épisode des aventures 'Horus et de Seth (P Chester Beatty I R° 11 1-13 1)' *Revue D'Égyptologie*, Tome 55, pp125-148.

Snape, Steven (1996) *Egyptian Temples*, Shire Publications, Princes Risborough, UK.

Shual, Katon, (1986) *Sexual Magick*, Mandrake of Oxford.

Stadelmann, R (1967) *Syrisch-palästinensische Gottheiten in Ägypten*, Leiden.

Steindorff, G (1903) Urkenden des ägyptischen Altertums; Section I, Sethe, K, *Urkunden des alten Reiches*, Leipzig 1903; Section IV, Sethe, K, *Urkunden der 18 Dynastie, historische-biographische Urkunden*, 4 vols, Leipzig, 1906-9; vol i, second edtion 1927-30; Section V, V H Grapow, *Religiöse Urkunden*, 3 parts, Leipzig 1925-17. This monumental work often appears in books on egyptology indicated by the abbreviation *Urk*.

Sweene, Deborah (2002) 'Gender and Conversational tactics in the Contendings of Horus & Seth' *JEA* Vol 88 pp 141-162

Te Velde (1967) *Seth: God of Confusion: a study of his role in Egyptian Mythology and Religion*, E J Brill (rev 1977).

Te Velde (1970) 'The God Heka in Egyptian Theology' *JEOL* 21 175-186 followed by unnumbered plate section.

Vercoulter, Jean (1970) *Mirgissa*, 3 vols, Paris.

Wainwright, G A (1923) 'The Red Crown in Early prehistoric times', *JEA* 9, pp26-33.

Wainwright, G A (1938) *The Sky Religion in Egypt: its antiquity and effects*, Cambridge.

Wainwright, G A (1961) 'The Earliest Use of the Mano Cornuto' *Folklore*.

Walker-John, B (1996) 'Set in His Own Right', *Twenty-Two*, High Wycombe.

Wente, E F (1972) 'Contendings of Hours and Seth' in Simpson, *The Literature of Ancient Egypt*, Yale.

Webb, D (1996) *Seven Faces of Darkness,* Runa-Raven.

Welsby, Derek A & Anderson, Julie R (2004) *Sudan: Ancient Treasure*, BM Press.

Whittaker, J C (1994) *Flint knapping: making and understanding stone tools*. University of Texas Press, Austin.

Wilkinson, Toby AH (2003) *Genesis of the Pharaohs: dramatic new discoveries that rewrite the origins of Ancient Egypt*, Thames and Hudson.

Williams, B B (1998) 'The wearer of the Leopard skin in the Naqada Period' in J Phllips, L Bel, BB Williams, J Jacok (eds) *Ancient Egypt, the Aegian and the North East, Studies in honour of Martha Thads Bell* pp.483-496.

Williams, R J, review of translations of 'Dialogue between a man weary of Life and his Soul'.

Winkler, H (1938) Rock drawing of southern Upper Egypt, EES.

Wreschner, E E (1980) 'Red Ochre and Human Evolution: A case for Discussion'. *Current Anthropology* vol.21 no. 5, pp631-633.

Glossary

Amon: The King of the Gods is represented as a human being (at times ithyphallic), wearing a mortarboard crowned with two plumes or, at times, with a ram's head, the animal dedicated to him. With the goddess Mut and the god Khonsu, they formed the Theban Triad. He was also identified with the god Ra and venerated under the name of Amon-Ra. The cult's principal location was in Thebes.

Anath: Canaanite-Phoenician goddess of Fertility and Victory

Ankh: 'Life' - in origin a loin cloth (not a sandal strap as was once thought) - perhaps used to secure the penis tubes of earlier times. See volume III for an investigation of genital augmentation in Ancient Egypt.

Ankh-tawi: Necropolis near Memphis, Ptah, south-of-his-wall was lord of Ankhtawy, Bast was called Lady of Ankhtawy

Anubis: A jackal-headed god who presided over mummification and accompanied the dead to the hereafter.

Apep, Apophis, demon of non-being, the opponent of Ra

Astarte: Canaanite goddess, called *Lady of Heaven* by the Egyptians.

Ate: Chieftain, sorcerer?

Atef: The double-feathered crown of Osiris

Banebdjedet: Ram-headed primeval deity of Djedet (Mendes).

Barque of the Millions of Years: Ra's Manjet boat, with which he sailed through the 12 provinces of day. For his night journeys, Ra used his Mesket boat.

Bebon: Also Baba, Bata - Seth

Beer, h.(n)k.t - Egypt beer came in many varieties and was brewed using sophisticated means different to the Mesopotamia method whereby loaves made from yeasted dough were lightly baked, crumbled then fermented. The Egyptians started from the grain, (Emmer [archaic] wheat or Barley). Various mixes, either of malted or ground grain were boiled, strained then mixed before fermentation. (Samuel & Bolt 1995).

Bull of Meroe: Amon-Ra

Bousiris: From the Egyptian, meaning "City of Osiris". A city in Lower Egypt where the worship of Osiris was born.

Canopic urns: These four urns contained the liver, lungs, stomach and intestines extracted from the body during mummification.

Cartouche: A loop of cord with a knot at its base, in the side of which the Pharaoh's name was written. The cartouche, the symbol of the Sun God's universal power - and thus the Pharaoh's - was reserved for the Pharaoh's nomen and pronomen.

Castles for millions of years: On Thebes' west bank, the Pharaohs of the 18th, 19th and 20th Dynasties had large religious monuments built, which were improperly called 'funerary temples'. In reality, they used them, during their liftime, to worship the deified pharaoh associated with Amon, the main Theban deity.

Cheth = CTh or Seth in Betz.

Coffin Texts: a term reserved for those spells which are peculiar to the early coffins and do not recur later, not at least until the Saite period, when some of them were sporadically revived. These Coffin Texts contain excerpts from the earliest Pyramid Texts, usurped by the nobility of the IX-XI dynasties for their own benefit (Gardiner: 1927:13).

Cubit: Approximately half a metre

Damanhur: 'Town of Horus', argued by some to be the original Behadit in the western delta, until its transfer to Edfu as the 'Behadit' of Upper Egypt.

Dead (western): The Land of the Setting Sun: this is the Kingdom of the Dead.

Dendara: The capital of the sixth Nome of Upper Egypt, and its necropolis contains tombs dug between the Predynastic period and the end of the Old Kingdom. This site's renown is due to the famous Temple of Hathor, which dates back to the Greco-Roman period. Dendara was dedicated to Hathor, one of the oldest Egyptian deities, represented as a cow or a woman with cow's ears.

Djed: A pillar, symbol of stability and duration; it represents Osiris' spinal column. It is also a protective amulet.

Decanal: 36 stars on the belt of the southern ecliptic, whose rising was used to mark the passage of the 'hours' during each cycle or 'week' of ten days.

Egyptian: A language of the Hamiti-Semitic group which includes Semitic, Berber, Cushitic and Hausa)

Epagnomal: see Intercalary.

Harpoon: The main weapons used for hunting hippos.

Histeriola: Divine precedent for a spell.

Hathor: This cow-headed deity (sometimes depicted as a woman with cow's ears) protected women and the dead, as she was likened to the Goddess of the Kingdom of the Dead; she was also goddess of music and intoxication.

Horus: God of the sky and protector of the pharaoh who was likened to him, Horus could be depicted as a falcon-headed man. As the son of Osiris and Isis, he was often represented as infant (Harpocrates) with a finger held to his lips; a gesture rather paradoxically interpreted in the Hermetic Order of the Golden Dawn, as 'the sign of silence.'

Iathath = (ie Seth) In Greek Magical Pap (Betz) Black 'blood' of Seth.

Ideogramme: A pictorial sign, that has no phonetic value but nevertheless helps define the meaning or sense rather than the sound of a word. Incidentally where the ideogramme follows one or more phonogrammes and ends the word, it is known as a determinative. The ideogrammes are historically the oldest part of the Egyptian language, the phonograms later prefixed to it for the sake of clarity (Gardiner 1926).

Intercalary: Twelve lunar months of 30 days equals 360, which leaves five extra or intercalary days, on which the priests of Heliopolis assigned the birth of five gods, almost as a supplement to their own theological system. The five gods said to be born on these days were: Osiris, Isis, Seth, Nephthys and Horus the child. This schema is known from Pyramid Text 1961 and Plutarch, Isis and Osiris, 12. Mercer (1949 : 277) states that the priests of Heliopolis had invented this calendar by 2781BC.

Ennead: A group of more or less nine deities, such as the Ennead of Heliopolis - Atum, Shu and Tefnut, Geb and Nut, Osiris and Isis, Seth, Nephthys.

Kiki: Seemingly the burning oil from the castor oil plant (ricinus communis) used in lamps.

Khmun: Hermopolis Magna in Middle Egypt, cult centre of Thoth.

Ladder of Seth: means by which the king's soul rises to the stars. (Budge BOTD lxxii). Made of iron that has fallen from the heavens. Jacob's ladder may also be a meteorite (see Wainwright).

Lettuce (Lactuca sativa): was considered an aphrodisiac in Egypt and Mesopotamia. Eaten by Min, god of fertility and Seth. Contain small amounts of an opiate later reduced by cultivation.

Meroe: Capital city of the kingdom of Kush (4th century BCE to 4th century CE).

Maat heru: Speaking true, which will get you through the gates after judgement (lxvi).

Maat: Divine personification of the cosmic order, secondarily connected to the concepts of truth and justice. She wears an ostrich plume on her head, the transcription of her name.

Mut: The wife of Amon, she was venerated in Thebes. Originally depicted as a vulture, she later took on a human form.

Naos: A small chapel of stone or wood inside the sanctuary, in which the god's effigy was kept.

Neolithic: Of or relating to the cultural period of the Stone Age beginning around 10,000BC in the Middle East and later elsewhere, characterized by the development of agriculture and the making of polished stone implements. See also Three Ages Source: Wikopedia

Neter: God or the Divine.

Nehes: Nubia; (later Kash: Kush), the derivation of 'Nubia' according to Baynes & Malek (2000) may be from 'Nub' - meaning gold.

Neith: Goddess of the hunt and war, cult centre at Sais.

Nome: One of forty-two administrative districts, significantly also the number of the judges of the dead. Interestingly each Nome coincides with one of the enormous temporary lakes caused by the annual Nile flood (Butzer 1976).

Nomen: The King's titulary consisted of five great names. The family name, called the nomen by Egyptologists, is introduced by epithet 'son of Ra'.

Pronomen: King's first cartouche or throne name.

On: Heliopolis

Onnophris: Osiris, about whom is said: He brings peace to the lands in his name of Sokaris, mighty is his reputation in his name of Osiris, he persists until the ends of eternity in his name Onnophris.

Onuris: Anhur, god of hunt and war, resident at This. He returns the Eye of the Sun as his consort Mehit.

Osiris: The husband of Isis; after having been killed by his brother, Seth, he fathered a son, Horus, who, grown to adulthood, avenged him. He is represented with his crown (atef), his scepter (bequa), and his flail, (nekhekh).

Palaeolithic: Of or relating to the cultural period of the Stone Age beginning with the earliest chipped stone tools, about 750,000 years ago, (incidentally same time as the Nile found its way out of Africa) until the beginning of the Mesolithic Age, about 15,000 years ago. See also Three Ages. source Wikopedia

Pega the gap: A Gorge in mountain beyond Abydos, gateway to the western lands of the dead.

Pluvial: A Rainy period or age.

Pre: also Phra - Ra. Ra was beholden to Seth for defending him against the demons who assailed him on his daily journey through the skies.

Pre-Harakhti: A combination of Re and Horus!

Ptah: The God of Memphis, where he was believed to have brought the universe into being; the husband of the Lion Goddess, Sekhmet, he was depicted wearing a mummy's shroud, holding in his hand a scepter. He was later likened to another Memphis god of death, Sokaris, and was worshipped in his syncretic form of Ptah-Sokaris.

Pylon: A monumental temple entrance, consisting of a portal between two enormous trapezoidal monoliths.

Tê: The underworld

Sais: Centre in western delta, where local rulers, decendents of 25th dynasty, became important in the conflicts of the 8th century.

Sekhmet: Lion-headed goddess, sometimes crowned with the solar disk. She protected the royal power; she can be likened to Hathor, Bastet and Isis.

Setna, Khamuas: Khaemwase, son of Ramesses II and Isis-Nefert. He died in the 55th year of the reign of his father. He was sem-priest of Ptah and chief artificer. Setme: also Setna - sem, the title of Khaemwase

Sycamore, Lady of the Southern : epithet of Hathor at Memphis, she had assisted Horus after he had been blinded by Seth.

Shed: 'Save', 'rescue', 'saviour' - used especially after the traumas
of the Amarna period. The Egyptian aspect of the semitic god
Reshef - or young saviour god used as an epithet of Horus.

Thebes: During the 18th Dynasty (ca.1550 - 1295BC), the city of
Weset was founded by Amenhotep I; better known by its Greek
name, Thebes, it became the heart of the country. It was at this
time that the Great Temple of Amon in Karnak became the
country's most important religious center and the royal
necropolises were excavated in the Valley of the Kings and the
Valley of the Queens. *Theban Triad*: Amon-Ra, Mut and Khonsu.
.

This: In the beginning of what is known as the Predynastic
period (3300 - 2920BC), the population had gathered in two
centers: one in the North, in the Delta region and the other in
the South, in Hierakonpolis, where we know of sovereigns such
as King Scorpion and Narmer. The last King of the Predynastic
period, he conquered Lower Egypt and unified the country, no
doubt after several wars. His successor, Aha - who can probably
be identified with the legendary Menes - founded the 1st Dynasty
(from the Greek: dynam(is) = power). The two first Dynasties
were called Thinite because, according to the Greek historian,
Manethon - to whom we owe a list of all thirty lineages of the
Egyptian sovereigns - the pharaohs of this period came from the
city of This, of which no trace was ever found, but which must
have been located in the Abydos area.

Three Age System: 'In organizing the extensive collection of
artifacts at the National Museum of Denmark, the 19th-century
Danish archaeologist Christian Thomsen proposed an innovative
system based on the assumption of a progression in human
technology from stone to bronze to iron. His insight that early
technology had developed in chronological stages rather than
concurrently at different levels of society proved essentially
correct, though ultimately of limited use in describing the various
progressions in other parts of the world. Once empirical study
of archaeological collections began, Thomsen's Three Age

system was rapidly modifed into four ages by the subdivision of the Stone Age into the Old Stone (now Palaeolithic) and New Stone (Neolithic) ages. Subsequent refinement has added Mesolithic (Middle Stone) and Chalcolithic (Copper and Stone) to the original terms, which are now known as periods rather than ages. Use of the full terminology—Palaeolithic, Mesolithic, Neolithic, Chalcolithic, Bronze, and Iron—is appropriate only for Europe, the Middle East, and Egypt, and even there it is not uniformly accepted among archaeologists today.' source: Wikopedia

Ursa Major: The Great Bear, The Plough, Meshketyu. Constellation associated with Seth.

Ursa Minor - 'Small Bear' another significant northern constellation, the location of the current pole star *Polaris*, the target of Seth's constellation *Ursa Major*.

Xois: city in the Delta, centre of the Amon-Ra worship

Wadj: A scepter in the form of a papyrus stalk, it was characteristic of female deities.

Index

Mandrake
Other Related Titles of Interest

Tankhem:
Seth & Egyptian Magick Vol I
By Mogg Morgan
£12.99, isbn 1869928865, 234pp,
second revised edition

The Typhonian deity Seth was once worshipped in Ancient Egypt. Followers of later schools obliterated Seth's monuments, demonised and neglected his cult. A possible starting point in the quest for the 'hidden god' is an examination of the life of Egyptian King Seti I ('He of Seth') also known as Sethos.

When looking for an astral temple that included all of the ancient Egyptian gods and goddesses, the temple of Seti I proved itself worthy of examination. Many secrets began to reveal themselves. The essence of the real philosophy of the Sethian and indeed what Satanism is, stems from the author's astral wanderings in this temple.

The temple is a real place, and like any temple no part of its design is accidental. It is a record in stone and paint of the Egyptian wisdom. It also fits quite well with the Thelemic mythos and tells lots of interesting things about the ancient Seth cult - if you have the eye to see it.

Contents: Prolegomena to Egyptian magick; Setanism; Tankhem; Egyptian Magick and Tantra; Sexual Magick; Twenty Eight; North; The Crooked Wand.

The author has published numerous articles, short stories and books, principally Ayurveda: Medicine of the Gods, The English Mahatma (a Tankhem novel) and as ('Katon Shual') Sexual Magick.

A complementary ebook (*House of Life*) with an introductory magical practice is available with the above title on request.

To contact the author direct log onto the *Tankhem* group at Yahoo groups: tankhem-subscribe@yahoogroups.com

For these & other titles contact:
Mogg Morgan, (01865) 243671
mandrake@mandrake.uk.net
web: mandrake.uk.net
PO Box 250, Oxford, OX1 1AP (UK)

Printed in the United States
34957LVS00002B/241-258

9 781869 928872